@WAR

THE RISE OF CYBER WARFARE

Also by Shane Harris

The Watchers: The Rise of America's Surveillance State

@WAR

THE RISE OF CYBER WARFARE

SHANE HARRIS

headline

First published in 2014
by HEADLINE PUBLISHING GROUP

1

Cataloguing in Publication Data is available from the British Library

Trade paperback ISBN 978 0 7553 6519 7
Hardback ISBN 978 0 7553 6517 3

Set in Minion Pro

Printed and bound in Great Britain by Clays Ltd, St Ives plc

Headline's policy is to use papers that are natural, renewable and recyclable products and
made from wood grown in sustainable forests. The logging and manufacturing processes are
expected to conform to the environmental regulations of the country of origin.

HEADLINE PUBLISHING GROUP
An Hachette UK Company
338 Euston Road
London NW1 3BH

www.headline.co.uk
www.hachette.co.uk

CONTENTS

For my husband, Joe de Feo

A NOTE ON SOURCES

I'VE COVERED cyber security and electronic surveillance as a journalist for more than a decade. This book is informed by the more than one thousand interviews I've conducted over the years with current and former government officials, military personnel, corporate executives and employees, subject matter experts, researchers, and activists. Over the past two years as I was working on this project, I conducted new rounds of interviews with many of these people, who are among my most credible and trusted sources. I also conducted interviews with some sources for the first time. For this book I relied especially on my interviews with current government officials and military personnel whose jobs deal directly with cyber security operations or policies. They are working in the trenches of this evolving terrain, not at its fringes. I'm grateful to them for taking the time to speak with me and for confiding in me on a subject that many in government still resist discussing publicly because too much of it touches on classified material and operations.

Many of the people I interviewed agreed to be quoted on the record, and in those cases I have listed their names either in the text or in the endnotes. Others requested that I not identify them by name and, in some cases, that I not identify the agency or company where they work. It's regrettable and frequently unavoidable when reporting on classified matters of national security that journalists cannot more fully identify their sources. I don't believe a single person I interviewed for this book has revealed information to me that would jeopardize national security or put lives at risk. But I granted these people's requests for two reasons.

First, the information they provided either was essential to the story and couldn't be obtained any other way or it amplified information from other on-the-record sources or documents in the public domain. (And a surprising amount of revealing information about cyber warfare and espionage has been made public or was never classified.) Second, these people spoke to me at significant risk to their professional livelihood and potentially their personal freedom. In discussing cyber warfare and espionage, it's often hard for sources to know if they're revealing classified information or getting close to the line. If the sources who discussed these matters were identified by name, they could lose their top-secret security clearances, which would make them effectively unemployable in their chosen profession of national security.

But these sources also risked criminal prosecution in talking to me. The Obama administration has been historically hostile to government employees who share information with journalists. The Justice Department has prosecuted more people for disclosing classified information than all previous administrations combined. Simply put, it is a dangerous time to talk to journalists. And this risk extends to former government employees and military personnel. Several former intelligence officials have told me that within the past year they were explicitly told by the intelligence agencies where they're still employed as contractors that they should stop talking to journalists if they want to continue doing business with the government. In cases where I refer to anonymous sources, I've done my best to explain why those people are credible and authoritative, while honoring my obligation not to reveal information that could identify them.

A significant portion of this book is based on documents in the public domain. These include government reports and presentations; congressional testimony; speeches by senior officials; and an ever-growing and highly detailed body of written analysis by private security researchers. When I began researching this book, a number of colleagues questioned how I'd be able to write about a subject as shrouded in official secrecy as cyber security. But I was surprised to learn that a very large amount of revealing and informative unclassified information exists in the public domain. There's a significant amount of knowledge out there, which tends to undermine the claims by many government officials that this subject is too sensitive to talk about publicly. I'm heartened that in the past few years more government officials and military leaders have decided to talk more openly about cyber warfare and espionage. The public cannot understand these issues, and governments can't make sound law and policy, without candid and frank discussion in the light of day.

PROLOGUE

THE SPIES HAD come without warning. They plied their craft silently, stealing secrets from the world's most powerful military. They were at work for months before anyone noticed their presence. And when American officials finally detected the thieves, they saw that it was too late. The damage was done.

The intruders had made off with huge amounts of technical and design information about the United States' most important new weapon, a next-generation aircraft called the Joint Strike Fighter. It was supposed to be the fighter to end all fighters, which would be flown by every branch of the armed forces and ensure America's aerial dominance for decades to come. Dubbed the F-35, the jet was the most complex military weapons system ever devised and, with an estimated total price tag of $337 billion, the most expensive.

All signs pointed to China's military as the culprit in a series of audacious raids that began in late 2006. It had the motive and the opportunity to steal the F-35's secrets, particularly details about how the fighter evaded enemy radar systems. For decades China had waged an aggressive espionage campaign against the US Armed Forces, its most formidable adversary. Beginning in the late 1970s, Chinese agents working in or visiting American universities, government research labs, and defense contractors made off with design information about weapons systems, including nuclear warheads.

But there was something strange about the Joint Strike Fighter theft. The spies weren't taking paper documents out of offices or eavesdropping on engineers in the break room. They were stealing information remotely, via a computer connection. The Joint Strike Fighter program had been hacked.

Computer forensics investigators at the air force, which was in charge of the F-35 program, started looking for the culprits. To understand how the hackers had gotten in, they had to think like them. So they brought in a hacker. He was an ex–military officer and a veteran of the military's clandestine cyber campaigns. He'd cut his teeth in some of the army's earliest information-warfare operations in the mid-1990s, the kind designed to get inside an enemy's head more than his databases. These were computer-age variants of classic propaganda campaigns; they required military hackers to know how to penetrate an enemy's communications systems and transmit messages that looked as if they came from a trusted source. Later the former officer's work evolved into going after insurgents and terrorists on the battlefields of Iraq, tracking them down via their cell phones and Internet messages. He was only in his mid-forties, but by the standards of his profession he was an old hand.

This much the air force knew about the Joint Strike Fighter breach: the data hadn't been taken from a military computer. It seemed to have come from a company that was hired to help design and build the aircraft. The spies had made an end run, targeting Defense Department contractors whose computers were full of highly classified information, including some of the same plans for the F-35 that were likely to be found on a military system. It was a shrewd tactic. Contractors are an indispensable part of the American military; without them, planes don't fly, tanks don't roll, and ships aren't built and repaired. But their computer systems were generally less defended than the military's top-secret networks, the most sensitive of which weren't even connected to the Internet. The hackers simply found another way in, targeting the firms to which the military outsourced so many of its key operations.

The air force investigators weren't sure which company was the source of the breach. It could be Lockheed Martin, the lead contractor on the F-35 program, or its two main subcontractors, Northrop Grumman and BAE Systems, or any one of the more than one thousand other firms and suppliers hired to work on the jet's many mechanical systems or its elaborate electronics. About 7.5 million lines of software code helped run the aircraft itself — more than three times the number in the service's current top-of-the-line fighter. Another 15 million lines of code ran the jet's logistics, training, and other support systems. For a spy, this was what the military would call a "target-rich environment." Anywhere he looked he might find secrets about the aircraft's navigation systems, its onboard sensors and surveillance equipment, and its weaponry.

The logical place to start the investigation was with Lockheed Martin, the primary contractor. Its own computers held vital information about the aircraft, but perhaps more important, it was in charge of the many subcontractors to whom various aspects of the F-35's development had been farmed out. But when the air force's hacker showed up at a Lockheed office to start his investigation, he was met not by fellow techies or military officers overseeing the F-35's construction. He was greeted by the company's lawyers.

The hacker requested a laptop. "Why do you need that?" the lawyers asked. He explained that he had to look at Lockheed's internal computer networks, for starters. Also, he wanted to know what software and applications a typical Lockheed employee's laptop was running. They might have flaws in software code or "backdoors," which allow a user (including a legitimate one, such as a systems administrator) to bypass normal security controls, like a user log-in and password screen, and gain access to the machine. An intruder could have used these access points to gain a foothold inside the company's electronic infrastructure. All the spy needed was a way in, a place to set up a digital beachhead and conduct operations.

The lawyers gave the hacker a laptop fresh out of the box; it had never been connected to a Lockheed network. It had never been touched by a Lockheed employee — other than an attorney. The hacker protested. This was like being asked to figure out how a house was burgled without being allowed to inspect the crime scene.

Why would Lockheed, which stood to make billions building the Joint Strike Fighter, not do everything it could to help find the spies? Maybe because a thorough investigation might reveal how poorly defended the company's networks were. Investigators might even find evidence of other breaches, on other military programs. Word that it had been infiltrated by spies who'd never set foot on company property could hardly help its business. Lockheed was the single-largest provider of goods and services to the US government. In 2006 it held at least $33.5 billion in contracts, more than 80 percent of which were with the Defense Department. And those figures don't include secret work for intelligence agencies, which surely totaled billions more. Lockheed couldn't afford to be seen as a poor steward of the government's most precious secrets — indeed, no defense contractor could. Lockheed was also a publicly traded company. Presumably, shareholders would react negatively to news that it couldn't protect the information at the core of its multibillion-dollar business.

Unsurprisingly, the hacker found nothing useful on the laptop. The top air force generals charged with seeing the Joint Strike Fighter to completion were furious about the breach, and they demanded that Lockheed, and all the other contractors involved, cooperate fully with the investigation. As they saw it, these companies didn't just work for the government. They were effectively part of the government, sustained by taxpayer dollars and entrusted with top-secret work. The air force expanded its investigation, and over the next several months the hacker and his colleagues scrutinized Lockheed's networks and those of other contractors working on the program.

The investigators discovered that this was no one-off break-in. Lockheed's networks had been breached repeatedly. They couldn't say precisely how many times, but they judged the damage as severe, given the amount of information stolen and the intruders' unfettered access to the networks. In the entire campaign, which also targeted other companies, the spies had made off with several terabytes of information on the jet's inner workings. In absolute size, that was roughly equal to 2 percent of the collection of the Library of Congress.

In another era, running a human spy inside an American corporation and planting a listening device would have counted as a heroic feat of espionage. Now one just had to infect a computer with a malicious software program or intercept a communication over the Internet and listen in from the other side of the world.

The more investigators combed Internet logs and computer drives, the more victims they found. The spies had penetrated the networks of subcontractors in several countries. Technicians traced the Internet protocol addresses and the techniques the spies had used. There was little doubt they were in China, and were probably the same group that has been linked to other break-ins aimed at the US military and large American companies, particularly in the technology and energy industries. The breadth, persistence, and sophistication of Chinese cyber espionage was just beginning to dawn on US military and intelligence leaders. Whether they feared embarrassment and ridicule or because they didn't want to tip off the Chinese that they were being watched, US officials didn't publicly reveal the extent of the espionage.

The spies were hunting for details about the fighter's mechanical design and how well it held up under the stresses of flight and aerial combat. This suggested that they wanted to learn the weaknesses of the aircraft — but also that they wanted to build one themselves. The implications were chilling. Presuming the spies were working for the Chinese military, American fighters might one day go into battle against their clones. American pilots might be flying against Chinese foes who already knew the F-35's vulnerabilities.

At the moment, the jet's sensors and flight controls, which allowed the aircraft to detect its adversaries or perform complicated maneuvers, appeared to be safe, because those plans were stored on computers that weren't connected to the Internet. But more than a year later, investigators were still discovering breaches that they'd missed earlier. One had to assume that the campaign might continue, and that even an offline computer was a target. The very fact that it wasn't connected to the public network suggested it contained the most sensitive information.

Investigators eventually concluded that the spies weren't initially looking for information about the F-35 at all but that they'd targeted another classified program. Perhaps they found it an easier target given how much information was lying unprotected on company networks. That they'd switched plans mid-heist hinted at the spies' audacity. Some officials marveled at how little care the intruders took to cover themselves. They didn't seem to care if they were exposed. It was like they were daring the Americans to come after them, believing they wouldn't.

The spies had made off with potentially useful intelligence, but they'd also set back the development of the F-35. US officials later said that rampant penetrations of subcontractors' computers had forced programmers to rewrite software code for the jet, contributing to a one-year delay in the program and a 50 percent increase in its cost. The Chinese might never have to fight the jet if it didn't get off the ground. But China also moved forward with its own design. In September 2012, during a visit by Defense Secretary Leon Panetta, Chinese officials leaked photographs of their newest fighter jet parked on an airfield. It bore a number of design similarities to the F-35, which was no coincidence, US officials acknowledged. The Chinese jet's design was based partly on information the spies had stolen from American companies six years earlier.

The CEOs weren't sure why they'd been summoned to the Pentagon. Or why they'd been granted temporary top-secret security clearances. Looking around the room, they saw plenty of familiar faces. The chief executives or their representatives worked for the twenty biggest US defense contractors: Lockheed Martin, Raytheon, General Dynamics, Boeing, and Northrop Grumman, among others. These were blue-chip companies in their own right, and collectively they had spent decades building the American war machine. Whatever had brought them all together at Defense Department headquarters that summer day in 2007, on such short notice, it couldn't be good news.

The executives gathered outside a "sensitive compartmented information facility," or SCIF (pronounced "skiff"), a room built to be impervious to eavesdropping. Their hosts began what had been billed as a "threat briefing," which didn't seem unusual, since military officers routinely talked to defense company chiefs about threats to national security. But this briefing was about threats to corporate security. Specifically, the corporations run by these executives.

Military personnel who'd investigated the F-35 breach described what they'd learned. A massive espionage campaign had targeted each of the companies' computer networks. The spies weren't looking just for information about the F-35; they stole as many military secrets as they could find. Spies had overrun the companies' weak electronic defenses and relayed classified information back to their home servers. They had sent employees working on secret projects innocuous-looking e-mails that appeared to come from trusted sources inside the company. When the employee opened such an e-mail, it installed a digital backdoor and allowed the Chinese to monitor every keystroke the employee typed, every website visited, every file downloaded, created, or sent. Their networks had been infiltrated. Their computers compromised and monitored. America's military-industrial complex had, in the language of hackers, been owned.

And the spies were still inside these companies' networks, mining for secrets and eavesdropping on employees' communications. Maybe they were monitoring the executives' private e-mails right now. "A lot of people went into that room with dark hair, and when they came out, it was white," says James Lewis, a prominent cyber security expert and a fellow at the Center for Strategic and International Studies, a think tank in Washington, who knows the details of the meeting.

These companies were the weak link in the security chain. Pentagon officials told the executives that responding to theft of military secrets was a matter of urgent national security. And for the companies, it was a matter of survival. Most of their businesses depended on the money they made selling airplanes, tanks, satellites, ships, submarines, computer systems, and all manner of technical and administrative services to the federal government. Officials were clear: if the contractors wished to continue in their present business arrangements, they would have to do a better job defending themselves.

But they wouldn't be doing it alone.

After the meeting the Defense Department began giving the companies information about cyber spies and malicious hackers being monitored by US intelligence agencies. At the time, the Pentagon was tracking about a dozen espionage campaigns — distinct groups of hackers that could be categorized based on their interest in certain military technologies, aspects of military operations or organizations, or defense contractors. This information about foreign spies was the fruit of American espionage, gathered by monitoring and studying attempts to penetrate military networks, but also by breaking in to the computers and networks of America's adversaries. US intelligence agencies were also monitoring huge flows of traffic over the global telecommunications networks for viruses, worms, and other malicious computer programs. Never before had the United States shared so much classified information with private individuals. The work of securing the nation had historically been the government's exclusive domain. But now government and industry formed an alliance against a common threat. The Pentagon gave the companies Internet addresses that were tied to computers and servers where the foreign spies were believed to be sending stolen information, as well as the e-mail addresses that were known to have sent those innocuous-looking messages that actually contained a virus or a piece of spyware. Government analysts shared the latest tools and techniques that they'd seen foreign hackers use against their targets. And they alerted companies to the types of malicious software hackers were using to pry into computers and pilfer files. Armed with these data points, known as threat signatures, the companies were supposed to bolster their own defenses and focus their attention on repelling the intruders before they compromised their networks again. The threat signatures were compiled by the National Security Agency, the government's largest intelligence organization. Its global network of surveillance plucks data out of tens of thousands of computers that the agency itself has penetrated and implanted with spyware — just like the Chinese spies who broke in to the defense companies' computers. Information gathered by the National Security Agency (NSA) is some of the most revealing about the capabilities, plans, and intentions of America's adversaries, and as such it is highly classified. Now the government was sharing it with companies under strict secrecy rules. The recipients were not to disclose that they'd received the threat signatures, and they were to keep the Pentagon apprised of any incursions into their own networks.

The Defense Industrial Base Initiative, as the intelligence-sharing program is called, started small, with just the 20 companies whose executives had gathered in the SCIF at the Pentagon. But within a year there were 30 members. Today there are about 100. Pentagon officials want to add as many as 250 new members per year to the secretive club, known by its members as the DIB (pronounced "dib").

But officials don't want only to protect military contractors. They see the DIB as a model for securing whole industries, from telecommunications to energy to health care to banking — any business, system, or function that uses a computer network. Which today means nearly everything. The DIB was the seed of a much larger and still evolving alliance between government and industry.

The leaders of the intelligence agencies, top military officers, and the president himself say that the consequences of another major terrorist attack on American soil pale in comparison with the havoc and panic a determined and malicious group of hackers could cause. Instead of stealing information from a computer, they could destroy the computer itself, crashing communications networks or disabling systems that run air traffic control networks. They could hijack the Internet-connected devices that regulate the flow of electrical power and plunge cities into darkness. Or they could attack information itself, erasing or corrupting the data in financial accounts and igniting a national panic.

In October 2012 then defense secretary Leon Panetta warned that the United States was on the verge of a "cyber Pearl Harbor: an attack that would cause physical destruction and the loss of life, that would paralyze and shock the nation and create a profound new sense of vulnerability." Five months earlier President Barack Obama wrote in a newspaper editorial that the wars of the future would be fought online, where "an adversary unable to match our military supremacy on the battlefield might seek to exploit our computer vulnerabilities here at home." Obama painted a dire and arguably hyperbolic picture. But his choice of imagery reflected the anxiety gripping senior leaders in government and business that cyberspace, which seems to hold boundless promise for the nation, is also its greatest unaddressed weakness. "Taking down vital banking systems could trigger a financial crisis," Obama wrote. "The lack of clean water or functioning hospitals could spark a public health emergency. And as we've seen in past blackouts, the loss of electricity can bring businesses, cities and entire regions to a standstill." FBI director James Comey has said the risk of cyber attacks and a rise in cyber-related crime — to include espionage and financial fraud — will be the most significant national security threat over the next decade. For the past two years the possibility of a crippling cyber attack has topped the list of "global threats" compiled by all seventeen US intelligence agencies in a report to Congress. Protecting cyberspace has become the US government's top national security priority, because attacks online could have devastating effects offline.

And yet the government is not telling us the whole story. Officials are quick to portray the nation as a victim, suffering ceaseless barrages from an unseen enemy. But the US military and intelligence agencies, often with the cooperation of American corporations, are some of the most aggressive actors in cyberspace. The United States is one of a handful of countries whose stated policy is to dominate cyberspace as a battlefield and that has the means to do it. For more than a decade, cyber espionage has been the single most productive means of gathering information about the country's adversaries — abroad and at home. The aggressive actions the United States is taking in cyberspace are changing the Internet in fundamental ways, and not always for the better. In its zeal to protect cyberspace, the government, in partnership with corporations, is making it more vulnerable.

The story of how securing cyberspace became so important for the United States starts with its efforts to control it, to use it as both a weapon and a tool for spying. The military now calls cyberspace the "fifth domain" of warfare, and it views supremacy there as essential to its mission, just as it is in the other four: land, sea, air, and space. The United States has already incorporated cyber attacks into conventional warfare, and it has used them to disable infrastructure in other countries — precisely the same kinds of malicious acts that US officials say they fear domestically and must take extraordinary measures to prevent. On the spectrum of cyber hostilities, the United States sits at the aggressive end.

The US military and intelligence agencies are fielding a new generation of cyber warriors, trained to monitor the computer systems of foreign adversaries, break in to them, and when necessary disable and destroy them. *Cyber warfare,* like *cyberspace,* is an amorphous term. But it applies to a spectrum of offensive activities. Just as espionage is an inextricable part of traditional warfare, so too is spying on a computer a prerequisite to attacking it. To be sure, the United States has spent far more time and money spying on computers and stealing information than it has taking down critical infrastructures and destroying physical facilities through a computer connection. But it has done that, too. And it will do it more often, and more effectively. Indeed, cyber warfare — the combination of spying and attack — was instrumental to the American military victory in Iraq in 2007, in ways that have never been fully explained or appreciated. The military, working with US intelligence agencies, used offensive cyber techniques (hacking) to track down people in the physical world and then capture or kill them.

But just as protecting cyberspace is not the exclusive domain of government, waging war in cyberspace is becoming a private affair. A burgeoning industry of cyber arms merchants and private security forces is selling its goods and services both to the government and to corporations that will no longer endure relentless espionage or the risk of cyber attack. The armies of nations will inevitably meet one another on the cyber battlefield. But the armies of corporations will meet there, too.

Governments don't operate in cyberspace alone. Defending computer networks, and launching attacks on them, requires the participation, willing or otherwise, of the private sector. The vast majority of computer networks in the United States are privately owned. The government cannot possibly protect or patrol all of them. But most of the world's communications travel through equipment located in the United States. The government has a privileged position to exploit those networks, and an urgent need to protect them. To those ends, a military-Internet complex has emerged.

Like the military-industrial complex before it, this new cooperative includes the makers of tanks and airplanes, missiles and satellites. But it includes tech giants, financial institutions, and communications companies as well. The United States has enlisted, persuaded, cajoled, and in some cases compelled companies into helping it fend off foreign and domestic foes who have probed the American electrical grid and looked for other weaknesses in critical infrastructures. The NSA has formed secret arrangements with marquee technology companies, including Google, to monitor private networks for threats. It has shared intelligence with major banks and financial institutions in order to prevent a catastrophic cyber attack on Wall Street.

But the government also has attempted to force some companies into letting the NSA place monitoring equipment on its networks. And it has paid technology companies to install backdoors in their products that it can use to spy on foreign intelligence services and monitor military movements. Those clandestine access points also allow the military to launch cyber attacks in foreign countries. Without the cooperation of the companies, the United States couldn't fight cyber wars. In that respect, the new military-Internet complex is the same as the industrial one before it. The government doesn't fight wars alone. It relies on companies to design weapons, move and feed troops, build and maintain aircraft, ships, and satellites. The United States became the most formidable military in world history through a mutually beneficial alliance with corporations. It aims to do so again in cyberspace.

The United States is rapidly building its capacity to dominate cyberspace. In 2014 the government planned to spend more than $13 billion on cyber defense programs, mostly to protect government computers and networks, and to share threat intelligence with private industry. To put that in some perspective, in the same year the government planned to spend $11.6 billion on direct efforts to combat climate change, which Obama has called "the global threat of our time." Over the next five years, the Defense Department alone plans to spend $26 billion on technology for cyber defense and offense. Precisely how much the United States intends to spend on the offensive component is classified. But in cyberspace, the line between offense and defense is blurry and constantly shifting. The same infrastructure that is being put in place to defend networks is the one that is used to launch attacks. Government officials prefer to talk publicly about defense, which is a strategic and a cynical calculation: it's easier to drum up funds and political support for repelling invaders than it is for building a cyber army to attack and spy on other countries. And yet, that is precisely what the

United States is doing, and using some of the billions of dollars nominally appropriated for "defensive" purposes to do so.

The business of cyber security is booming. Companies and individuals around the world spend $67 billion a year protecting their computers and networks. Many of the experts they hire learned their trade in the military or an intelligence agency. Indeed, the Pentagon has become a training ground for private cyber sentries, who can double or even triple their salaries when they jump to a private security firm. The same defense contractors that were once the target of cyber spies now sell the expertise to protect networks and wage war on them to their customers, including utilities and banks — the very companies that the government had set out to protect in the first place.

The struggle to control cyberspace is defining American national security in the twenty-first century. But the response to cyber threats promises to change the shape of cyberspace more than the threats themselves do. The decisions that government and business leaders make today will have profound implications not just for Americans but for people around the world, who are increasingly united in their reliance on a broad, distributed, and often hard-to-define space that is neither entirely a commons nor the property of one corporation or government. That threats exist in cyberspace is undeniable. Answering them is a befuddling and often perilous exercise, but one in which we all have a stake.

PART I

ONE

The First Cyber War

BOB STASIO NEVER planned to become a cyber warrior. After he graduated high school, Stasio enrolled at the University at Buffalo and entered the ROTC program. He majored in mathematical physics, studying mind-bending theories of quantum mechanics and partial differential equations. The university, eager to graduate students steeped in the hard sciences, waived the major components of his core curriculum requirements, including English. Stasio never wrote a paper in his entire college career.

Stasio arrived at Fort Lewis, Washington, in 2004, when he was twenty-two years old. His new brigade intelligence officer took one look at the second lieutenant's résumé, saw the background in math and physics, and told Stasio, "You're going to the SIGINT platoon."

SIGINT, or signals intelligence, is the capture and analysis of electronic communications. Like all branches of intelligence, it's a blend of science and art, but it's heavy on the science. The brigade intelligence officer had worked at the National Security Agency and recognized that Stasio's physics training would come in handy, because so much of SIGINT involves the technical collection of radio signals, fiber-optic transmissions, and Internet packets.

Stasio's military training in college focused on how to use a rifle and lead a squad. But he had spent six months learning the basics of intelligence gathering and analysis at the army's intelligence school at Fort Huachuca, Arizona. When he came to Fort Lewis, Stasio was assigned to a Stryker brigade, a mechanized force designed to be light on its feet, capable of deploying into combat in just a few days. It was Stasio's job to locate the enemy on the battlefield by tracking his communications signals. And he was also supposed to divine his adversary's intentions by eavesdropping on the orders a commander gave to troops, or listening for the air strike that a platoon leader was calling in from behind the lines. Stasio would join the Fourth Brigade, Second Infantry Division, "the Raiders," and deploy to Iraq. He'd be working with a team of linguists, who would be essential, since Stasio didn't speak Arabic. But when it came time to meet them, Stasio started to worry: nearly all of the linguists spoke only English and Korean.

The army had designed its signals intelligence system for the Cold War. Thousands of troops still served on the Korean Peninsula. They were still trained in how to fight a land battle with North Korean forces, in which the physics of SIGINT — locating tanks and troops — would be central to the mission. But the Raiders were going off to fight a network of Iraqi insurgents, volunteer jihadists, and terrorists. These guys didn't drive tanks. They didn't organize themselves according to a military hierarchy. And of course, they didn't speak Korean.

Stasio decided that his intelligence training would be mostly useless in Iraq, where the US occupation was coming unglued. Army casualties were mounting, the result of a well-orchestrated campaign of roadside bombings by insurgents. The soldiers who didn't die in these attacks were coming home with limbs missing, or with severe brain injuries that would impair them physically and emotionally for the rest of their lives. SIGINT wasn't preventing these attacks. Indeed, it was hardly being used at all. In October 2004 the military's top signals intelligence officer estimated that as much as 90 percent of all information in Iraq was being supplied by a network of human spies and informants — and they weren't helping the Americans reduce the bombing attacks and insurgent strikes.

Stasio read as much as he could about insurgencies, noting in particular how they organized themselves using a network model, with many independent nodes of people working in teams, separate from a central controller. This was the opposite design of a vertical, military bureaucracy, with orders filtering down from the top through several layers of officers. In principle, the intelligence discipline in which Stasio was trained should still work. He was expected to locate his enemy using electronic signals and figure out his next move. But the tools the army had supplied to do this were ill suited to the shadowy, urban battlefields of Iraq. The Raiders used a collection "platform" known as the Prophet system, a rugged truck affixed with a tall, roof-mounted radio antenna about the size of a streetlamp. The older officers in the brigade liked the Prophet because it told them what enemy forces were in their immediate area of operations. It was a tactical device, and they controlled it, driving it to wherever they wanted to collect intelligence.

But the Prophet was designed to collect radio waves, and on a wide-open and relatively flat area of battle. Stasio knew that the enemy fighters in Iraq were communicating using cell phones and e-mail and through videos they'd posted on the Internet. They were moving in small groups through the dense concrete maze of Baghdad and other crowded Iraqi cities. The Prophet wasn't the most useful tool. Indeed, when Stasio finally got to Iraq, he saw that the military intelligence units that had come before him were using the Prophet not to collect signals but to transport food and other supplies around the base.

There was another reason the old-timers liked the Prophet — it was theirs. They could drive it wherever they wanted. They had control over the collection and analysis of intelligence. Stasio thought that his more senior officers generally distrusted intel that came from back in the States, frequently from Washington, DC, and the national intelligence agencies such as the CIA and the NSA, which, from the battlefield, looked like big, lumbering bureaucracies filled with software engineers and computer geeks who were too removed from the on-the-ground tactical needs of forces in Iraq.

But Stasio knew the national agencies, and in particular the NSA, had something he needed: data. Namely, servers full of electronic communications and signals collected by the agency's listening posts around the world. Stasio thought that if he could tap into SIGINT from Iraq, he might be able to understand something about the size and shape of the insurgent networks by piecing together their communications records. This was painstaking work, and it would require hours sitting in front of a computer, probably in some air-conditioned trailer, not driving a Prophet through dusty streets. Stasio was a fan of the HBO series *The Wire*, and he was particularly fond of one character, Lester, who uncovers a network of drug dealers in Baltimore by tracking their cell phone calls. Stasio wanted to do the same thing in Iraq.

He pleaded with his brigade intelligence officer at Fort Lewis: instead of sending him out to the rifle range to practice infantry techniques and study the bulky Prophet, let him and a few of his fellow intelligence officers spend time in the state-of-the-art intelligence facility on the base, learning how to use software for diagramming networks and digesting Internet and cell phone traffic. These tools had been largely overlooked by tactical military intelligence units, Stasio argued. But they could be enormously helpful in Iraq.

The officer agreed.

Stasio and a fellow lieutenant devised their own training regimen, which hinged on a concept called "reachback." The idea was that in the field, small military intelligence units would set up their own computers and local networks, but they would reach back to the massive databases at the NSA and other agencies that were collecting useful intel from across the entire spectrum of military and intelligence operations, including satellite images, tips from informants, summaries of interrogations of captured fighters, even political forecasts produced by CIA analysts. To Stasio, no single piece of data was insignificant. But a single piece on its own was of little use. The information had to be "fused" into a nuanced picture.

For someone who grew up using many different modes of communication — phone, e-mail, text messaging — on many different devices, this method of intelligence analysis was intuitive. Stasio and the members of his platoon trained for two and a half years before they finally headed out to Iraq. He took four of the Korean linguists in his platoon and sent them to a one-year crash course in Arabic. He didn't need them to be fluent, but with some language proficiency they could work with local translators to write intelligence reports. The rest of the linguists he sent to learn intelligence analysis.

Stasio arrived in Iraq in April 2007 — without the Prophet in tow — as part of a new "surge" of American troops. He might have wondered if they arrived too late. Stasio and his team found US forces under relentless assault from insurgents, roadside bombers, and mortar attacks. Iraq was collapsing amid an escalating civil war. Foreign fighters were pouring into the country from neighboring Syria and Iran, and a ruthless terrorist network, known as al-Qaeda in Iraq, ran a brutal campaign of attacks against US and coalition forces, the Iraqi government, and Iraqi Shiites — fellow Muslims and innocent civilians. The terror group aimed to break the back of the fledgling government with a theocratic dictatorship. *Maybe,* Stasio thought to himself, *I should have spent more time learning to fire my rifle.*

But he didn't know — couldn't have known — that his ideas about intelligence-supported warfare were about to be tested on a massive scale. US forces were going to attack their enemy in a way they'd never attempted. And Stasio would be on the frontlines.

Mike McConnell had one hour to sell a war.

In May 2007, as Lieutenant Stasio was taking in the parlous situation on the ground in Iraq, the newly appointed director of national intelligence sat down in the Oval Office with President Bush and some of the top members of his National Security Council. In addition to the president, McConnell faced Vice President Dick Cheney, Defense Secretary Robert Gates, Treasury Secretary Henry Paulson, and the president's national security adviser, Stephen Hadley. Rarely did this much political firepower gather in one room. But for the plan McConnell had in mind, their presence was required.

The last of the five additional brigades Bush had sent to combat the insurgency in Iraq was deploying that month to an area southeast of Baghdad. There were now thirty thousand additional troops on the ground. McConnell wanted to give them a new weapon. He told the president about particular capabilities the National Security Agency had developed that would allow a team of highly skilled computer hackers to penetrate the communications systems the Iraqi insurgents were using to coordinate their attacks and plan roadside bombings. Once inside those communications networks, the American hackers would use powerful software to spy on the enemy and obtain vital intelligence, such as who was leading a particular cell and where they intended to strike. This information could help forces on the ground target their enemies, tracking their location and, hopefully, interceding before they could set off a bomb or mount an ambush.

But the hackers could also manipulate the insurgents, controlling their cell phones, sending misleading text messages or fake calls that would appear to come from fellow fighters. They could wave insurgents off targets or even direct them into the sights of awaiting US forces. Once inside the insurgents' computers, they might be able to find out who was uploading gruesome videos of beheadings, which had become a cheap and effective way of attracting followers and terrifying the Iraqi public. The American hackers would implant spyware on the enemies' computers and copy any e-mail addresses and cell phone numbers being used by other fighters. They could track every word their enemy typed, every website visited, every e-mail sent. And they could capture all the passwords the enemy used for logging in to web forums where fighters planned attacks.

McConnell was proposing to subvert the insurgents from the inside, using their own resources against them. In principle, it may have sounded like straightforward espionage, hardly the kind of operation that needed the president's personal authorization. But this mission would rely on hacking techniques and tools, including malicious computer viruses, that were considered some of the most innovative and unpredictable weapons in the American arsenal. Once a piece of malicious software, or malware, was unleashed against a computer, there was always a risk that it wouldn't stay on that machine. Worms are self-replicating programs designed to burrow into other machines to which their hosts are connected. And viruses, as their name implies, could spread rapidly from host to host. In the months leading up to the 2003 invasion, military leaders had called off a planned cyber strike on Iraq's banking system for fear the malware might migrate from Iraqi computer networks to those used by banks in France. Owing to the interconnected architecture of the Internet, the two countries' financial systems were linked. American officials imagined front-page news stories of cash machines shutting down across France, the result of errant US strikes.

The risk of collateral damage from cyber weapons was great. And under McConnell's plan, the NSA would have to infect not just insurgents' phones and computers with malware but potentially many other innocent Iraqis' devices, too. The plan called for providing total awareness of the battlefield, and that meant distributing spyware widely, and capturing as many Iraqi communications as possible, to see with whom the terrorists and insurgents were communicating. Because the malware had to be distributed so widely, there was even a chance it could come back to infect their own forces.

Though they were not lethal in the sense that traditional weapons were, cyber weapons could be very dangerous and disruptive far beyond the intended target. In this way they had a lot in common with nuclear weapons. And like nukes, cyber weapons required presidential "release authority" before they could be used. That's what McConnell had hoped to get in his hourlong meeting with Bush and the top members of his national security team. It was a momentous request, and a politically sensitive one. Only eighteen months earlier, in December 2005, the agency had been pilloried for monitoring the communications of Americans inside the United States without a court's permission. Now the NSA would be breaking in to communications networks and gathering information not just on insurgents but on tens of millions of innocent people as well. Some of these networks were privately owned, and the NSA wouldn't be asking the companies for permission to siphon their data. Now the agency would be spying on an entire country and unleashing cyber weapons against it. The president had to sign off.

McConnell knew that Bush was not technically savvy; this was the man who'd once said he used "the Google" on occasion, mostly to look at satellite pictures of his ranch in Texas. Not that Bush's predecessor was a technophile. Bill Clinton sent only two e-mails during his eight years in office, a period that witnessed the birth of the contemporary Internet and a telecommunications revolution.

But McConnell knew that he had the trust of the most important people in the room. Six months earlier, Cheney had called McConnell in his personal office at the government contractor Booz Allen Hamilton to say that he and the president wanted McConnell to take the intelligence director job, a position that had been established only two years earlier, paid a fraction of McConnell's seven-figure salary, and was still ill defined and lacked bureaucratic muscle. And it was Gates, McConnell's longtime friend and bureaucratic ally, whom McConnell had called first for advice, and who pledged his personal and political backing for whatever decisions the would-be spymaster made. McConnell also had an important ally in General Keith Alexander, current director of the NSA. It would fall to Alexander to execute the plan in Iraq.

Alexander relished the opportunity. He was building an intelligence empire at the NSA, the country's largest spy agency, with 35,000 employees working at sites across the United States and in allied countries around the world. Alexander had amassed an unrivaled set of intelligence-gathering authorities and astonishing technical capabilities to spy on phone calls, text messages, e-mail, and Internet traffic on the world's communications networks. The NSA was the single largest contributor of intelligence to the president's daily briefing about national security threats, which gave it tremendous political clout. It was also the only agency coming up with reliable and consistent leads on the whereabouts of wanted terrorists. The CIA, by contrast, had practically no human sources capable of providing information from the inner circles of al-Qaeda. The war on terror was driven mostly by surveillance. The Iraq operation was a chance for the NSA to show the power of cyber warfare, which was inextricably linked to surveillance. To manipulate or disable a computer or a phone, one had to locate it on the network and then get inside it. Alexander had spent his two years in office building up his spying forces. Now they'd finally be unleashed for war.

Bush was a quick study. Despite his own lack of familiarity with technology, he seemed to immediately grasp the relationships between computers and people, how surveillance would help manipulate not just machines but the humans using them — and how it could be used to track and capture or kill someone. The president had already okayed a separate, covert effort to infect the computer systems that regulated an Iranian nuclear plant with a worm that would cause its enrichment centrifuges to break down. Faced with few viable options for halting Iran's progress in building a nuclear bomb, Bush's intelligence advisers and some of his top generals had offered up an idea. Why not disrupt Iran's ability to enrich uranium — the key ingredient of a weapon — by sabotaging the mechanical process? They suggested a target: the enrichment facility at Natanz. And they proposed a weapon: a complex computer program that would commandeer the electronic equipment regulating the facility's thousands of centrifuges, the tall, tubular machines that spin gaseous uranium at incredibly high speeds and turn it into weapons-grade material. Centrifuges were the heart of Iran's nuclear program. Without them, the country couldn't enrich nuclear material to put into a bomb or a warhead.

Bush approved the mission, and the United States' top hackers and security experts set out to create a first-of-its-kind cyber weapon. It would come to be known by a single name, a combination of words contained in its thousands of lines of code — Stuxnet. But the operation, which began in earnest later that year, was designed for stealth, not total destruction. The Americans, working with Israel, wanted to slowly degrade and frustrate Iran's ability to build a bomb, all the while giving no hint that a cyber weapon was the cause. Stuxnet was designed to close valves that regulated the flow of gas inside the centrifuges. The more pressure was increased, the closer the centrifuge was brought to its breaking point. Such a tiny failure could be attributed to any number of causes, including faulty equipment or the ineptitude of engineers and workers at the plant who could be blamed for improperly installing and operating the centrifuges. The computer systems that regulated the centrifuges sat behind an "air gap," meaning they weren't physically connected to the outside Internet, so a human spy or some other remote means of insertion would have to be employed to deliver Stuxnet inside the plant. This was to be a quiet and delicate operation.

What McConnell was proposing now in Iraq was something very different. It would involve the widespread use of viruses, spyware, and hacking techniques. And its purpose was to kill people, not stymie mechanical processes. Stuxnet was an act of sabotage. This was an act of war.

Bush was also growing to trust McConnell implicitly, asking him to deliver the daily briefing in the Oval Office every morning, a task that previous spymasters had relegated to subordinates. The two had hit it off when they met at Bush's ranch shortly before the president announced McConnell's nomination, in January. The ex-spy and re-tired navy admiral found the president's down-home demeanor both affable and familiar. McConnell had grown up in South Carolina, and he never shed his aw-shucks charm. Sitting on Bush's porch, the two men watched a thunderstorm gathering in the distance. Not a good omen, they said, laughing.

Now McConnell had asked for an hour of the president's time to make the case for cyber war in Iraq. Bush gave the green light after only fifteen minutes.

Stasio arrived in Iraq at Forward Operating Base Taji, a flat, dusty expanse in a rural area north of Baghdad that once served as a Re-publican Guard base and a chemical weapons production facility. Taji was nestled in the violent Sunni Triangle, the epicenter of resistance to US forces. The base and its troops were hit with mortars and impro-vised explosive devices, or IEDs, about 150 times a day. Every time the troops went on patrol, a thatch of fighters or a roadside bomb awaited them. And Taji was not unique. Across Iraq the violence was reaching a zenith. The prior year had been one of the bloodiest yet for coalition forces, with almost 900 killed, and 2007 was on track to break the record. The month Stasio arrived saw the most fatalities since January 2005. Nearly all the dead were Americans. Iraqi civilian deaths, which were more difficult to track, were also at all-time highs, by one reliable estimate approaching 30,000 per year from 2006 to 2007, more than double what they'd been at the start of the war.

The new surge troops were to secure Baghdad and the most violent surrounding areas, freeing up additional forces to go after the insur-gent fighters and protect the civilian population. General David Pe-traeus, the man whom Bush had tapped to implement the last-ditch effort, envisioned a two-prong plan of attack: forge alliances with those fighters who could be persuaded to help the Americans, or at least lay down their arms, and capture or kill the rest. Petraeus called that latter group "the irreconcilables."

The surge was slow-going and confusing at first. Stasio's bosses at Taji seemed not to know what to do with this sudden rush of new soldiers. But Stasio and a fellow analyst from Fort Lewis reverted to their training. They set up shop in an old munitions warehouse and got in touch with the units they'd replaced, who had already gone back home and were working in the intelligence center at Fort Lewis. They became one of his "reachback" points. Stasio connected to them via a secure computer network, and then he plugged in to the national intelligence databases, which were now swimming in new data. The massive surveillance dragnet being placed over Iraq was producing new signals, new leads. Finally, he could emulate Lester from *The Wire*.

Stasio began by building network diagrams of the fighters in the area, using their cell phone signals to connect members to one another and help determine their location. He fed those reports back to Fort Lewis, then pulled more data from the national sets. At the same time, the team in Fort Lewis would go to work on big-picture reports. What was the tribal makeup of the region in which Taji was situated? Who was loyal to whom? Where could the US forces exert some leverage and try to break alliances, turn one group against another, or persuade others to come over to their side?

The Iraqi cell phone network was a potential intelligence gold mine. Cell phone contracts were among the first business deals struck in Iraq after Saddam Hussein was driven from power. Wireless was cheaper than wired communications, and cell phones were proliferating. By September 2004, only eighteen months into the US occupation, the NSA had developed a secret technique that US special operations forces called "the find," which allowed them to locate a cell phone even when it was switched off. Members of one special operations unit estimated years later that they found thousands of new targets this way, including members of al-Qaeda's branch in Iraq.

The NSA had access to foreign telecommunications networks through agreements struck with the United States–based carriers that operated them. These companies were paid handsomely—each receiving tens of millions of dollars annually, according to one former company executive—to give the spy agencies privileged access to their networks and the data coursing through them. Some of the carriers were partially owned by foreign investors. In exchange for the federal government granting the company a license to operate in the United States, they had to sign a contract that guaranteed US intelligence agencies uninterrupted access to the networks, so that phone calls could be logged and recorded. One agreement, with Level 3 Communications, even included a "kill switch" provision, stating that if ever directed by the US government, the company must be able to immediately sever all communications traveling through its undersea cables into the United States. This was a protective measure, meant to block the network from delivering malicious software or traffic in the event of a cyber attack.

In some cases a foreign communication could be intercepted from inside the United States. (In fact, this kind of capture was routine for e-mail traffic, much of which flowed through United States–based cables and routers.) When the NSA didn't have permission to tap a line, it simply stole the communications. In a revealing article for a trade magazine in 2005, an ex-marine turned intelligence agency contractor noted that cell phones and wireless technology were the means by which hundreds of millions of people around the world were accessing the Internet. "This trend presents an unprecedented exploitation opportunity for allied forces with the means to collect packets moving through the airwaves," he wrote. "Western intelligence assets have the capability to monitor these services by setting up rogue access points and conducting targeted war-driving collections and site survey analyses. Wireless collections provide the unique opportunity of conducting operations without host nation cooperation."

Translation: wireless communications networks were a spy's dream. And the dream was coming true in Iraq.

Stasio knew nothing of the fateful meeting in the Oval Office or President Bush's decision. But he would soon see its fruits. With access to the telecommunications networks running in and out of Iraq, the NSA began scooping up and storing every phone call, text message, and e-mail sent in and out of the country. It was a key pillar of the new strategy: collect all the data, then use it to map out the networks of terrorists and insurgents.

The enemies' phones also became tracking devices. Signals emitted by the cell phone itself could be plotted on a map. Few places in Iraq needed this kind of precise, tactical intelligence more than Taji, the base where Stasio had been assigned. A key supply road, known as Route Tampa, ran through the base and north toward Balad in the Sunni Triangle. Tampa was the most important artery for delivering cargo and fuel to US forces, and it was a prime target for insurgents. American soldiers nicknamed it IED Alley.

Stasio drew maps of Route Tampa, dividing it into sections based on reports of insurgent activity. He drew network diagrams that, combined with reports from human spies or US troop patrols, showed where in the area IED cells were most active. He could flag certain zones as especially risky and try to predict where, based on previous attacks, the insurgents were likely to go next. He cross-referenced the bombings based on the type of device used. Did it employ a timer, or was it set off by a nearby attacker using a remote trigger? If the latter, the attacker was likely to be in the area after his device went off. Stasio kept track of what type of artillery rounds were used in some IEDs, in hopes that he could trace the source of the bomb makers' materiel.

Stasio systematically mapped out the bomber networks. And then other soldiers systematically destroyed them. Armed with the new tactical intelligence, American patrols would take down entire bombing networks in one night. They targeted not just the top man in the cell, but his designated number two, and then the third and fourth man in the order of succession. Three platoons were assigned to focus on IED networks using the intelligence that Stasio and his colleagues were providing. The Raiders were now in the man-hunting business.

Stasio and his team were also able to trace the funding sources of their enemies and discover tribal chiefs who were aiding the attackers. (Other former officials said that money also came from corrupt Iraqi officials.) Over the next fifteen months they took 450 insurgents off the battlefield. They only had to kill two, who shot back. The rest were taken prisoner and interrogated. The information they provided was shared with intelligence officers across the country. By the time Stasio was ordered to leave Taji for a new mission, IED attacks in the area had decreased by 90 percent. Route Tampa was safe.

A sudden and dramatic success like that could not go unnoticed for long. David Petraeus, the top US commander in Iraq, visited Taji and told the brigade they were needed farther north in Baquba, at Forward Operating Base Warhorse, in the restive Diyala Province. They arrived in October 2007. Baquba was a midsize, ethnically diverse city. Stasio, who a month earlier had been promoted to captain, knew it had been the scene of fierce fighting in close, urban quarters. Tracking insurgents and terrorists hiding among civilians posed a much tougher challenge than finding bomb makers along a single stretch of road.

But the new intelligence machine was built for just this type of work. And in Baquba it went into overdrive.

Stasio and his team went from taking out cells of fighters to taking out entire networks of them. They found the man responsible for building many of the suicide vests that terrorists used, tracking him down to his workshop. When the troops kicked open the door, they found a woman being fitted with her lethal garment. The bomb maker and the would-be bomber were arrested.

The team uncovered a cache of several thousand explosively formed projectiles, the largest they'd ever seen in Iraq. EFPs were designed to be fired at a distance and to penetrate the armored vehicles — the ones that soldiers drove to protect them from traditional roadside bombs. The EFPs were hidden in a compartment under an unassuming-looking house. Stasio and his analysts discovered that a foreign national was training people in Iraq to make the deadly projectiles. He too was arrested.

Stasio was just a young officer. But in his new role as an analyst, he had to understand where the bombs were, who was making them, and who was financing the production. Every time his boss went into a meeting with a sheikh or local leader, Stasio had to brief him on the political backstory, the complexities of the interlocking and sometimes interchangeable alliances that US sources hoped to exploit in their effort to win more "hearts and minds" among Iraqis.

Never in war, as far as he knew, had such a low-ranking officer been required to know so much tactical and strategic information, to understand not just the battlefield on which he fought but the geopolitical realities of the war. Usually that kind of analysis was done by a guy with stars on his shoulders.

His fellow officers kidded him: "Bob, did you brief the president today?"

He took it as a compliment.

Stasio was just one member of a vast hacking enterprise, the vanguard of a new cyber war. After Bush gave his order, daily strikes in Iraq were being carried about by a hybrid military and intelligence unit that brought together soldiers and spies. Their center of operations was a concrete hangar at the Balad Air Base, north of Baghdad, which had once housed Iraqi fighter jets. Most of the planes here now were unmanned drones. Their pilots worked alongside NSA hackers, FBI cyber forensics investigators, and special operations forces — the military's elite commando squads. They all broke off into clusters, working with a seamless, almost organic precision. The hackers stole information from the enemy's electronic devices and passed it to the analysts, who drew up target lists for the troops. As they went off on raids, the drone pilots watched overhead, giving eye-in-the-sky warning to the troops on the ground, thanks to sophisticated cameras and other sensors developed by the CIA. Sometimes the drone pilots themselves made the kill with a missile shot.

When an attack was finished, the troops gathered more intelligence from the site or from the fighters they captured — cell phones, laptop computers, thumb drives, address books, scraps of paper called "pocket litter" that might contain nothing more than a name, a phone number, or a physical or e-mail address. The troops brought the information back to the base and gave it to the analysts, who fed it into their databases and used data-mining software to look for connections to other fighters either in custody or at large. They paid close attention to how the fighters were getting money for their operations, including sources outside Iraq — in Syria, Iran, and Saudi Arabia.

Every day the unit netted between ten and twenty fighters. Whole terrorist networks were illuminated in this way, by US forces who were starting to think and act like their enemy. They structured themselves not in vertical hierarchies but in networks, each member responding to conditions on the ground. They were making it up as they went along, and creating a new kind of warfare.

The NSA had already built the infrastructure to tap into communications networks. After the 9/11 attacks, the agency set up new listening posts and collection points to monitor cyberspace for terrorist phone calls, e-mails, and other digital communications. Many of these new access points were inside the offices and switching stations of the United States' major telecom network carriers. Analysts tracking a particular insurgent's cell phone could see when it was logged on to the network. The analysts relayed that information to troops on the ground, who intercepted the wireless signal. (Aircraft and satellites were also used to grab the signal if ground forces weren't close by.) All that data was quickly collated to locate the target, down to the exact street, building, and even apartment from which he was calling or texting.

To the casual visitor at the intelligence fusion center in Balad, it might seem to house an unlikely crew. Contract analysts sporting nonregulation ponytails worked alongside squared-away soldiers and officers dressed in combat fatigues. But if he looked up at the huge computer screens suspended from the ceiling of the hangar, which were streaming surveillance video from drones, and then glanced down to the civilian-military teams pecking away at laptops and speaking to one another in a shorthand apparently all their own, he would realize he was standing inside a war room.

There was another pillar to the new intelligence strategy. In addition to collecting all electronic communications in Iraq, and using it to pinpoint the location of fighters and financiers, the NSA began to manipulate the methods of communications themselves — the insurgents' phones and computers — just the scenario Mike McConnell had described to President Bush.

The US hackers sent fake text messages to insurgent fighters and roadside bombers. The messages would tell the recipient, in effect,

"Meet at this street corner to plan the next attack," or "Go to this point on a road and plant your device." When the fighter got there, he'd be greeted by US troops, or perhaps the business end of a Hellfire missile fired from a drone aircraft thousands of feet above.

The hackers and analysts at the NSA, working with forces on the ground in Iraq, infiltrated al-Qaeda's network of websites and servers, which the Americans called Obelisk. This was effectively al-Qaeda's corporate intranet. The terrorists published propaganda videos to Obelisk, as well as marching orders and plans for waging holy war. They even posted mundane administrative materials, including expense accounts and personnel memos. Obelisk was the insurgency's command-and-control system. And once inside, NSA hackers implanted malicious software in jihadi forums, tricking readers into clicking on links that installed spyware on their computers. Obelisk gave the spies access to al-Qaeda's secrets, and the means to infiltrate its ranks.

In September 2007 a US raid in the Iraqi village of Sinjar, ten miles from the Syrian border, turned up a massive intelligence cache, including al-Qaeda operatives' names, e-mail addresses, and phone numbers, as well as the web addresses and passwords for secret al-Qaeda chatrooms. This cache became an essential component of the intelligence efforts to track down fighters and capture or kill them. Once inside the chatrooms, analysts could see the rhetoric and images al-Qaeda was using to recruit new fighters. Armed with that insight, they developed counterpropaganda. They sprinkled messages throughout different conversation threads, questioning whether al-Qaeda was violating the tenets of Islam by killing other Muslims.

US spies also began to target individual propagandists. Gruesome videos of fighters beheading their captives — sometimes American contractors working in Iraq — had become a powerful recruitment tool. Videos of roadside bombs ripping into US armored vehicles were set to jihadi anthems. The American hackers could have blocked the propagandists' access to the Internet. But that wouldn't put them out of business permanently. Instead, they located the computers uploading the videos by their unique Internet address. Then special forces were sent out to capture or kill the video maker.

This was an exceptionally difficult task — much more so than locating a fighter via his local cell phone signal. The Internet offered a cloak of anonymity. Anyone could set up an e-mail address with a fake name using Google or Hotmail, which had millions of customers and kept their data in repositories located around the world. Those people were hard enough to find. But more sophisticated adversaries knew how to route their traffic through servers or computers in different countries, making it nearly impossible for them to be tracked to their actual physical location.

In the years before the surge, the NSA had been intensely focused on building and buying software that could locate people based on their Internet addresses. At the time, the agency was interested not so much in finding insurgents as in finding hackers who stole classified information from government and corporate computers and threatened to disable critical facilities, such as power plants and financial systems. By the time the surge began, the agency had sharpened its techniques for finding people in the haze of cyberspace. So-called network forensics tools could help peel away layers of anonymity and unmask an adversary. But human analysts had to apply some old-fashioned investigative work as well. The NSA began studying the telltale techniques that certain hackers used — what malware they favored, what publicly available toolkits they used to break in to systems. The NSA bought forensics software from Computer Associates, an established technology company based in New York, as well as a new entrant into the market called NetWitness, which had set up shop not in the tech corridors of Silicon Valley but in Reston, Virginia, to be near the Pentagon and US intelligence agencies just down the road in suburban Washington, DC. The spy agency took these and other software, some of which engineers devised in-house, and devoted years of energy to solving the so-called attribution problem so they could positively locate someone in the real world based on his Internet activity. The NSA sleuths honed those techniques in Iraq. And in the years to come they would deploy them in a global hunt for hackers.

The cyber warriors in Iraq also turned their focus to new networks being set up in the country. Insurgents gravitated to Internet cafes that sprouted up after the fall of Saddam Hussein, whose regime had tightly restricted access to foreign media. Cyber warriors with the air force penetrated Internet cafe computers and watched what the insurgents were posting and with whom they were communicating. Going to the cafes made the insurgents vulnerable because they had to come into the open to use them, and the computers were not under their constant control and supervision. Every time they logged on to a public machine, they risked being tracked.

The NSA also developed a tool called Polarbreeze for tapping wirelessly into nearby computers. An American intelligence officer or agent would sit in the cafe, pretending to check e-mail or talk on the phone or send a text message, when really using a kind of remote data-sucking device, aimed at computers in the room only a few feet away.

Sometimes it was easier to shut down a web server than try to track someone through it. On several occasions US hackers disabled the infrastructure that fighters were using to send e-mail and Internet-based communications, forcing them onto the phone network, where they could be more easily tracked.

As the operations picked up pace and began to pay dividends, the NSA called in its most skilled cyber warriors. They worked in a unit called Tailored Access Operations, or TAO. As their name implies, they devised bespoke tools and techniques for breaking in to computers. The stealthiest of all US hackers, they were also the rarest — only a few hundred worked for TAO, and many of them had undergone years of NSA-devised training, sometimes through colleges and universities where the spy agency had helped write the curriculum.

In one successful operation, the TAO hackers set their sights on the Islamic State of Iraq, an insurgent group that had formed in 2004, pledged allegiance to al-Qaeda, and then fallen under its banner. The group fought US soldiers, but it also terrorized and murdered civilians. In 2007 alone this al-Qaeda branch killed two thousand Iraqis and seized control of the Dora neighborhood in southern Baghdad, where it tried to install Islamic law and set up a new "emirate" to govern the people. Local Christians who had lived in Dora for decades fled their homes rather than live under such harsh religious rule. A member of the new emirate knocked on the door of one Christian man and told him that if he wanted to stay, he could pay a tax or convert to Islam. Otherwise, he must abandon his house; the al-Qaeda members offered to help remove his furniture.

TAO hackers zeroed in on the leaders of the al-Qaeda group. Centering their operations in Baghdad, they scooped up e-mail messages that the terrorists had left in draft form in their personal accounts, where they could be picked up by fellow fighters without having to be sent over the Internet. This was a common trick terrorists used to avoid detection. TAO had been on to it for years.

The TAO hackers joined forces with troops on the ground as part of a major offensive, Operation Arrowhead Ripper, that aimed to rout the al-Qaeda branch from neighborhoods in Bequeath, where it had established a foothold. The operation began in June 2007 and included about ten thousand soldiers, the bulk of them from Forward Operating Base Warhorse. The offensive included an Iraqi army brigade and about five hundred police officers. Operations began with a ground and air strike on Baquba. United States–led forces killed nearly two dozen fighters on the first day. Meanwhile, in Anbar Province, troops rounded up six terrorists suspected of being tied to senior al-Qaeda officials. And they apprehended three would-be roadside bombers in Fallujah, as well as three more suspected terrorists in the town of Tarmiyah.

US intelligence had gotten very good at locating these fighters, linking them to al-Qaeda, and understanding how the terrorist group was recruiting and carrying out its attacks.

For TAO, hacking into the communications network of the senior al-Qaeda leaders in Iraq helped break the terrorist group's hold on the neighborhoods around Baghdad. By one account, it aided US troops in capturing or killing at least ten of those senior leaders from the battlefield. When Arrowhead Ripper concluded in mid-August, Baquba had been reclaimed, and most insurgent activity in the area had ceased. By November, al-Qaeda had left the Dora neighborhood.

The intelligence machine continued to win victories. There were 28 bombings and other attacks by al-Qaeda in Iraq reported in the first six months of 2008, down from 300 such attacks in the previous year. And the number of civilian casualties attributed to the terror group plummeted, from 1,500 in 2007 to 125 in the first half of 2008. A former military intelligence officer likened the cyber assault on the top echelons of al-Qaeda to "cutting the head off a snake."

"We took operations to get inside the communications systems and the command-and-control structure that allowed terrorists and insurgents to coordinate attacks against US forces," he said. "That's the key to *any* successful operation."

For the first time in the now four-year-old Iraq War, the United States could point to a strategy that was actually working. The overall success of the surge, which finally allowed US forces to leave Iraq, has been attributed to three major factors by historians and the commanders and soldiers who served there. First, the additional troops on the ground helped to secure the most violent neighborhoods, kill or capture the "irreconcilables," as Petraeus called them, and protect Iraq's civilians. The cities became less violent, and the people felt safer and more inclined to help the US occupation. Second, insurgent groups who were outraged by al-Qaeda's brutal, heavy-handed tactics and the imposition of religious law turned against the terrorists, or were paid by US forces to switch their allegiances and fight with the Americans. This so-called Sunni Awakening included eighty thousand fighters, whose leaders publicly denounced al-Qaeda and credited the US military with trying to improve the lives of Iraqi citizens.

But the third and arguably the most pivotal element of the surge was the series of intelligence operations undertaken by the NSA and soldiers such as Stasio, authorized by Bush in that fateful Oval Office meeting. Former intelligence analysts, military officers, and senior Bush administration officials say that the cyber operations the president authorized opened the door to a new way of obtaining intelligence, and then integrating it into combat operations on the ground. The information about enemy movements and plans that US spies swiped from computers and phones gave troops a road map to find the fighters, sometimes leading right to their doorsteps. This was the most sophisticated global tracking system ever devised, and it worked with lethal efficiency.

Petraeus credited this new cyber warfare "with being a prime reason for the significant progress made by US troops" in the surge, which lasted into the summer of 2008, "directly enabling the removal of almost 4,000 insurgents from the battlefield." The tide of the war in Iraq finally turned in the United States' favor. The intelligence operations, which were later exported to Afghanistan, "saved US and allied lives by helping to identify and neutralize extremist threats across the breadth of both battlefields." Later the NSA integrated the techniques it had developed on the battlefield into its other intelligence operations used to track terrorists, spies, and hackers around the world. That alliance between the spy agency and the military, forged in Iraq, would forever change the way America fights wars.

TWO

RTRG

THE 2007 SURGE marked the first time US military and intelligence agencies tested the theories of cyber war on the battlefield. But the lethally efficient system they set up in Iraq was born of an earlier battle, and one of the darkest periods in the NSA's history.

On September 11, 2001, Lieutenant General Michael Hayden, then NSA director, had been at work for two hours when he got a call telling him that a plane had crashed into one of the Twin Towers in New York. A few minutes later a second plane hit. Hayden called his wife, Jeanine, asked her to track down their three children, and then prepared for a lockdown of the agency's 350-acre campus at Fort Meade, Maryland, about twenty-five miles outside downtown Washington.

Hayden ordered all nonessential personnel to evacuate. Guards carrying machine guns and directing bomb-sniffing dogs fanned out. Near the top floor of a high-rise, workers in the agency's counterterrorist center started tacking blackout curtains to their windows. The NSA's headquarters had moved from Washington to its present location in 1957, because the fort was far enough outside the city to survive the blast of a nuclear explosion. No one had imagined that terrorists might attack it with commercial airliners.

Hayden went first to the counterterrorist center, where he found employees in tears. It was clear to everyone that the NSA had missed some very important signals in the terrorist "chatter" that its vast network of global data interceptors was so good at snatching up. The agency had electronic ears on its targets, but it failed to understand their true intentions. Investigators would later discover that on September 10, 2001, the NSA had intercepted a phone conversation from a known terrorist, warning in Arabic that "tomorrow is zero hour." It sat in the agency's databases, untranslated into English, until September 12.

Hayden's immediate concern was stopping any follow-up attacks. On September 14 he approved "targeting," or electronic monitoring, of communication links between the United States and foreign countries where terrorists were known to be operating — principally Afghanistan, where al-Qaeda had a sanctuary, thanks to the theocratic Taliban regime. The NSA was to look for telephone numbers associated with terrorists. In practice, that meant that any telephone number in Afghanistan that contacted a number in the United States was presumed to have foreign intelligence value, and therefore could be monitored. But when it came to spying on numbers in the United States, Hayden was more circumspect. Only preapproved telephone numbers were allowed to be monitored on communications links that originated inside the United States. Hayden knew that the NSA was prohibited from spying inside the country. But, as he later recalled, he made a "tactical decision" to use his existing authority to monitor foreign intelligence, albeit more aggressively than before. Hayden reasoned that so long as one end of the communication was outside the United States and involved foreign terrorist groups, it was fair game. The nation was in crisis, and at the time no one would have begrudged him a more expansive view of his agency's mandate. The NSA's general counsel determined that Hayden's orders were legal.

But almost as soon as the NSA started spying on new targets, Hayden and his staff discovered what they thought were significant limitations on the agency's ability to cast a wider surveillance net and ensure it was doing all it could to prevent another attack. The White House wanted to know what more the NSA could do. So, Hayden asked his senior managers and the NSA's signals intelligence experts, what would they put on their wish list?

For starters, they said, there was a huge so-called international gap. The NSA was monitoring foreign threats. The FBI handled domestic ones. But no agency was following the foreign threats as they came into the United States. In part that was to prevent US intelligence agencies from spying on Americans. But that sensible prohibition, enshrined in more than two decades of law and regulation, now seemed like a suicide pact.

The NSA also wanted to tweak the existing rules so they could intercept communications that transited the United States as they traveled from one foreign country to another. Under current law, if the agency wanted to capture a foreign terrorist's e-mail, it might have to get a warrant if that e-mail was stored on a server located in the United States. This was obviously foreign intelligence, it just happened to move over a fiber-optic cable or end up in a corporate database on US soil. NSA staffers argued that the agency should be allowed to grab that without asking for permission from a court, just as it could legally do if the message were stored on a server in a foreign country.

But the NSA also wanted to analyze more domestic communications. The staff proposed an idea first conceived in 1999, in preparation for the threat of terrorist attacks during millennium celebrations. The agency wanted to conduct "contact chaining" on US phone numbers. This was a painstaking process of figuring out who someone had called, who those people had called, who *they* had called, and so on, all based on analyzing phone records. The NSA wouldn't see the names associated with those phone numbers, but they believed the contact chain would help identify people of interest in a possible terrorist network. The Justice Department had ruled at the time that even monitoring this so-called metadata required a warrant, because the data was associated with people presumed to be Americans or legal residents. Now the NSA wanted to start contact chaining on phone numbers in the United States to see who was in contact with terrorists — whether they were abroad or already here. Hayden himself pointed out to administration officials that metadata wasn't considered "content" under

US law, and therefore wasn't subject to the Fourth Amendment's prohibition on warrantless surveillance. Indeed, the US Supreme Court had ruled in 1979 that the government didn't need a warrant to capture a phone number, because a person voluntarily gave up the privacy of that information the moment he dialed the number and it was recorded by the phone company.

For all the items on the wish list, the NSA believed that current surveillance law was insufficient because it hadn't kept up with technological change. When the legislation governing intelligence operations against Americans, the Foreign Intelligence Surveillance Act, was signed into law in 1978, there was no data-mining software to allow contact chaining. There was no global communications network using US soil as a transit point. And there was no threat of international terrorism inside the United States. Now the obvious next move for the administration was asking Congress to change the law, to allow the NSA to do many of the things that Hayden and his staff were certain needed to be done.

President Bush's advisers, however, were in no mood to seek Congress's permission for intelligence activities that they believed were within his discretion. Vice President Cheney, in particular, was loath to allow lawmakers to start directing NSA operations against al-Qaeda. The White House was also concerned that a public debate about changes in surveillance law would tip off terrorists to what the NSA was doing to track them.

Cheney took Hayden's list of ideas and, working with the NSA director and other White House staff, came up with a plan to give the agency broad new authorities under executive order. The task of writing up the order itself fell to David Addington, Cheney's legal counsel and his right-hand man in the White House. The NSA would now be allowed to monitor communications inside the United States, so long as one end of that communication was outside the country and the communication was reasonably believed to be associated with terrorism. The NSA would not have to seek permission from a court to monitor individual phone numbers or e-mails, a legal process that historically had taken four to six weeks. Now it could engage in hot pursuit of as many communications as it pleased, so long as they fit within the boundaries of the executive order — and the NSA's computer systems could process them all.

Bush signed the order on October 4, 2001.

The NSA was going to war, and it set to work right away on its new campaign. A twenty-four-hour watch center was set up, called the Metadata Analysis Center, or MAC. It was situated in the Signals Intelligence Directorate, the part of the NSA that steals or intercepts digital communications. A group of experienced NSA analysts and engineers were put on the new team; they all had to sign nondisclosure agreements. They were given office space. And the program was given a code name, or "security compartment": Starburst. A new name, Stellar Wind, would come a few weeks later, on October 31, 2001. The program also got a hefty dose of new hardware: fifty computer servers to store and process all the new data Starburst collected. The agency didn't want a record of it suddenly buying a lot of new equipment. So officials asked a server vendor to divert a shipment intended for another recipient to the NSA instead, and to tell no one. The servers arrived at Fort Meade under police escort on October 13.

Hayden told the new Starburst team members during meetings on October 6 and 7 that the emergency, warrantless collection of communications involving people in the United States was temporary. But that was belied by the program's $25 million budget, a large amount of money to spend on a program that was only supposed to last thirty days.

Nearly ninety NSA employees were cleared for access within the first week of the program's operations. Two staffers in the NSA's Office of General Counsel reviewed the program — after Bush signed the order — and determined that it was legal. The office didn't document its opinions or legal rationale.

By October 7, three days after Bush had signed the order, the MAC was running twenty-four hours a day, seven days a week, crunching metadata sucked up by NSA's electronic filters. Twenty analysts and software developers worked in three shifts. Many of the MAC employees had manually built call chains of Russian intelligence targets during the Cold War. Now this process was being automated and applied to al-Qaeda and its affiliates, its financial and political supporters, and would-be recruits.

The contact chain of an individual target could stretch into the millions of people if an analyst wanted to look at every single person in that target's contact list, along with all *their* contacts. The analysts called each link in the chain a "hop." Following one hop to the next, to see who might be connected to the original target, was reminiscent of the game Six Degrees of Kevin Bacon, in which players try to connect the prolific actor to some other actor who appeared in one of his films or TV shows. Hayden got a briefing from the MAC once a week, and his deputy got one every night, a measure of its supreme importance in the new intelligence war on terrorism.

The MAC had other partners at the NSA and outside the secret confines of Fort Meade. The spy agency set up a counterterrorism "product line" to send specific tasks to the MAC and conduct analysis of what was found in the contact chains. The FBI and the CIA got involved, providing leads to the MAC, which conducted contact chaining inside the United States. Telephone and Internet companies also started sending the NSA content — the recorded words of a phone call or the written text of an e-mail or Internet communication. The task of collecting this data, which was in the hands of corporations, was managed by the NSA's Special Source Operations group, its primary liaison and conduit to the telecommunications companies, Internet service and communications providers, and other companies that moved and stored the information that the NSA wanted. The agency set up equipment at the companies' physical facilities and installed surveillance devices on computers and networks that they controlled. One crucial participant, AT&T, which managed huge swaths of the telecom network, had a secure facility not far from the NSA's Fort Meade headquarters where it had historically provided mostly foreign communications for the intelligence agency. The company also allowed the government to install monitoring equipment at an office in San Francisco as part of the new domestic collection regime.

The companies were not powerless to resist — one major firm, Qwest Communications, rebuffed the agency's requests for telephone metadata because the government lacked a warrant. But most companies complied with the administration's requests, owing largely to assurances that the president had authorized the collection, which, officials argued, made it legal. The companies became indispensable partners in a new global surveillance system. Only a handful of executives within each firm even knew that the NSA had spy portals inside their facilities. Corporate employees were cleared into the program on a strictly need-to-know basis, meant to limit the risk of exposure of the NSA's clandestine mission. NSA employees were handpicked to work on the program. The product line grew rapidly. Thirty days after Bush had signed the emergency order, the new surveillance program was fully up and running. The military-Internet complex was born.

As significant as the NSA's new authorities to listen in on phone calls and read e-mails were, it was the bulk collection of phone and Internet metadata that put the most power in Stellar Wind's sails. A human analyst would never have enough time to listen to all those calls and read so many messages, and presumably the terrorists would mostly be communicating in code and not explicitly stating where they planned to attack and when. But contact chaining could illuminate the network based on how targets were connected to one another.

Metadata was pouring into the agency's computers and databases, faster than it could be analyzed in real time. Eventually, the agency would start to run out of storage space to keep its intelligence haul and electricity to power the computers that churned the information into intelligible graphs. And *intelligible* was a debatable term. NSA analysts created bigger contact chains than ever before. They fed the metadata into a massive graphing system that displayed connections as a bewildering array of hundreds of overlapping lines. Analysts called it the BAG, for "big ass graph."

The FBI and the CIA also used the metadata NSA obtained. These agencies either sent the NSA a specific request for information about a particular phone number or e-mail address — what the NSA called a "selector" — or they asked more broadly for information about a target's contacts. These were known internally at the NSA as "leads." The FBI and the CIA could submit leads in order to discover more leads, and then investigate those people. The NSA sent back reports, known as "tippers," which contained the contact-chaining analysis that related to terrorism or potential terrorist links.

The intelligence cycle didn't always run smoothly. FBI agents complained that many of the leads the NSA supplied were dead ends — particularly the telephone numbers of suspected terrorists whom the agency believed were in the United States or had contacts there. But this team spying was a primitive model for the fusion center that was set up in Iraq six years later. Contact chaining was also the same method of analysis that the soldier-spy team at Balad used to hunt down Iraqi insurgents and terrorists. The system was even used on targets in Iraq before the first US boots hit the ground. In 2003, prior to the United States–led invasion, Bush authorized the NSA to spy on members of the Iraqi Intelligence Service whom the CIA had determined were engaged in terrorist activity that threatened the United States. (The same claim was later used to help publicly justify the United States' case for war, along with the CIA's conclusion that Iraq had been manufacturing and stockpiling chemical weapons. Both claims were later proven false. The NSA stopped spying on the Iraqi Intelligence Service under the Stellar Wind program in March 2004.)

As the months passed, NSA's contact chaining became more automated. Analysts developed tools that would send alerts about new people in the chain that they might want to examine. Anyone who had direct contact with an individual already on the NSA's list could be reported to the FBI or the CIA. Usually, the analysts would move out two hops from a target. It was up to them to determine whether the information was reportable — that is, whether the names of people they were finding in their digital nets could be included in intelligence reports and sent around the government. This was a crucial step. If an analyst discovered that an e-mail or a phone number was connected to a US citizen or a legal resident, the law usually demanded that he stop the analysis and obtain a warrant before going any further. If a communication of one of these so-called US persons was referred to even tangentially in an intelligence report, the NSA was supposed to use an anonymous designation: "US Person 1," for instance. This process, called minimization, was meant to keep innocent Americans' names from ending up in covert intelligence reports and being associated with terrorists or spies. It was also meant to prevent the NSA from building dossiers on Americans.

But it wasn't data on Americans that the NSA was most curious about. What Hayden called "the real gold of the program" was the entirely foreign communications that the NSA intercepted as they passed through telecommunications lines and equipment in the United States. The agency could spy on the world without leaving home.

From the start of the program until January 2007, the NSA collected content from 37,664 telephone and Internet selectors, of which 92 percent were foreign, according to a report by the agency's inspector general. This does not account for metadata collection, but as with content, that too was mostly focused on foreign targets. Precisely what portion of the mix was represented by Iraqi communications is unknown. But by the time the 2007 surge began, NSA had put in place the spying infrastructure to collect every piece of electronic data going in and out of the country — every phone call, every text message, every e-mail and social media post. The infrastructure of Stellar Wind, with its pipes and monitoring equipment connected to the switching stations and offices of the United States' biggest telecommunications providers, gave the NSA several entry points into the global network. From there it could scan and copy communications. And it could also launch cyber attacks. The spying paths created by Stellar Wind equipment for electronic eavesdropping were the same ones used to provide access to Iraqi phone and computer networks and implant malware.

Few people have ever known — and it has never been publicly reported — that the key to winning the war in Iraq was a spying program set up to win the war on terror. It was a network of cyber surveillance meant to keep tabs on Americans that allowed US forces to track down Iraqi insurgents.

When this massive intelligence-processing machine was exported to Iraq for the surge, it was given a new name: the Real Time Regional Gateway, or RTRG. In the litany of NSA code words known for their absurd inscrutability — Pinwale, EgotisticalGiraffe, Nevershakeababy — the RTRG stood apart because its name actually described what it did. It produced intelligence reports and found connections among data in real time, that is, as soon as analysts queried the system; it was focused on a geographic region, in this case Iraq; and it *was* a gateway of sorts, a portal through which a user stepped into a virtual space in which all the connections were visible.

General Keith Alexander was the driving force behind the RTRG. The system represented a culmination of his career-long efforts to bring high-level national intelligence directly to "the warfighter" (much like Stasio had envisioned when he first joined the army). The key to the RTRG's success was its ability to fuse all that data coming in from raids, intercepted communications, interrogation reports, drone footage, and surveillance cameras into a single, searchable system. It was like a private Google for the new soldier-spies.

The RTRG had a few fathers. The prototype was designed under a contract to SAIC, a longtime Defense Department contractor. Headquartered in California, the company had such deep and historic ties to the spy business that it was often called NSA-West. An army colonel named Robert Harms, who worked in the Military Intelligence Corps, managed the program at NSA. He would join SAIC after his retirement in 2009.

Also among the developers was one of the most enigmatic spies of the late twentieth century, a retired air force colonel named Pedro "Pete" Rustan. His storied and secretive career gave some insight into how important the RTRG was to intelligence and military leaders such as Alexander and Petraeus, who believed it would be pivotal to the war in Iraq. After the 9/11 attacks Rustan, who had fled communist Cuba as a college student in 1967, left a lucrative career in private business and returned to government service at the National Reconnaissance Office, an agency more secretive than even the NSA, where he led projects to build spy satellites for the military and the CIA. Career intelligence officers who knew Rustan were tight-lipped about what precisely he did, but they described him as one of the true living legends in the spy business, and someone whose work had saved lives. In the 1980s, Rustan designed technology to protect air force jets that were hit by lightning. It worked flawlessly — the service never lost a jet to a lightning strike after it implemented Rustan's design. In the early 1990s, Rustan managed a joint Defense Department and NASA program to build an experimental spacecraft, called *Clementine,* to explore the surface of the moon. It took only twenty-two months to conceive of the satellite and get it to the launch pad, a remarkable feat of engineering and project management that reinforced Rustan's reputation for working brilliantly under tight deadlines.

His work after the 9/11 attacks was closely linked to the new intelligence war. Rustan made frequent trips to the front lines and was known and liked among the clandestine warriors of the Joint Special Operations Command. After a Navy SEAL unit killed Osama bin Laden in Pakistan, they presented Rustan with a flag that flew at their base in Afghanistan. When Rustan died in 2012, Michael Hayden told the *Washington Post,* "This is the kind of guy the public never hears about but who is so responsible for keeping Americans safe."

In a 2010 interview with a trade publication, Rustan said no one agency in government had been looking for "patterns" in intelligence by putting together disparate pieces of data. The RTRG was designed to do that. He explained:

Imagine that you are in Iraq. You have insurgents. They are on the telephone, making phone calls. That signal would be intercepted by ground [antennas], by the aircraft network and by the space network. If you're smart enough to combine all that data in real time, you can determine where Dick is out there. He's in block 23 down there, and he just said he's going to place a bomb. . . . The information from those three devices come[s] into a location where somebody can actually say action is needed, and the tank or the truck or the warfighters [are] right here in this location. He's a colonel, and he can say, "We have verification that this bad guy is in this location: Go and get him."

The RTRG was unique for the way it brought together not only intelligence but people — the top levels of the military brass and the intelligence community, the brightest minds from across government, and the expertise of private industry. It was a rare example of successful collaboration within the byzantine federal bureaucracy.

The NSA got so good at managing big data — huge data, really — by abandoning its traditional approaches. Rather than trying to store all the information in the RTRG in central databases and analyze it with supercomputers, the agency tapped into the emerging power of distributed computing. Silicon Valley entrepreneurs had developed software that broke big data sets into smaller, manageable pieces and farmed each one out to a separate computer. Now the burden of analyzing huge data sets didn't rest on one machine. Working together, the computers could accomplish tasks faster and cheaper than if one central machine took on the workload. This revolution in data management is what allowed Facebook, Twitter, and Google to manage their own data stores, which were growing exponentially by the late 2000s. NSA used the same distributed computing technology for the RTRG. The system was like Google not only on the front end but on the back end as well. In fact, the NSA later developed its own distributed computer software, called Accumulo, based on technology from Google.

But the collection of huge amounts of electronic data by the NSA had proven controversial before. In the spring of 2004 the Justice Department's Office of Legal Counsel reviewed the program and found that one method of collection in particular was illegal under current law. It had to do with the bulk collection of so-called Internet metadata, including information about the sender and recipients of e-mails. The NSA thought since President Bush's order allowed them to search for keywords and other selectors in Internet metadata, it also implicitly authorized the bulk collection of that data. In the view of the agency's lawyers and its director, Michael Hayden, no one had "acquired" the information until it was actually looked at. A computer gathering up the data and storing it didn't count as acquisition under the law, and it certainly didn't meet the agency's definition of "spying."

When the president went ahead and reauthorized the program over the Justice Department's objections, senior officials in the department threatened to resign, including the head of the Office of Legal Counsel, Jack Goldsmith; the director of the FBI, Robert Mueller; and the attorney general, John Ashcroft, along with his deputy, Jim Comey, whom President Obama would later choose for Mueller's replacement as head of the FBI.

The threat of mass resignation was a unique moment in the history of the Bush presidency. Had they stepped down, their reasons would eventually become known through press leaks and congressional inquiries. The American people would have discovered not only the existence of a domestic spying program but that top law enforcement officials had resigned because they thought a part of it was illegal.

But for all the high drama surrounding the Internet metadata collection program, it turned out to be only a momentary hiccup in NSA's insatiable consumption of intelligence. Only seven days after Bush ordered the NSA to stop collecting Internet metadata in bulk, Justice Department officials told the NSA's Office of General Counsel and officials in its Signals Intelligence Directorate to find a new legal basis for restarting the program. This time they were to seek permission from the Foreign Intelligence Surveillance Court — the same body that Bush had bypassed when he authorized warrantless surveillance after the 9/11 attacks. Justice Department officials worked closely with a judge on the court to come up with a legal foundation for the program. Hayden personally briefed her twice on what capabilities the NSA needed to acquire bulk Internet metadata. The court issued an order specifying the data links from which NSA could collect information and limiting the number of people with access to what was acquired. Less than four months after President Bush had ordered the agency to stop collecting bulk Internet data, the NSA was back in business. The future foundations of the RTRG were secured.

As the RTRG grew, its regional scope expanded too. Analysts started looking outside of Iraq in a hunt for the insurgents' and terrorists' financial backers. They traced many of the worst attacks back to an individual in Syria who was funneling money to the bomber cells and helping to provide safe passage for replacement fighters through Iran. When Petraeus learned that his forces had pinpointed the Syrian, he took the evidence to a council of President Bush's top advisers, who met every week via video teleconference. Petraeus insisted to Stuart Levey, the Treasury Department's undersecretary for terrorism and financial intelligence, that the department freeze the Syrian's assets and lock him out of the international financial system. Everyone on the call knew better than to deny Petraeus's requests, because if they did, the general would take his complaints directly to President Bush, with whom he had his own weekly videoconference, every Monday morning at 7:30 Washington time.

The intelligence operation also found evidence of Iran's support of Shiite extremists in Iraq. But this information was used to wage a different kind of war — one of ideas. The United States wasn't about to invade Iran or launch secret commando raids to target Iraqi backers. So, it gave the intelligence to the Iraqi government and shared it with local officials in face-to-face meetings.

"Clearly establishing in the eyes of the Iraqi people that Iranian elements were supporting members of the most violent Shiite militias also helped turn some Iraqis against Tehran's meddling in their country," Petraeus recalled in 2013. The Americans were using intelligence for propaganda purposes of their own, and it worked.

When the last US troops left Iraq in December 2011, the nine-year war had taken nearly forty-five hundred American lives. But it had also given birth to a new way of fighting. The combination of NSA intelligence with special operations forces was repeated over and over. In May 2011, when a team of Navy SEALs descended upon the Abbottabad, Pakistan, compound of Osama bin Laden, they were directed there by NSA spies. The agency's elite hacker unit, Tailored Access Operations, had remotely implanted spyware on the mobile phones of al-Qaeda operatives and other "persons of interest" in the bin Laden operation. The CIA helped find the geographic location of one of those phones, which pointed investigators to the compound.

The successful bin Laden mission was just the most famous of hundreds over the years. And it was fairly recent evidence of what America's soldier-spies had long known. Wars would be fought differently now. Hacking and virtual sleuthing would be integrated into all future operations, as indispensable as the weapons and ammunition soldiers carried into battle.

THREE

Building the Cyber Army

I T TOOK ALMOST a decade to build the cyber force that proved so effective in Iraq. Success may have many fathers, but if one person could claim credit for introducing the senior leaders of the United States government to the concept of cyber warfare, it would be Mike McConnell.

More than a decade before he convinced George W. Bush to authorize cyber attacks in Iraq, McConnell was a three-star admiral running the NSA, where he set up the first "information warfare" unit in 1996. At the agency's Fort Meade headquarters, intelligence and military personnel worked together developing new technologies for defending computer networks — and breaking in to them.

The NSA had spent the Cold War becoming expert at snatching satellite transmissions, tapping undersea telephone cables, and breaking the secret codes of US adversaries. But now, with the Soviet Union gone and the emergence of the World Wide Web, officials were panicked about a new, faceless menace. Already, they knew, foreign intelligence services were trying to penetrate the classified government computer networks. In 1996 the National Defense University held a war game to imagine possible doomsday scenarios, such as computer attacks aimed at banks or electrical grids in the United States. That year the secretary of defense ordered all DOD components to start planning for an "information warfare attack" on the networks that the Pentagon used but didn't actually run, particularly the public telephone network and the Internet, of which the Defense Department was not only an early adopter but the inventor.

Information warfare — the term "cyber warfare" had yet to be widely adopted in military jargon — was an obvious job for the NSA to take on. The agency's eavesdroppers and interceptors pried and peered into the world's networks. Their supercomputers spun twenty-four hours a day trying to break codes that encrypted data sitting on foreign computers. The NSA knew how to break in to networks. Once inside, it could also destroy them.

McConnell was a natural leader for that mission. During Operation Desert Storm in 1991 he was the intelligence adviser to the chairman of the Joint Chiefs of Staff, Colin Powell, and his performance made him a celebrity in the ranks of military intelligence officers. McConnell was credited for predicting Saddam Hussein's invasion of Kuwait by one day. His foresight didn't stop Iraq's attack on its neighbor, but it sure got the attention of his bosses. McConnell was adroit at using satellite imagery and intercepted communications — the fruits of intelligence gathering — to paint a picture of what was happening on the ground. Where the enemy was moving. Where he was likely to go next and what he was likely to do when he got there. McConnell, a native of South Carolina, had a plainspoken delivery and an affable demeanor. He performed so well in private briefings that Powell put him in charge of the daily press briefings, covered by reporters from around the world.

In 1992 the job of NSA director was about to become vacant — Admiral Bill Studeman, himself a widely admired military intelligence officer, was nominated by President George H. W. Bush as the next deputy director of the CIA. Powell and Secretary of Defense Dick Cheney supported McConnell for the NSA directorship. The position could only be filled by a military flag officer with three stars, and McConnell, then in his late forties, had just one. Powell and Cheney made sure he got promoted.

Under McConnell's leadership, the NSA first began to grapple with the complexities, the risks, and the potential advantages of cyber warfare.

The NSA's early cyber warriors were also building a kind of arsenal, looking for vulnerabilities in networks, software, and hardware that they could use to hijack the system, and then inject viruses or install hidden backdoors for use in future operations. The NSA hid these vulnerabilities from the manufacturers of the technologies they were exploiting. If it had disclosed them, the manufacturers could have patched the holes, making the technology safer for others to use. But that would deprive the NSA of its secret access. At least eighteen separate organizations within the agency were collecting vulnerability information, according to an internal newsletter, and they were even keeping secrets about their work from one another. "Intelligence operatives wish to protect their sources and methods," wrote one anonymous NSA author. "No one really knows how much knowledge exists in each sector." Without that knowledge, there could be no "large-scale national" approach to cyber war, which was not only something NSA wanted, it was something the agency had been directed to prepare for by the Pentagon.

Under McConnell there was a certain breathlessness to the advent of cyber warfare. The NSA was at once captivated by the strategic advantage the United States could have if it penetrated the information networks that were then spreading around the globe. And yet officials were anxious that the very kinds of cyber weapons they were developing could be used against the United States. The NSA was full of brilliant cryptographers and computer scientists, but they knew there was a low barrier to entry on this new battlefield. The knowledge to exploit networks was advancing as fast as the networks themselves. Cyber warfare would not be the province of nations alone.

Soon the cyber war fever spread beyond the NSA. By the late 1990s the air force was creating offensive cyber teams, under the direction of a task force that was initially set up to defend the service's networks. The army got in on the action, too, and began researching "ways to knock out the lights in Tehran," as one former officer puts it.

McConnell had left the NSA in 1996 and gone to work for the government contractor Booz Allen Hamilton, where he made millions off his expertise and connections. He built an intelligence unit at Booz that specialized in — what else? — cyber security. Everything he'd learned at the NSA he was now selling back to the government.

On December 23, 2006, a decade after McConnell had left public service, his secretary walked into his expansive corner office at Booz, twenty miles outside downtown Washington.

"The vice president's on the phone," she said.

"The vice president of what?" McConnell asked.

"The vice president of the United States."

McConnell jumped to his feet and grabbed the phone. His old patron Dick Cheney informed McConnell that President Bush wanted to nominate him for director of national intelligence. It was a thankless job, and one that McConnell knew more powerful men than he had turned down, most famous among them Robert Gates, the former CIA director and an old friend of McConnell's, who was now the secretary of defense.

McConnell told Cheney he needed to think about it and that he'd give him an answer after Christmas. He hung up and called Gates, who already knew the nomination was in play. McConnell said he'd only take the job if he had a free hand to make some big changes in the way the intelligence community was run, and if he had Gates's support. Gates promised that he did.

When McConnell had left the NSA, cyber war was in its infancy. In his absence, it entered adolescence. Now he would take it into adulthood.

McConnell's tenure as director of national intelligence, the chief of all the government's intelligence agencies, lasted just under two years. But the mark he left on the office, espionage, and warfare was profound.

It was McConnell, of course, who convinced President Bush to sign off on the cyber warfare tactics the NSA and the military used in Iraq. But he also spearheaded a major overhaul of the law that governs many of the NSA's operations, the Foreign Intelligence Surveillance Act. As it happened, when McConnell was coming into the job, a federal judge on the FISA court, set up to oversee electronic spying, had ruled that the government needed a warrant to intercept communications between foreign individuals who were outside the United States if the surveillance was performed on equipment located there. McConnell spent the months of June and July explaining to lawmakers that most of the world's communications traffic moved through cables, routers, and switches inside the country. But when the NSA tapped that equipment for foreign intelligence purposes, it shouldn't need a warrant, he argued — it wasn't spying on any Americans, after all.

McConnell told lawmakers that if the NSA were no longer allowed to monitor wholly foreign communications on United States–based equipment, it would lose its coverage on many foreign people, including members of al-Qaeda and insurgents in Iraq. As he saw it, this was not the time to lose access to the very technological infrastructure on which the United States was fighting a new kind of war.

Congress's summer recess was approaching, and Democrats, who ran the House and Senate, risked looking weak on counterterrorism if they failed to enact the changes required to keep NSA operations up and running. Most lawmakers didn't know about the cyber warfare operations, but the administration had long said publicly that surveillance activities by the agency were essential to preventing terrorist attacks in the United States.

McConnell seized the opportunity and pushed for more than just a tweak in existing law. He wanted to rewrite FISA to allow broad searches on whole groups of individual targets — say, all the telephone traffic coming out of Yemen. This was an unprecedented expansion. The Constitution had never been used to justify warrants against whole groups of people. The Fourth Amendment required the government to name the person and the place it wanted to search. And while FISA could accommodate spying on an individual whose identity the government might not know, it still required the government to point to that one person as the target. Now McConnell wanted authority for dragnet surveillance.

The truth was, the NSA already had it, as long as it was conducting the surveillance overseas and not spying on American citizens or legal residents. But a change in the law, critics feared, would allow the broad surveillance to be conducted inside the United States. It would give the

NSA license to demand access to huge volumes of data from US technology companies by broadly invoking the need to protect national security.

Which is exactly what happened. In August 2007, Democrats, who believed they'd been backed into a corner by McConnell and the White House, reluctantly signed on to the bill. Just over a month later the NSA ramped up a new collection system, called Prism, which obtained large numbers of e-mails and other Internet communications from US companies. The first company to come on board was Microsoft, on September 11, 2007. Yahoo joined the following March. Over the next four years, some of the biggest names in American business were added to the Prism list, including Google, Facebook, YouTube, and Apple. There were nine companies under Prism surveillance by October 2012. Today those companies are responsible for huge portions of Internet traffic and usage in the United States. Google alone accounts for a quarter of all traffic moving through Internet service providers in North America. YouTube is responsible for almost 20 percent of all download traffic in the United States. (Its closest rival is Netflix, the video streaming service, which accounts for about one-third.) The companies' e-mail services also attract billions of people around the world. Three years after Google was added to the Prism program, the company announced that 425 million people were using its Gmail product. (More recent figures aren't available.) Yahoo claimed 281 million users of its mail service as of December 2012. And as of February 2013, Microsoft says 420 million people were using its Outlook e-mail system. Apple, which was the last known company added to Prism, in 2012, said that year it had sold 250 million iPhones.

As vast as the Prism program was, the government still needed an individual warrant if it wanted to obtain the contents of an American's communications. The rest of the world, though, was more or less fair game. Judges who approved FISA surveillance were now being asked to sign off on "authorizations," prepared by senior administration officials, that listed broad categories of surveillance targets and gave highly technical and complex explanations for how the NSA would ensure it was collecting only on the categories it had specified. That sounded workable in theory, but really, the agency often didn't know how much data it was collecting, on foreigners or Americans. That's because it's exceptionally difficult to know the nationality and location of the sender or recipient of an e-mail, which is sent over the Internet not as a discrete communication but as a series of packets, broken up and dispersed through the network on the fastest and most efficient path, then reassembled at their destination. Frequently that end point is not the recipient's computer but the servers of whatever e-mail service the recipient is using, such as Microsoft's Hotmail or Google's Gmail. Since the NSA might not know where the sender and recipient are, or who they are, it can't always be certain that it's spying on only foreigners.

On the surface, the changes to the surveillance seemed only to expand the NSA's ability to spy. But it also gave the agency more access points to the physical infrastructure of the Internet, from which it could conduct cyber warfare operations. And with access to the systems of major e-mail and Internet companies, the NSA could gather more intelligence about its adversaries and craft messages that looked trustworthy but were actually loaded with viruses and other malware. The Internet was a battlefield, and the new law gave the NSA more ways to enter it.

As the NSA's powers grew, it cast its net wider, tapping into the undersea cables that carry communications between continents. The agency started filtering the content of all e-mails going in and out of the United States, scanning them for the names, phone numbers, or e-mail addresses of suspected terrorists. And it managed to penetrate the defenses of Google and Yahoo, stealing communications as they traveled between the companies' overseas private data centers and the public Internet.

McConnell's second big contribution to the burgeoning cyber battle came toward the end of his tenure, in 2008. After Senator Barack Obama won the presidential election in November, McConnell flew to Chicago and met with the soon-to-be commander in chief in a secure facility at the FBI field office. There he explained the contours of the new battlefield. McConnell put special emphasis on how weak the United States' own defenses were, and described some of the steps the Bush administration had taken to shore them up. Later, in a private meeting with Bush, Obama learned that the president had authorized a covert set of cyber attacks on an Iranian nuclear facility, using the computer worm that later came to be known as Stuxnet. Bush told Obama that the sabotage operation, code-named Olympic Games, was one of two intelligence missions that he believed the new president shouldn't relinquish. The other was a CIA program to kill suspected terrorists and militants in Pakistan using armed aerial drones.

Obama agreed on both counts. And for the cyber program, he ordered up a new round of Stuxnet attacks in 2009. Unlike Bush, who had opted to quietly degrade and frustrate the Iranians' capability to make a nuclear weapon, Obama wanted to cause massive damage inside the Natanz plant. The United States deployed a new variant of the worm designed to make the rotors inside the centrifuges spin at dangerous speeds. The worm also carried multiple novel attack codes designed to penetrate different software programs through hidden flaws that the Iranians hadn't detected. The new features made it a more destructive weapon. Researchers generally credit Stuxnet with destroying one thousand centrifuges between 2009 and 2010. This was only about 20 percent of the total number operating at the plant, and the Iranians had more centrifuges in reserve to replace the damaged equipment. But Obama administration officials have said that Stuxnet set back Iran's weapons program by up to two years. That's precious and valuable time if, as appears to be the case, Stuxnet was designed to forestall a war, not to start one.

But those aggressive programming features also increased the chances that Stuxnet would be discovered, which eventually it was, in June 2010, when an obscure security company in Belarus discovered the first evidence of a computer virus that would later be dubbed Stuxnet. Researchers initially speculated that a flaw in the worm's code (which of course was now more complex, and thus more prone to error) had allowed it to "escape" beyond the confines of its initial target's networks, perhaps after an engineer at Natanz connected a laptop to an infected machine, then took it home or to the office and connected to the Internet. But what's not generally known is that this leaping aspect was perhaps not a bug but a feature. In addition to breaking centrifuges, Stuxnet was also designed for reconnaissance. It sent the

Internet address and host names of infected computers back to its command center. Why would any of these features be necessary for a weapon that was built to attack machines behind an air gap, where they were separated from the Internet? The obvious answer is that Stuxnet's designers knew it wouldn't stay behind the air gap for long. And perhaps they didn't want it to. Stuxnet was also designed to scout out networks and computers inside Natanz as it looked for the right target to attack. The contractors inside the plant worked for other clients as well. If their laptops became infected with Stuxnet, and they carried those computers to their other work sites, the worm might perform this reconnaissance function at other nuclear facilities in Iran. Stuxnet could tell the United States who those nuclear contractors were working for, where other nuclear facilities in Iran were located, and perhaps how far along those plants might be on their respective enrichment paths. It could potentially give the Americans more insight into Iran's nuclear program than any human spies ever had. Obama's decision to escalate the Stuxnet attack wasn't without risk, but the potential upside to US intelligence-gathering efforts was too tempting to ignore. No wonder McConnell and Bush took so much time to explain cyber warfare and its benefits to the new commander in chief.

As McConnell was nearing the end of his time in office and preparing to return to Booz Allen Hamilton, he felt he had one task left to do. The NSA had made great strides in cyber warfare. The military was developing its own capabilities. But there was no commander in charge of all their work. The military runs on a rigid hierarchy, the core philosophy of which is that in war the armed forces fight jointly. The army and the air force don't head into battle with separate missions and agendas. They make plans and then fight together. So should it be in cyber war, McConnell thought.

He wanted to establish a new cyber command, designed along the lines of the military's combatant command structure, which divided the world up into geographic regions — Pacific Command, European Command, Central Command for the Middle East, and so on — and also around specific missions. The special operations forces, JSOC, which had worked so closely with the NSA in Iraq, fell under the direction of US Special Operations Command. And the Strategic Command conducted operations in outer space and managed the United States' nuclear weapons.

Cyber needed its own command, McConnell thought, so that the unique expertise and capabilities of each branch of the armed forces could be harnessed. Military leaders and administration officials were coming around to the idea that future wars would be fought on the Internet as well as in the physical domains. But a new command would make it clear that cyber warfare was not a passing fashion. McConnell thought there was no better way to establish cyber's staying power than to enshrine it in the military's command-and-control structure.

As it happened, in late October, less than two weeks before the election, a computer worm had infected military networks, a major breach that persuaded the Pentagon brass that their cyber defenses were lacking. The NSA had quickly neutralized the intrusion and was leading the cleanup through the remainder of Bush's term. McConnell conferred with his old friend Bob Gates, who had agreed to stay on as secretary of defense under the new administration. Gates agreed there should be a new cyber command. It wouldn't happen while McConnell was in office. Official Washington would be consumed by the ritual of the presidential transition, as Bush administration officials handed off the keys to the incoming crew and explained in detail everything they'd been working on. But Gates took the baton. In June 2009 he ordered the commander of US Strategic Command to establish a new Cyber Command, or CyberCom. Strategic Command seemed like an obvious home — it had nominal responsibilities for coordinating information warfare across the military services. But by now the NSA was effectively in charge of that mission. Therefore, the NSA director should run CyberCom, Pentagon officials reasoned. The plan was to keep it as a subordinate command temporarily, let it grow, and then elevate CyberCom to full combatant command status.

In ways that few could discern at the moment, the current NSA director, army general Keith Alexander, had been groomed for the role of cyber commander his entire military career. Over time he would be revealed as an erudite technologist, a cunning warrior, and one of the most politically skillful generals in recent memory. For now, though, as the new Cyber Command got on its feet, he was one of its strongest supporters on Capitol Hill, in the military ranks, and at the White House.

At an "activation ceremony" on May 21, 2010, at Fort Meade, Alexander was sworn in as the first commander of US Cyber Command. Gates attended, along with David Petraeus, who was then in charge of Central Command. The only man missing from the bunch of founding fathers was McConnell. But his work was done. The United States had officially entered the age of cyber war.

The military-intelligence alliance proved it was very good at attacking bands of insurgents and terrorists in Iraq. But what would happen when the United States met a large, organized national military on the battlefield of cyberspace — and it fought back?

To find out, on May 7, 2010, around six hundred people showed up at Nellis Air Force Base, on the outskirts of Las Vegas, for the annual Schriever Wargame. Every year the game was premised on some hot-button issue of strategy currently vexing US forces. (In 2012, the participants fought pirates around the Horn of Africa.) The name Schriever, in addition to being attached to the base in Colorado that administered the game, was an important one in air force history: Bernard Adolph Schriever, or Bennie, was a German immigrant who became a US general in 1961 and was a pioneer in space and ballistic missile research.

The participants for the 2010 game included senior military officers, representatives from all the combatant commands, and military and civilian cyber security experts from more than thirty US government agencies — including the NSA, the Homeland Security Department, and the National Reconnaissance Office, which runs a network of spy satellites and is arguably the most secretive of all the spy agencies. Executives from technology companies also showed up, along with policy wonks, official delegations from Australia, Canada, and Great Britain — the United States' three closest allies — as well as one former member of Congress, Tom Davis, whose district included many of the biggest Defense Department and spy agency contractors. For the war game, Davis played the role of president of the United States.

The year was 2022. A "regional adversary" in the Pacific — it was never named, but everyone seemed to pretend it was China or North Korea — perceived a military provocation from a US ally. In response, the adversary launched a crippling cyber attack on the ally's computer networks. The ally invoked its mutual defense agreement with the United States. Washington had to respond.

Before the US forces could decide on their first move, the adversary struck preemptively, attacking "aggressively, deliberately, and decisively" to block the US forces' access to the computer networks they would need to communicate and send orders, according to a senior US general who participated.

"Red blockades Blue," the players were informed.

Blue had trained for a blockade on water, not on the Internet. They knew how to signal to an adversary, "We see you — back off." They could hail him over a radio frequency. Flash lights. Sound sirens. They could summon other ships to the area as a show of force. There were assertive but nonlethal steps a commander could take, short of actually firing on the enemy's ship, to halt his advance.

But in cyberspace, the only thing the players knew how to do was attack the enemy's network and destroy it, skipping all the posturing and signals and heading straight to full-on combat. There was no cyber equivalent, that they knew of, for summoning all hands to battle stations. It was either attack or don't. The traditional deterrence strategy was useless.

It also wasn't clear that the other side had a deterrence strategy of its own, or even believed in the value of one. Military planners liked to compare cyber weapons to nuclear weapons, because they both could cause massive, strategic-level damage and required presidential authorization to use. But with nuclear hostilities there was a series of clear, mutually understood actions each side could take that stopped short of using the weapons. Throughout the Cold War, the United States and the Soviet Union helped keep a fragile peace in large part by making clear how they could — and would — destroy each other. The Soviets test a new missile, the Americans show off one of theirs. They talk of deploying missiles closer to targets in Europe, the US president talks openly about the possibility of using nuclear weapons, and says he hopes it never comes to that. In this back-and-forth, full of chest thumping and heated words, both sides implicitly agreed they were trying to avoid a nuclear war, not cause one. Signaling their hostile intent gave each side time to back down, cool off, and save face.

But now, in the game, the regional adversary continued attacking in unpredictable ways. After hitting the US forces' computer networks, it sent "grappler" satellites to latch on to US satellites, pushing them out of their orbit and disabling them.

Over the next four days, military commanders struggled to come up with a response short of full-scale war, which they were convinced would result in enormous casualties on both sides. Senior leaders in the Defense Department and at the White House got involved. The US forces discovered they had no cyber war agreements with their foreign allies, so there was no road map for an international response. Military leaders turned to the corporate executives for help. What technology did the companies have to send some kind of signal to the enemy to change its tactics? Was there such a thing as a non-hostile cyber attack? No one was sure.

The enemy had already made a decision that cyber and space attacks were the best way to counter the perceived aggression from its neighbor and fend off a US response. They had already set their red line. And they had already gamed out the US response, which got bogged down as more and more senior executives weighed in about what moves would be effective, or even legal. The mighty superpower was reduced to a bunch of confused and disorganized players. Worse, in the words of one participant, this appeared to be exactly what the enemy wanted. "We were unwittingly and obediently following a script that the adversary had already written for the campaign, and our military actions to deter would have no effect on their decision calculus."

All war games start with a set of premises; the risk for the players is that they presume those facts will hold true in real life and fail to consider alternatives. The Schriever Wargame was designed so that China or North Korea would preemptively launch a cyber attack. Of course, they might not. Maybe in a real standoff they would fear a cyber counterstrike by the United States — or worse, a nuclear one. Arguably, one lesson of the war game was that the military should reexamine its premises and assess how likely another country was to launch a first strike in cyberspace, given the mutually assured destruction that the military believed would follow.

Instead, the game reinforced the military's natural disposition toward war. And it convinced senior military and Pentagon leaders that if a cyber war ever did break out, it would happen "at the speed of light," with practically no warning. From now on, whenever they testified before Congress or gave public speeches and press interviews, they warned about the instantly devastating nature of cyber warfare. It became an article of faith when it came to their planning. The United States, they said, had to prepare now for the inevitability of this conflict, and take extraordinary measures to strengthen its forces — for defense and offense.

As unnerving as the war game proved to be, there were threats closer to home that had US officials worried. In May 2009, in a speech in the East Room of the White House, President Obama revealed that "cyber intruders have probed our electrical grid and that in other countries cyber attacks have plunged entire cities into darkness." Obama didn't say that foreign hackers had actually turned off the lights in the United States. But privately, some intelligence officials claimed that Chinese hackers were responsible for two major blackouts, in 2003 and 2008. The first blackout was the largest in North American history, covering a 93,000-square-mile area including Michigan, Ohio, New York, and parts of Canada. An estimated 50 million people were affected. The ensuing panic was so severe that President Bush addressed the nation to assure people the lights would come back on. Within twenty-four hours, power was mostly restored.

One information security expert who was under contract to the government and large businesses, dissecting Chinese spyware and viruses found on their computers, claimed that in the second blackout, a Chinese hacker working for the People's Liberation Army had attempted to case the network of a Florida utility and apparently made a mistake. "The hacker was probably supposed to be mapping the system for his bosses and just got carried away and had a 'what happens if I pull on this' moment." This expert thought the hacker triggered a cascade effect, which shut down large portions of the power grid in Florida. "I suspect, as the system went down, the PLA hacker said something like, 'Oops, my bad,' in Chinese."

The companies that operated the networks and the power plants vehemently denied the accusations and pointed to public investigations that concluded the blackouts were triggered by natural causes, including overgrown trees that had shorted out strained power lines. No government official ever offered verifiable evidence that the Chinese were behind the blackouts. But the persistent rumors of the country's involvement were a measure of Washington's paranoia and dread about cyber attacks.

After a possible attack on US power grids, officials' next greatest concern is relentless theft of intellectual property and trade secrets from US companies, particularly by hackers in China. Alexander, who became the Cyber Command chief in 2010, called rampant Chinese industrial espionage "the greatest transfer of wealth in history." By 2012, Congress finally felt compelled to act. It was six years after lawmakers' own computers were found to have been infected with spyware that was probably implanted by Chinese hackers. Computers in several committee offices in the House of Representatives also were infected, including those overseeing commerce, transportation and infrastructure, homeland security, and the powerful Ways and Means Committee. The Congressional-Executive Commission on China, which monitors human rights and laws in China, was also hit. Most committee offices were found to have one or two infected computers. The International Relations Committee (now called the Foreign Affairs Committee), which oversees US foreign policy, including negotiations with China, had twenty-five infected computers and one infected server.

In 2012, proposals wound their way through Congress that, among other things, would give the government more authority to gather information about cyber intrusions and reconnaissance of networks from affected companies. The idea was to share information about potential threats but also to force companies to step up their own security. But some companies balked, fearful that the legislation marked a new wave of expensive and intrusive regulation. Companies were also worried that they might get sued by their customers for working with the government. Internet service providers wanted legal assurances that if they transmitted information about attacks in real time to the Defense or Homeland Security Departments, they wouldn't be held liable for any personal data those warnings might contain, such as the identities or Internet addresses of people whose packets had been intercepted or whose computers had been compromised.

The US Chamber of Commerce, a powerful trade association with deep pockets and a history of supporting Republican candidates for office, said legislation would give the government "too much control over what actions the business community could take to protect its computers and networks." At a moment when conservative officeholders in particular had been denouncing President Obama's health care law as government intrusion into citizens' private lives, the Chamber became the most vocal opponent of cyber legislation as another example of government excess. GOP lawmakers closed ranks behind them, and any chance for a comprehensive cyber law died.

In lieu of Congress acting, President Obama signed an executive order in February 2013 that made it US policy "to enhance the security and resilience of the Nation's critical infrastructure." That term, *critical infrastructure,* was intentionally broad, in order to encompass a multitude of businesses and industries. The president defined it as "systems and assets, whether physical or virtual, so vital to the United States that the incapacity or destruction of such systems and assets would have a debilitating impact on security, national economic security, national public health or safety, or any combination of those matters." By that definition, a power plant was certainly critical. But so was a bank. And a hospital. So were trains, buses, and trucking companies. Was UPS a critical infrastructure? To the extent that businesses depended on shipping and timely delivery of goods and services, maybe it was.

With the executive order, the Obama administration told Congress and businesses that it wasn't going to wait for a new law to extend government influence over the Internet. The order instructed federal agencies to start sharing more cyber threat information with companies; authorized the Commerce Department and the National Institute of Standards and Technology to come up with a "framework" of security standards that companies would be encouraged to adopt; and told the secretary of Homeland Security to draw up a list of critical infrastructures "where a cybersecurity incident could reasonably result in catastrophic regional or national effects."

The White House was still prepared to fight for a new cyber law. But in the meantime, Obama's order did something profound: it gave the military the green light to prepare for cyber war.

Obama's executive order, along with a classified presidential directive signed five months earlier and not released publicly, made it clear that the military had the lead in defending the nation during a cyber attack. Just as the armed forces would swing into action if the United States were invaded by a foreign army, or if missiles were flying toward US cities, the country's cyber forces would get the call to defend against a digital attack — and to retaliate.

The executive order made it easier for the Defense Department to expand its classified threat intelligence sharing program beyond the defense industrial base to more of those "critical infrastructure" sectors that the government would define. And the separate directive, known as PDD-20, spelled out how the military would go to cyber war, under what circumstances, and who may give the orders.

Any cyber strike has to be ordered by the president. But during an emergency the president can designate that authority to the secretary of defense. If a power plant, for instance, were under imminent attack, and there was no time to get the president's approval for defensive actions — which could involve a counterstrike on the source of attack — then the secretary could give the order.

But PDD-20 isn't really about cyber defense. It instructs the military to draw up a list of overseas targets "of national importance," where it would be easier or more effective for the United States to attack with a cyber weapon than a conventional one. These are the equivalent of Cold War–era, high-priority targets in the Soviet Union, where bombers would drop their payload in the event of a war. PDD-20 does not name individual targets, but those of national importance would naturally be communications systems; command-and-control networks used by military forces; financial networks; air defense and traffic control systems; and critical infrastructures, such as electrical grids. These are the same kinds of targets that a foreign army would draw up on the United States for a cyber war.

The directive also instructs other government departments and agencies, including the State Department, the FBI, the NSA, the Treasury Department, and the Energy Department, to make plans for retaliating against "persistent malicious cyber activity against US Interests" when "network defense or law enforcement measures are insufficient or cannot be put in place in time." The military would carry out those attacks as well, at the president's instruction.

PDD-20 is seen by military commanders and civilians as the rules of the road for cyber war, a crucial document that spells out lines of authority and command, responsibilities, and broad principles. It says the United States will conduct cyber warfare consistent with the international law of armed conflict: strikes must be designed to cause minimal collateral damage and must be waged in proportion to the threat or the attack on the United States. The military must also be cautious not to disrupt or destroy networks that may be connected to the ones they're targeting. A virus or worm designed to attack a power plant in Iran must not be allowed to destroy a plant in China. "We don't want to start World War III," says Ann Barron-DiCamillo, a senior official at the Homeland Security Department who works with the Defense Department to coordinate responses to cyber attacks in the United States.

As important as these rules are, PDD-20 does something more fundamental to the way the United States will fight wars in the future: it elevates cyber operations to the status of traditional combat, and instructs the armed forces to integrate offensive cyber warfare "with other US offensive capabilities," on land, in the air, at sea, and in space.

The military has three principal cyber war missions, and three kinds of forces with which to conduct them.

The first mission, and the largest force, runs and defends the military's networks around the world—everywhere from the battlefields of Iraq and Afghanistan to the waters of the Pacific, where the combined forces of the army, navy, air force, and marines would be the first line of attack in any war with China. These "cyber protection forces," as the military calls them, try to keep foreign adversaries and hackers out of those military networks. Attempted intrusions occur several thousands of times a day, but these are mostly automated probes, not really attacks, and they can be fended off with automated software. The Defense Department also limits the number of points where its networks connect to the public Internet, which helps fortify the military's defenses. Filters scan every piece of information that moves through those points, looking for worms, viruses, and other indicators of an attempted intrusion, such as traffic coming from Internet addresses suspected of being used by foreign militaries and intelligence services.

This is everyday defense. The protection forces would really earn their stripes in the event of a full-scale war, when a US adversary would bring out its most sophisticated cyber weapons and best warriors in order to disable the military's command-and-control networks or corrupt information inside them. These cyber strikes might happen before the first exchange of gunfire, as a prelude to more traditional combat, or as part of an active "kinetic" operation. For instance, during the war in the Balkans in the 1990s, US hackers penetrated Bosnian air defense systems and tricked controllers into thinking that invading aircraft were coming from one direction, when really they were coming from another.

The military's defense mission is constrained by the fact that it doesn't actually own and operate most of its network infrastructure: 99 percent of the electricity and 90 percent of the voice-communications services the military uses come from privately owned cables, routers, and other infrastructure. Protecting the military's networks "is not getting any easier because of our reliance on key networks and systems that are not directly under DOD's control," says Major General John Davis, the Pentagon's military cyber security adviser.

So, the cyber protection forces have created "hunt teams" that work with the cyber spies at the NSA and the Defense Intelligence Agency to find potential threats in military networks before they strike. As part of those efforts, the military has access to a database containing dossiers on every known hacker in China, according to an official with a Pentagon contractor that provides tracking services. The dossier notes which kinds of malware the hacker likes to use, what systems he has been known to target, and where he is believed to be operating. In some cases the dossier also includes a photograph, obtained by intelligence operatives in China or purchased through private intelligence companies whose employees follow hackers on the ground. By knowing who the hackers are, the military can raise defenses against their preferred targets. But it can also attempt to lure the hacker into a system with false or misleading information, known as a honeypot, and then track his movements in a controlled environment. The longer he stays inside, trying to steal what he believes to be important documents, the longer the US spies can study his craft and develop ways to counter it.

An NSA unit known as the Transgression Branch specializes in this kind of track-the-hacker work and takes things one step further. The branch watches a hacker break into another country's computer system, then follows him inside. In a 2010 operation called Ironavenger, the Transgression Branch saw e-mails containing malware being sent to a government office in a hostile country — one that the NSA wanted to know more about. Upon further inspection, the branch discovered that the malware was coming from a US ally, whose own intelligence service was trying to break in. The Americans let their allies do the hard work and watched silently as they scooped up passwords and sensitive documents from the adversary's system. The Americans saw everything the allies saw and got some inside knowledge about how they spied.

The second of the military's cyber missions is supporting the armed forces in combat. These are the cyber warriors fighting alongside their traditionally armed compatriots. They comprise teams that conduct defense and offense, and they are spread out across the armed forces. Each one has a separate focus, depending on its branch of service. For instance, the air force is training its cyber warriors to hack into enemy air defense and traffic control systems, while the army is focused on land operations, penetrating command-and-control systems of artillery, for instance.

In a remarkable shift from the earlier days of cyber war, cyber attacks in battle no longer require the approval of the president in every instance. According to the Joint Chiefs of Staff's official guidance on targeting, much of the decision making about who and what to attack is up to the head of US Cyber Command. "Targeting for cyberspace generally follows the processes and procedures used for traditional targeting," the guidance states. In other words, the military now thinks cyber weapons are not so different from missiles, bombs, and bullets. Military commanders are cautioned to remember "the unique nature of cyberspace as compared to the traditional physical domains"—that is, the possibility that a cyber weapon could cause widespread collateral damage.

The skills of these support teams are overlapping, which means that in future wars, an army hacker could hop over to an air force mission with little trouble. During the Iraq War, army operators cracked the cell phones of insurgents and sent them misleading messages, because the army was on the ground fighting the insurgents. But air force cyber warriors also have the skills to conduct that kind of deception operation, and there's no reason they couldn't step in if the army was tied up fighting other battles. Likewise, a navy cyber warrior, who is trained to hack the navigation systems of an enemy submarine or fry a ship's radar, could wreak havoc on a commercial telecom network.

The third mission is protecting the United States itself, using what the military calls the Cyber National Mission Force. This force only conducts offensive operations. It would get the call from the president or the secretary of defense if China were trying to disable an electrical power plant or Iran were attempting to alter the databases of major banks or financial transaction systems. The members of the National Mission Force are trained to reroute malicious traffic away from its target, breaking in to networks if necessary, or to strike back at the source and take it offline. It reports to US Cyber Command, which is linked to the National Security Agency and its crack Tailored Access Operations unit. The Cyber National Mission Force represents a tiny portion of the overall military cyber force—probably about 1 percent, though the precise number is classified.

The Pentagon is "at full speed working our way through how the services will implement" the three-tiered structure of US cyber forces, Davis says. Beginning in 2011, the military began conducting regular cyber war games at Nellis Air Force Base, where the pivotal Schriever

Wargame took place. Officials have set up joint cyber operations centers in each of the military's combatant commands, which are organized according to regions of the world and are run by a four-star general or admiral. There is now an emergency conference-call system so that in the event of an imminent or ongoing cyber attack on the United States, military, Defense Department, intelligence, and law enforcement officials can be looped in with the president and the National Security Council — constituting a kind of cyber war cabinet — to decide how to respond. A command-and-control system for US cyber attacks is also in place. There is even an emergency communications line from Washington to Moscow, the cyber equivalent of the Cold War red phone.

The core infrastructure for fighting a cyber war has been created. Now the United States is raising an army.

To build a cyber force, the military first has to recruit the best warriors. Each branch of the armed forces has developed aptitude tests, molded on those used by corporations, to determine whether someone might be suited to network maintenance and defense or shows promise for the rarer, more sophisticated offensive missions. The service branches are beginning to introduce basic cyber security training for all new officers; in the air force it's already mandatory. And the five military service academies now include cyber warfare as a field of study. Every year since 2000, the best hackers from each academy have competed against one another in a war game sponsored by the NSA. The simulation is meant to pit the schools against one another but also to test their mettle against the government's best cyber warriors.

"We build a network, all from scratch, then defend it against a team from NSA," says Martin Carlisle, professor of computer science at the Air Force Academy and director of its Center for Cyberspace Research. The battle lasts for two and a half days. In 2013 the academy fielded a team of fifteen computer science and engineering majors who squared off against an NSA "red team," — war game code for the aggressor — of about thirty military officers, civilians, and contractors from the NSA. The agency's team was not allowed to use any classified hacking techniques, but they ran operations against the cadets that they would likely see if the United States ever fought a cyber war with a foreign military. The NSA red team attempted to get inside the air force network and modify crucial data, so that the cadets could no longer trust its veracity. They launched known computer viruses against the cadets' network and tried to install backdoors in their systems.

The air force won the 2013 competition, its fourth victory since the game began in 2001, and its first consecutive win.

Future air force cyber specialists take special training at Keesler Air Force Base, on the Gulf Coast of Mississippi. Just like pilots have to pass flight school, the would-be cyber warriors have to run a gauntlet before they can wear the cyberspace badge — a pair of silver wings crossed by a lightning bolt centered on a globe.

The next and most important step in the education of cyber warriors is on-the-job training, "where you have your hands on the keyboard," says Lieutenant General Michael Basla, chief of information dominance and the chief information officer, or CIO, of the air force. Basla's dual titles reflect the air force's approach to its cyber warfare mission. "Information dominance" encompasses propaganda, deception, and computer operations. And a CIO, generally, is the head techie in an organization, responsible for keeping the networks up to date and running. The air force lumps its network maintenance staff with its defenders, as well as those who conduct offense. It's one big techie pool.

About 90 percent of the air force's cyber force (which consisted of approximately 12,600 people in 2013) works on defense. They are guarding networks, patching vulnerabilities, and trying to keep abreast of changes to hardware and software that might create more holes for an intruder to use. Less than 1 percent of all air force cyber warriors are engaged in what Basla calls the "exquisite" work of penetrating an enemy's computer systems.

There are two big reasons for this mismatch. First, offense is a lot harder than defense. The tools and principles to do both are essentially the same in many ways. But asking a defender to go out and break in to a highly protected enemy computer would be like asking an auto mechanic, however talented, to fix the engine on a jet fighter. He may understand the principles of the task, but the application is an order of magnitude more difficult.

The second reason the offense side is so much smaller is that the military has only recently begun to make cyber warfare a priority. Protecting military networks and computers, which have proliferated in the past fifteen years, has long been part of its mission. That emphasis is changing now, as cyber warfare becomes integrated into military doctrine.

But if they ever go to war, US cyber forces will face an adversary just as skilled, and many times larger, than they are.

Groups of hackers have been operating in China for more than a decade. Some of their first handiwork was on display in 1999, after US forces inadvertently bombed the Chinese embassy in Yugoslavia during the Kosovo War. Outraged "patriotic hackers" hijacked the websites of the US Departments of Energy and the Interior and the National Park Service. The hackers took down the sites' usual content and replaced it with anti-American messages: "Protest the USA's Nazi action! Protest NATO's brutal action!" The White House also came under a heavy denial-of-service attack, in which an aggressor floods a server with traffic in an attempt to knock it offline. The White House took down its website for three days as a precaution.

Today these Chinese hacker groups, who were once motivated by their sense of national pride and opposition to foreign military action, are taking their orders from China's military and intelligence leaders. They weren't conscripted so much as brought under the banner of the People's Liberation Army, which has both clandestinely supported their work and officially ignored their existence. Lately that work consists mostly of stealing information. Chinese hackers have penetrated or tried to compromise classified computer systems of every department and agency of the federal government. They have broken in to countless corporate databases to steal trade secrets. Just like the hackers who broke in to US defense contractors in 2007, they are looking for any piece of information — however big or small — that will give

China a military or economic edge and advance the country's global strategy.

The Chinese hackers are skilled and relentless. They are also shameless. They've taken far fewer precautions than their American adversaries to cover their tracks. In part this is because they know the US government has been loath to call out one of its most important trading partners and lenders as the source of a global espionage campaign. But the Chinese also view cyber espionage and warfare as a set of tactics that helps them compete against more advanced economies, militaries, and intelligence organizations. They have little compunction about breaking in to competitors' systems because they know it's one of the few capabilities they have to gain some advantage over their adversaries. China has no blue-water navy capable of doing battle on the world's oceans. But it does have a cyber force that can wreak havoc on US targets from the other side of the planet.

Chinese cyber forces, along with their counterparts in Russia, have designed technologies to hack into US military aircraft. The Chinese in particular have developed a method for inserting computer viruses through the air into three models of planes that the air force uses for reconnaissance and surveillance. The attack is launched via the electromagnetic spectrum and targets the onboard surveillance systems that emit a signal. It's an ingenious tactic, and a potentially devastating one: such a strike could disrupt the aircrafts' controls and cause them to crash.

But these advances were predictable. For centuries the Chinese have employed a strategy of asymmetry, overwhelming a larger enemy by attacking his weaknesses with basic weapons. Cyber espionage and warfare are just the latest examples in a long and, for the Chinese, proud tradition.

To speak of the Chinese hackers as a group is a bit of misnomer. They don't operate entirely as a collective, and how they're organized is still a mystery — unlike the Americans, the Chinese don't publicize their cyber warfare hierarchy and command structure. But for the purposes of developing countermeasures, US security officials often view the hackers as one entity, because they are united by a set of characteristics — national pride, the belief in economic espionage as a tool for national advancement, and a strategy of asymmetric force. American security experts have given the Chinese cyber horde a name — the advanced persistent threat, or APT. It is responsible for a global spread of malware that has infected or attempted to infect every computer system of consequence in the United States, US officials say. Any American company operating abroad doing business with or in China or with any of its competitors can safely assume that it has been a target. Many of them don't even know that. On average, at least a month passes before most companies ever learn they have an intruder on their networks.

The precise number of Chinese cyber warriors is not known, but experts uniformly agree on two things: it is very large, likely in the tens of thousands, and unlike those in the United States, the Chinese cyber warriors are mostly focused on offense.

Joe Stewart, director of malware research at Dell SecureWorks, has tracked twenty-four thousand Internet domains that he believes Chinese cyber spies have either rented or hacked and use as bases of operations against the US government and American companies, he told *Bloomberg Businessweek* in 2013. The precise number of hackers is hard to gauge, but Stewart identified three hundred types of malware and hacking techniques that the Chinese used, double the number he saw in 2012. "There is a tremendous amount of manpower being thrown at this from their side."

In 2013 the computer security research firm Mandiant released a groundbreaking report that identified and gave the location of one suspected APT group, known as Unit 61398 — a Chinese military cover name — based in Shanghai. One of its main centers of operations is a twelve-story, 130,000-square-foot building capable of holding as many as two thousand people. The security company studied Unit 61398 going back to 2006 and discovered it had broken in to the systems of nearly 150 "victims." Mandiant judged the unit to be one of the most prolific cyber spying outfits in China. And other computer security experts linked the group to an incursion in 2012 on the networks of the Canadian arm of Telvent, which designs industrial control software used to regulate valves and security systems for oil and gas pipeline companies in North America. Telvent has acknowledged that the intruders stole project files. Hackers could use those to map out the networks of oil and gas companies and find their weaknesses.

Unit 61398 was formidable, and clearly interested in potential attacks on critical infrastructure. But it was just one of twenty hacker groups that Mandiant was tracking. Chinese hackers in general are mostly engaged in espionage. But it would be easy for its members to switch into cyber warfare mode and start taking down systems, corrupting data and information, or launching malware against critical infrastructure, such as power plants and communications facilities. If each of those twenty groups was just half as large as Unit 61398, the Chinese APT would consist of more than twenty thousand people.

The United States has a long way to go to match the size of China's cyber force. In 2013 there were only about three hundred people working for Tailored Access Operations, the NSA's elite hacker core. The US Cyber Command, which is responsible for coordinating all the cyber components of the military services, employed only about nine hundred people total in 2013, including administrators and officers who aren't actively engaged in hacking. The Defense Department plans to grow the ranks to six thousand by the end of 2016. If the Chinese military stopped growing its cyber forces today, it would still be at least five times larger than the Americans'.

To expand the US cyber force, commanders plan to retrain network defenders to be warriors. In the air force, for instance, the vast majority of the cyber staff are support staff and systems administrators — its version of the help desk.

But they're all the air force has got for now. There are no plans to add new cyber positions. Indeed, the overall active-duty air force is the smallest it has ever been, and it will shrink even more, owing to mandatory spending cuts that were enacted in 2013. US Cyber Command, which oversees all military cyber operations, also plans to pull from the ranks of support staff. Officials want to automate much of the military's IT support functions, theoretically freeing those personnel for offensive operations.

"There aren't enough of the most critically skilled professionals to go around," says Major General John Davis, senior military adviser for cyberspace policy at the Pentagon. The military can't pay its personnel what they'd make in the private sector, where the most highly trained military hackers could easily double their salaries working for a government contractor. "The air force will never win a bidding war" with businesses, says Mark Maybury, the service's chief scientist. The same goes for the other branches of the armed forces. And there's no obvious solution to this labor problem. There's not much money in the military to hire more cyber warriors. And there's little appetite in Congress for raising the salaries of the existing force.

The military has urged colleges and universities to teach cyber warfare, like the air force does. A few undergraduate institutions do. But most regard computer hacking as unsavory business. "Universities don't want to touch [it], they don't want to have the perception of teaching people how to subvert things," Steven LaFountain, an NSA official who helps develop new academic programs, told a reporter. And by the time some students reach the agency, officials discover they haven't always been trained to NSA standards. "We have to teach them the technical skills we thought they should have gotten in school, and then we have to teach them the specific skills related to their mission," LaFountain said.

The NSA has teamed up with a handful of universities to help write their curriculum. (Students who want to enroll have to pass a background check and obtain a top-secret security clearance. Part of the coursework includes classified seminars at the NSA.) The agency will also help pay for some students to get a bachelor's degree in computer science and take courses in basic security—the agency even gives them a laptop and a monthly stipend. In exchange, they go to work for the agency when they graduate. Most of these schools—which range from Princeton University to small community colleges in nearly every state—don't teach cyber offense. The NSA takes care of that part of the education when the student shows up for work.

Even before students reach college, the military sponsors cyber defense clubs and competitions for school-aged children, such as the CyberPatriot program, a nationwide competition for middle and high schoolers. The program is cosponsored by defense contractors, including Northrop Grumman and SAIC, the company that built the proto-type for the RTRG. The competition partners with Boy Scout troops and the Boys & Girls Clubs of America as well as Junior ROTC pro-grams, Civil Air Patrol squadrons, and Naval Sea Cadet Corps units. Davis calls the program "a way [for young people] to contribute to the national and economic security of this nation."

But to attract the best talent the NSA has to compete with private industry. It recruits from the best computer science schools, including Stanford University and Carnegie Mellon. And it sends representatives to the most important annual hacker conventions, Black Hat and Def Con, in Las Vegas. In July 2012, Keith Alexander, NSA director, gave a speech at Def Con, calling on the assembled hackers to join forces with his agency, either by coming to work there or by collaborating with his team. Many of the hackers worked for security companies, but some were freelance operators who made their living discovering holes in systems and then alerting the manufacturer or developer, so they could be patched. To appeal to his audience, Alexander shed his army uniform in favor of a pair of jeans and a black T-shirt. "This is the world's best cybersecurity community. In this room right here is the talent our nation needs to secure cyberspace," he told the hackers, any number of whom US law enforcement agencies might regard as criminals. "Sometimes you guys get a bad rap," Alexander said. "From my perspective, what you're doing to figure out vulnerabilities in our systems is great. We have to discover and fix those. You guys hold the line."

But Alexander wasn't the only one in Las Vegas on a recruitment campaign. On the convention floor, executives and employees from cyber security firms were handing out brochures and T-shirts of their own. Among them were former NSA employees, whom the agency had trained to become top-tier hackers.

Alexander's recruitment challenge became harder the following summer, after documents leaked by a former NSA contractor — whom the agency had trained to be a hacker — revealed extraordinary amounts of detail about clandestine efforts to spy on systems around the world, including a program that allows that agency to collect every telephone record in the United States, and another one that gathers data from some of the world's more important technology companies, including Google, Facebook, and Apple. It was hardly a secret that the NSA was in the espionage business, but the scale of the spying caught some hackers by surprise (as it did many in the public at large). Def Con rescinded an invitation for Alexander to give another keynote speech. He appeared instead at Black Hat, where he was heckled by audience members.

FOUR

The Internet Is a Battlefield

BY THE TIME he was named commander of US Cyber Command, in 2010, Keith Alexander had had five years to master the signals intelligence domain as the director of the NSA. He was an adept technician. "When he would talk to our engineers, he would get down in the weeds as far as they were. And he'd understand what they were talking about," says a former senior NSA official. Then, when surveillance laws were changed in 2007 and 2008 to allow broader access to communications networks, Alexander seized the political moment and turned the NSA into the undisputed spymaster of the Internet. The agency was given the authority and the money to build up a hacker force. Technically speaking, they were intelligence agency employees, instructed only to monitor networks. But when they linked up with Cyber Command, they became warriors. The hackers flowed freely from one mission to the other and blurred the lines between espionage and combat. And one group of hackers in particular became the NSA's secret weapon.

The agency's best-trained and most skilled hackers work in its Tailored Access Operations office, or TAO. Estimates on the number of personnel assigned there vary, from three hundred on the low end to perhaps as many as six hundred, but this latter number may include analysts and support personnel as well.

Within TAO, different groups carry out a range of espionage and attack operations. One conducts surveillance to map out the computer networks of its targets and find their vulnerabilities. Another unit researches the latest hacking tools and techniques for penetrating secure computer networks. Another builds penetration tools tailored just for telecommunications networks. Within that group are hackers who develop tools for commandeering video cameras, particularly on laptop computers, and industrial control systems, devices that control and regulate power grids, nuclear reactors, dams, and other infrastructure. And yet another unit carries out computer network attacks in conjunction with a CIA group called the Technology Management Office, which helps the NSA break in to hard-to-reach networks where a person might be required to manually insert a virus or piece of spyware with, say, a USB thumb drive.

TAO's offices are located in a secure building at Fort Meade, Maryland. To get inside, employees must pass a retinal scan and enter a six-digit code outside a large steel door manned by armed guards. The hacker unit is one of the most secretive organizations in the intelligence community. Few NSA employees have the high levels of security clearance necessary to know about what TAO does or step foot inside its fortified chamber at Fort Meade.

The TAO hackers have only one job: to get inside adversaries' networks, by hook or by crook. They steal or crack passwords, implant spyware, install backdoors, and work with CIA's networks of human spies, all in a broad effort to obtain information. There are two purposes for this espionage. One is to obtain the secrets of the United States' competitors — whether friend of foe. The other is to gather information on how to destroy those computer networks and the infrastructure attached to them should the president ever give that order. On the Internet battlefield, TAO is surveilling potential targets. Were an order to attack ever given, they would help lead the charge.

US officials and intelligence experts estimate that TAO has implanted spying devices in at least 85,000 computer systems in 89 countries, according to classified documents that were released by former NSA contractor Edward Snowden. In 2010, TAO conducted 279 operations. The unit has cracked the encryption that underpins widely used e-mail systems, including BlackBerry, in order to spy on computer users around the world. It has even gone so far as to divert the shipments of its targets' computers to an NSA facility and then implant spyware inside the computers. A TAO PowerPoint presentation detailing its exploits boasts a modified version of the familiar Intel logo. It reads, "TAO Inside."

In most cases the infected machine's owner has no idea that TAO hackers are watching it. That's because the unit relies on a stockpile of so-called zero day vulnerabilities, which are essentially flaws in a computer system known only to the hacker. The agency buys these vulnerabilities on a gray market from hackers who have discovered them, sometimes for several thousand dollars each. In other instances the NSA pays software and hardware companies not to disclose vulnerabilities or backdoors in their products, so that the spy agency and the TAO hackers can exploit them.

Once inside those computers, a hacker can read and copy all unencrypted documents on the machine, including text files, e-mails, audiovisual files, presentations, contact lists — everything. Encrypted information is harder to read, but not impossible. Part of the NSA's mission, after all, is code breaking, and it's been the best in the business for more than sixty years.

About the only thing that the TAO hackers can't do is spy on a country with restricted access to the Internet. That's why North Korea has generally been beyond the elite group's reach. The country's connections to the outside world are so limited, and so tightly defended and monitored, that TAO has very few points of easy entry.

The same cannot be said for China.

China is the most important target for NSA surveillance and cyber warfare planning. And although Chinese officials have gone to great lengths to control access to and activity on the Internet from inside the country, China is a large, technologically evolving nation, and that makes it vulnerable.

The intelligence historian and journalist Matthew Aid learned that TAO "has successfully penetrated Chinese computer and telecommunications systems for almost 15 years, generating some of the best and most reliable intelligence information about what is going on inside the People's Republic of China." Indeed, it was TAO that gave US officials the evidence that China had penetrated the computer networks of defense contractors and other US companies. Classified NSA documents show that the agency has targeted the networks of Huawei, the world's biggest telecommunications maker, which is based in China. US intelligence officials and some lawmakers have suspected for years that Huawei is a proxy for the Chinese military and intelligence services. US regulatory agencies have blocked the installation of Huawei telecom equipment, including switches and routers, in this country for fear they'll be used as a conduit for cyber spying.

Edward Snowden told Chinese journalists that the NSA broke in to computers at Beijing's Tsinghua University, one of the country's top education and research institutions. Snowden described the hacking as extensive. On one day in January 2013, the NSA had penetrated at least sixty-three university computers or servers, according to documents Snowden showed the journalists. Those documents proved the NSA had done as he claimed, Snowden said, because they showed Internet protocol addresses that could have been obtained only by someone with physical access to the computers.

Why would the NSA be interested in hacking a Chinese university? The journalists Snowden talked to noted that Tsinghua is home to the China Education and Research Network, a government-run system from which "Internet data from millions of Chinese citizens could be mined." That may be one reason the NSA wanted inside. But US analysts and investigators believe that Chinese universities are a major talent pool for the government. Unit 61398, the People's Liberation Army cyber outfit based in Shanghai, "aggressively recruits new talent from the Science and Engineering departments of universities such as Harbin Institute of Technology and Zhejiang University School of Computer Science and Technology," according to the computer security firm Mandiant. "The majority of 'profession codes' describing positions that Unit 61398 is seeking to fill require highly technical computer skills."

It's also possible that by hacking into computers at Tsinghua, the NSA was trying to get the names of Chinese recruits or learn more about how they're trained. Tsinghua's own computer science and technology department offers undergraduate-, master's-, and PhD-level classes. According to one international study, Tsinghua is the top computer science university in mainland China and ranks twenty-seventh in the world. The university publicly bills itself as a leading institution. The NSA and the military maintain a database of all known hackers working in China. If the NSA wanted to identify future Chinese hackers when they are just getting into the business, Tsinghua would be a logical place to look.

China is the biggest target of late, but it's not the only one on which TAO hackers have set their sights. They assisted in tracking down hundreds of al-Qaeda terrorists and insurgents during the 2007 surge in Iraq. That year they also were recognized with an award from NSA leadership for their work gathering intelligence about the capabilities of Iran's nuclear weapons program. Matthew Aid writes that TAO "is the place to be right now," according to a recently retired NSA official. Personnel who want to get promoted or win professional awards try to get transferred to TAO, where they have many opportunities to show off their electronic spying skills. One NSA official, Teresa Shea, got her job as the head of NSA's Signals Intelligence Directorate — one of the most prestigious and senior posts in the agency — thanks to the work she did as the chief of TAO, gathering intelligence that most agencies in the government could not.

Service in the crack unit also gives members an impressive credential and sophisticated training that they can parlay into a more lucrative job doing cyber security operations for businesses. Former members of TAO have gone on to work for government contractors, including the software maker SAP and Lockheed Martin, and for brand-name corporations, including Amazon; they have formed their own private cyber security companies, conducting hacker-for-hire operations against companies and foreign groups that are trying to steal information from the private firms' clients.

If TAO represents the elite of NSA hackers, a unit within it gathers together the elite of the elite. Its official name is the Remote Operations Center, but insiders call it simply the ROC—pronounced "rock."

The ROC is home to the most highly skilled and experienced hackers in the government, working at Fort Meade or at outposts in Colorado, Georgia, Texas, and Hawaii, beyond the reach of senior policymakers in Washington. In fiscal year 2013, the ROC was authorized to spend $651.7 million to break in to computer systems around the world, according to the NSA's classified budget. That was twice as much as the entire intelligence community spent defending US military and classified computer networks from attack.

Technically, US Cyber Command is supposed to work with the military combatant commands to conduct cyber war. In reality, the ROC and Cyber Command work hand in hand on surveillance and attack operations, and the ROC is usually in the lead. The ROC's work is inseparable from cyber warfare—surveillance is an essential precursor to attack. The ROC is authorized to scout out systems and networks and provide targeting information to the Cyber Command. And since the two organizations are overseen by the same person—the director of NSA, who is "dual-hatted" to run Cyber Command—they can work together with relative ease.

The regional centers are particularly active when it comes to tracking the United States' foreign enemies—and its allies. In the second half of 2009, a small team at the Hawaii center conducted targeting operations against high-priority al-Qaeda targets. The hackers broke in to the terrorists' electronic devices, as during the cyber operations in Iraq, in order to lead military forces to them.

The regional centers are also home to some of the most sensitive spying operations against US allies. In May 2010, members of a team in San Antonio, Texas, reported that they'd successfully broken in to an e-mail server used by the president of Mexico and his staff. In a top-secret summary of the operation, dubbed Flatliquid, TAO members crowed that they'd gained "first-ever access to President Felipe

Calderón's public e-mail account." The team worked with the CIA and spy teams in US embassies in Mexico as well, to surveil phone calls and text messages on Mexican networks.

The same e-mail domain that the NSA compromised also was used by Mexican cabinet officials. The American spies now had access to "diplomatic, economic and leadership communications which continue to provide insight into Mexico's political system and internal stability." Calderón, a reliable US ally, had been secretly turned into "a lucrative source."

It was an especially treacherous mission, because Calderón had been so close to US intelligence, military, and law enforcement officials as they worked together to combat Mexico's violent drug cartels, which had assassinated law enforcement officials and practically taken over entire Mexican towns during their reign of terror. Whenever senior US intelligence officials spoke about United States–Mexican relations, they were quick to praise Calderón and the way he'd opened up his government to work with the Americans, who provided intelligence about the drug cartels, including communications intercepted by the very same agency that was spying on the Mexican president.

It wasn't that US officials doubted Calderón's commitment to the drug war. But they apparently wanted to be sure that he was doing all he'd promised on his side of the border, and that there weren't threats against him that he either couldn't see or couldn't deter. It was paternalism mixed with condescension — the country was too unstable for Calderón to manage on his own, officials seemed to think.

But it was in America's self-interest to spy on Calderón too. American officials thought that the cartels could extend their violent reach over the border into the United States, and that they might even topple Calderón's government or weaken it so much that Mexico effectively became a failed state. In the summer of 2012 the NSA accessed the e-mails of then presidential candidate Enrique Peña Nieto, who took office in December of that year. The agency intercepted his cell phone calls, too, along with those of "nine of his close associates," as well as more than 85,000 text messages sent by Nieto and his associates, the top-secret NSA document states. The spies used a graphing program that displayed who was in touch with whom, then determined which sets of communications indicated significant relationships among those being monitored. Those people were watched more closely.

To say that the NSA has a tin ear for the political sensitivity of its work is to misinterpret what it does. Though the spying operations against US allies are obvious betrayals of trust, they are standard practice in the espionage business — and in that business, NSA officials and employees insist they are only following orders from the president, his cabinet, and top policymakers. In fact, twice a year they craft and approve a document that lays out the topics on which they want intelligence from the NSA and other agencies. Monitoring the inner workings of the Mexican government was essential to preserving the security of both countries, Obama administration officials decided. The NSA didn't choose to spy on Mexico — it was assigned that task.

The way that Tailored Access Operations and the ROC blend expertise and personnel from the spy agencies and the military points to one of the key features of cyber warfare: it blurs the lines between pure intelligence and military operations. Intelligence agencies, under US law, are allowed to engage in covert operations that violate other countries' laws and sovereignty and are designed to obscure the United States government's involvement. Military operations are conducted under international laws of war and, while not exactly done out in the open, are arguably more transparent and accountable than intelligence operations. When the two are put together, it creates challenges for lawyers and agency officials to know when an operation is being conducted under intelligence laws and regulations or under military ones. In practical terms, the decision is made by NSA officials, up to and including the director, who himself switches back and forth between running the agency (where he is a spy) and running Cyber Command (where he is a warrior).

This fungibility between spy and soldier mirrors what has happened in the world of special operations forces, in which military commandos, trained to fight wars, are sent out on covert intelligence missions. The operation that killed bin Laden was run in fact by the head of the Joint Special Operations Command, Admiral Bill McRaven. But in law it was overseen by the director of the CIA, Leon Panetta. In practice, that meant that Panetta sat in a room in Langley, Virginia, declared himself nominally in charge, and then told McRaven to run the show. No one doubted that McRaven was calling the operational shots, and that his soldiers were in charge of their own mission. But the legal distinction was important. For starters, it would give the United States government the ability to deny knowledge of the operation were it ever discovered. Second, it allowed the United States to skirt certain laws of war — namely, that a country cannot invade another, in this case Pakistan, where bin Laden was hiding, if the two countries aren't at war. Turning soldiers into spies is a common practice when boots are on the ground. So it is in cyberspace.

Indeed, the NSA couldn't carry out all of its hacking missions without the CIA's help. CIA personnel have conducted more than one hundred so-called "black bag jobs" to break in to physical facilities and install malware or surveillance equipment on the computer systems of foreign governments, militaries, and corporations — particularly telecommunications and Internet services providers. These computers are too hard for the NSA to reach remotely.

These secret break-ins are conducted by the Special Collection Service, a joint CIA-NSA office headquartered near Beltsville, Maryland, about a ten-minute drive from the NSA. The group earned a reputation for derring-do at the height of the Cold War, bugging Communist Party officials of the Soviet Union and Eastern bloc. Its members have been compared to the stealthy, acrobatic break-in artists of the *Mission: Impossible* TV series and movie franchise. Reportedly, they used lasers aimed at windows to record conversations inside offices. They even tied surveillance devices to pigeons that perched on the windowsills of the Soviet embassy in Washington, DC.

Today the Special Collection Service works out of sixty-five locations, or "listening posts," in US embassies and consulates. Its new targets are terrorists in remote areas, where it's difficult to place a listening device, and on foreign governments building up their own cyber armies, particularly in China and East Asia. (Alexander sent some members of the service to work with cyber forces in Iraq to hunt down insurgents and terrorists.) The group plays an indispensable role in helping NSA establish the digital beachheads it needs to listen in on hard-to-reach communications networks and devices and, should the need arise, to launch cyber attacks to destroy or disrupt those systems. A few years ago the Special Collection Service reportedly got access to the switching center that services several fiber-optic trunk lines in a South Asian country. It gave the NSA the ability to intercept the communications of the country's top military commanders and also created a vital access point to its communication arteries. These kinds of operations result in an intelligence twofer — surveillance and a base of operations for cyber attacks. The NSA secretly commandeers computers in these countries as well, and can use them to launch malicious software, so that it can't easily be traced back to the United States. Several dozen clandestine CIA officers trained for the black-bag operations to implant this spyware now work full-time at NSA headquarters in Fort Meade.

The CIA has also set up its own hacker force, known as the Information Operations Center, or IOC. According to a budget document leaked by Edward Snowden, this CIA group has grown in size in recent years and now employs hundreds of people, making it one of the agency's largest groups. The IOC launches cyber attacks and recruits foreign spies to help conduct its operations, according to the document.

The Internet has become a battlefield. In recent years the alliance between soldiers and spies has grown stronger, and they have expanded the terrain on which they fight together.

They've exported to Afghanistan the hunting techniques that proved so effective in Iraq. NSA hackers went into the war zone and worked alongside combat forces rounding up or killing Taliban fighters. Under a program called Shifting Shadow, the agency collected communications and locations information on cell phones in Afghanistan, tapping into what a classified document calls a "foreign access point." But other data was pumped into the analysis machine, including public-opinion polling, vehicular traffic reports, and even the price of food staples in the marketplace. Analysts were trying to gauge the public's mood and seeking connections between, for example, spikes in the prices of potatoes and the outbreak of violence. Results were mixed. One US official claimed the system could "predict the future," and credited it with determining the time and location of Taliban attacks with 60 to 70 percent accuracy. Others derided the system as a bloated and expensive data-mining experiment that never really provided the useful results that its backers claimed.

But whatever the degree of effectiveness, senior military leaders in Afghanistan believed that cyber warfare made a major contribution, and as the war dragged on, they opened a window on those usually secretive operations. "I can tell you that as a commander in Afghanistan in the year 2010, I was able to use my cyber operations against my adversary with great impact," said marine lieutenant general Richard P. Mills during a speech at a technology conference in Baltimore in August 2012. "I was able to get inside his nets, infect his command-and-control, and in fact defend myself against his almost constant incursions to get inside my wire, to affect my operations." At the time, Mills had been the highest-ranking marine in Afghanistan, where he led combat forces in the southwest. In his public remarks he was describing the same techniques and tactics that had been used in Iraq.

Over the course of two wars, the NSA deployed more than six thousand of its personnel to combat zones. Twenty of them died. No one could say that a cyber war was entirely without risk to those who fought it.

These cyber warriors were sent into smaller, shorter wars as well.

During US military operations in Libya in 2011, which led to the ouster of Muammar Gaddafi, the NSA worked with the navy's cyber warriors to track targets in Libya and help create "strike packages." The hackers found targets on the ground via their electronic devices and radio signals, then passed along the coordinates to an aircraft carrier strike group, led by the USS *Enterprise*. Those cyber operations were conducted in the navy's Information Operations Command, which is based at Fort Meade along with the NSA.

It was hardly the first time the navy and the NSA had worked together. During a six-month project directed by the secretary of defense in 2010, the navy's Information Operations Command worked with the NSA and its Special Source Operations division, which monitors US communications companies, including those who provide information to the Prism system. Certain details remain classified, including whether it was aimed at a government or a terrorist network. But according to a participant, the operation led to the real-time tracking of more than 600 individual targets in at least fourteen countries and generated nearly 150 written reports. It marked a further evolution in cyber warfare and espionage that a branch of the armed forces was working with an intelligence agency to tap into information held by US companies. Historically, the military had refrained from conducting operations inside the United States. And while their targets were not there, the tools they were using to fight this new war were. At moments like this, the Internet seems to be a borderless battlefield.

The cyber warriors have also racked up victories against terrorist groups, which themselves recognize no borders. The ROC has infiltrated various websites and forums that al-Qaeda operatives use to communicate. One internal communication among ROC hackers claimed that they could infect "pretty much anyone" who visited a particular web forum with a piece of spyware or a virus.

US cyber warriors have scored impressive victories against the remnants of al-Qaeda and its affiliates. In August 2013 a senior airman — the equivalent of an army corporal — at the air force's Seventieth Intelligence, Surveillance and Reconnaissance Wing was sifting through troves of intercepted communications when he noticed what seemed like a suspicious communication. The wing, which reports up to US Cyber Command at Fort Meade, regularly breaks in to other countries' communications networks to steal information about weapons, monitor compliance with treaties, and scramble command-and-control information. But this communication wasn't about a nation-state. The airman, a linguist by training, had spotted information that alerted the military to a "conference call" of al-Qaeda leaders, who were planning an attack. He alerted his senior officers, who ran the information all the way up the chain of command to President Obama.

The information prompted the State Department to temporarily close embassies in twenty-two countries across the Middle East. The terror alert was one of the biggest in recent memory, and it put the intelligence community, the military, and Americans abroad on heightened alert to the possibility of a major attack targeting US embassies and other government facilities abroad.

The conference call was conducted not via phone but on an encrypted Internet messaging system. Based on reporting by *The Daily Beast,* which first broke news of the meeting, as well as statements by a senior air force general, we can conclude that the airman discovered minutes of the meeting, uploaded as text documents to a series of encrypted accounts by an al-Qaeda courier. It now appears that the airman deciphered those documents and translated them, giving the United States the ability to intercept future documents and also locate the courier, who was later arrested by Yemeni authorities with help from the CIA. The courier was carrying a recording of another Internet-hosted meeting of more than twenty senior al-Qaeda leaders around the world.

Life on the frontlines of the cyber war has changed America's soldiers and opened their eyes to a world of threats they'd never appreciated. After he returned from Iraq, in 2007, Captain Bob Stasio found himself at lunch one day at the NSA's headquarters in Fort Meade, sitting next to a three-star general. The room was filled with men and women in uniform, and Stasio listened as one of them read a citation extolling the work that Stasio and his fellow cyber warriors had done in Iraq. How a small, 35-member signals intelligence platoon had made possible the capture of 450 high-value targets — an astonishing number for any outfit, but particularly for one platoon. How the number of attacks dropped 90 percent in less than a year. For their efforts, Stasio and his colleagues were being given the prestigious Director's Award, the highest honor bestowed in signals intelligence. At the time, Stasio's was the smallest unit ever to win it.

As the speaker read Stasio's name and the audience applauded, the three-star general sitting next to him smiled and gave him a gentle nudge. "Good job," said Keith Alexander, NSA director.

It was just the beginning of their new relationship. Alexander brought Stasio to work for the Commander's Action Group, Alexander's "A-team." Stasio reported to a senior officer who reported directly to Alexander. Stasio did some of the early work helping to set up the new Cyber Command. In 2009 he took command of a company in charge of army cyber operations at the NSA. He was overseeing seventy soldiers and more advanced and expensive equipment than he'd ever seen in one place. He pulled double duty as a watch officer, in a computer network operations center that he thought resembled the Mission Control room at NASA's Johnson Space Center. Stasio eventually left the army, but he stayed at NSA as a civilian and became the chief of operations at the NSA's Cyber Center.

There Stasio worked in what he describes as "constant crisis mode." He could see now how military networks were constantly being probed and scanned by hackers looking for a way in. But also how the whole Internet was filled with people trying to steal information, commandeer computers, or damage information networks and the infrastructure attached to them. The job opened Stasio's eyes to a world of threats that, he thought, few people truly appreciated or were prepared to address. Stasio knew the damage that hackers could do — because he'd done it. Sometimes, when he heard a story on the news about a train derailment, he'd wonder, *Did a hacker cause that?*

Stasio spent the years to come waiting for a catastrophic cyber attack on the United States. After leaving the NSA he started his own cyber security company, Ronin Analytics, and listened to corporate executives praising their sophisticated cyber defense operations and the resilience of their networks. Swearing that they were well protected. That they were safe.

He'd shake his head and think, *You don't see what I see.*

FIVE

The Enemy Among Us

THE INTERNET WAS a battlefield. But the enemy was hiding in plain sight. Everywhere Keith Alexander looked in cyberspace, he saw threats. To banks. To the power grid. To military and intelligence computer networks. How would the NSA's cyber warriors ever find them all?

The year after Alexander arrived at the NSA, he warned his staff that "the fight on the network" was coming. The agency had to evolve from its counterterrorism mission, which had been running full steam since after the 9/11 attacks, toward finding and fighting hackers, whether they were working with terrorist organizations, criminal rings, or nations. Alexander sent a memo to NSA personnel assigned to a secret program known as Turbulence. It was an early attempt to monitor hackers and malware around the world using a network of sensors, and in some cases to launch cyber attacks to neutralize a threat. Alexander informed the Turbulence team that there was "nothing more important in this agency" than their work.

To accomplish the mission, the NSA had to become more aggressive about implanting surveillance and monitoring devices on computers around the world. American hackers who had sworn an oath to defend the nation from cyber threats would start to think like their adversaries; they must be cunning and devious. Many of the same tactics they were trying to defend against, they would adopt. The cyber warriors were about to enter a gray zone, where in their quest to secure the Internet they would undermine its very foundations.

As the NSA's cyber warriors scanned the horizon for threats, they realized that certain key attributes of cyberspace would become impediments to their mission. So they decided to remove those obstacles. Among the first they set their sights on was a popular routing system, called Tor, that allows people around the world to connect to the Internet anonymously. Tor isn't a criminal enterprise, nor is it run by enemies of the United States. It was actually developed by the US Naval Research Laboratory in 2002, and it's used today by democracy activists and dissidents to evade the surveillance of oppressive regimes. But it's also favored by malicious hackers, spies, and crooks who use it to shield their location when conducting operations. Tor also provides an avenue to darker corners of the Internet, where people anonymously buy and sell illicit goods and services, including drugs, weapons, computer viruses, and hacking services, even murder-for-hire.

Anonymity is the bane of NSA's cyber war operations. The hackers can't hit a target if they don't know where it is. So it was hardly surprising that the NSA began trying to undermine the anonymizing features of Tor as early as 2006. And it has kept trying for years.

Users of Tor, which stands for "The Onion Router," download a free piece of software to their computer. Say a user wants to anonymously connect to a website. The software automatically directs him through a network of thousands of relay points, run mostly by volunteers. Traffic inside Tor is encrypted as it passes through various layers of the network — hence the onion metaphor. Once the user connects to the site, his data has been encrypted so many times, and he's been bounced around so many different relay points, that it's nearly impossible to know where he's located. Anyone can use Tor — drug traffickers, child pornographers, hackers, terrorists, and spies, all of whom have found it a viable means for achieving anonymity online and evading detection by law enforcement and intelligence agencies.

For six days in February 2012, the NSA joined forces with its British counterpart, the Government Communications Headquarters, and set up eleven "relays" in the Tor system. A relay, also known as a router or node, receives and directs traffic in a system. The government-installed relays were dubbed Freedomnet.

Trying to set up a spying station in Tor seemed like a better alternative than attacking the Tor nodes outright and taking them offline — although the NSA hackers considered that, according to a top-secret briefing document. They decided against it, since they couldn't always be sure whether a node was in the United States or abroad, and attacking equipment inside the United States posed a host of legal problems. Removing the nodes was also a foolhardy endeavor, since there are thousands of relays in Tor, and they could be brought back up in different locations. So, the NSA attempted to identify users once they were inside the network by tricking them into using its relay points. The NSA hackers also sent potential Tor users spear-phishing e-mails, messages that were designed to look as if they came from a trusted source — a friend, or someone in the users' contacts list — but that actually contained a virus or a link that would take the victim to a website where spyware was implanted.

The hackers also considered trying to "disrupt" the Tor system, according the briefing document titled "Tor Stinks." Maybe slow it down, or "set up a lot of really slow Tor nodes (advertised as high bandwidth) to degrade the overall stability of the network." They contemplated making it harder or "painful" for someone to connect to Tor. The NSA would be like a gremlin, mischievously futzing with the machine.

The agency also tried to attack Tor users from outside the network, infecting or "tagging" computers with a kind of electronic marker as they went in and out of Tor. The NSA's hackers looked for different avenues to break in to computers that might be using the network — or might not. Once, they discovered a particular weak spot in a version of the Internet browser Firefox, which made it easier to tag computers using that browser. Never mind that the same weakness, if left unprotected, could be used to harm people who'd never heard of Tor and had no desire to cover their online footprints.

• • •

The NSA's anti-Tor campaign was exposed in 2013, through top-secret documents leaked by Edward Snowden. Those documents also revealed that the campaign was largely a failure. The NSA identified or located only a few dozen people using Tor. That was a testament to how well Tor worked. But the NSA's attacks were still a measure of just how far the agency would go to get an advantage over its adversaries, regardless of the costs. Given that the NSA can't always know the location of computers using Tor, it was almost certainly infecting computers used by Americans. Tor estimates that about four hundred thousand users are connecting directly to the system in the United States.

The NSA's tactics also put it at odds with US foreign policy. Over the past few years the State Department has given millions of dollars to support Tor and has encouraged its use by activists and dissidents abroad, including rebels in Syria fighting a grueling civil war to overthrow the strongman Bashar al-Assad. The NSA knew that the State Department was promoting Tor, and it attacked Tor anyway. The United States now has two competing and directly opposed policies: trying to prop up Tor and at the same time tearing it down.

Former NSA director Michael Hayden put the dilemma in particularly blunt, NSA-centered terms. "The Secretary of State is laundering money through NGOs to populate software throughout the Arab world to prevent the people in the Arab street from being tracked by their government," he said in 2012 at a Washington think tank, before NSA's operations against Tor were disclosed. "So on the one hand we're fighting anonymity, on the other hand we're chucking products out there to protect anonymity on the net."

US efforts to promote democracy and free access to the Internet are set back as a result of NSA's actions. "The United States government is incredibly large with lots of diverse programs . . . and the employees shouldn't all get lumped together as aligned with the NSA's view of the world," says Dan Meredith, director of Radio Free Asia's Open Technology Fund, a private nonprofit that has received an annual grant from the United States for Internet anticensorship projects, including work with Tor. "You'll try to explain that to activists in Sudan, but they don't always take it that way. Sometimes I'll spend fifteen minutes with people trying to convince them that I'm not [a spy]."

The NSA doesn't work alone to undermine the Internet's key security and privacy pillars. Under a secret program called the SIGINT Enabling Project, it strikes deals with technology companies to insert backdoors into their commercial products. Congress allocated $250 million for the project in 2013. Working in conjunction with the FBI, the NSA got inside knowledge about a feature in Microsoft's e-mail product, Outlook, that could have created obstacles to surveillance if left unaddressed. The agency also got access to Skype Internet phone calls and chats as well as Microsoft's cloud storage service, SkyDrive, so that NSA analysts could read people's messages before they were encrypted.

Classified documents also show that the NSA invites makers of encryption products to let the agency's experts review their work, with the ostensible goal of making their algorithms stronger. But the NSA actually inserts vulnerabilities into the products, to use in its espionage and cyber warfare missions. One document states that this work allows the agency "to remotely deliver or receive information to and from target endpoints." In other words, steal information from or implant malicious code on computers.

These footholds in technologies sold and used around the world allow the NSA to spy without being detected and, if need be, disable the technologies themselves. The Stuxnet computer worm that destroyed centrifuge equipment in the Iranian nuclear facility relied on a previously unknown weakness in a control system used by Siemens. Computer security experts have questioned whether the company knew about the vulnerability and agreed to keep it undefended. In any event, the NSA clearly had inside knowledge of some kind about the weakness and rolled it into Stuxnet's design.

The military also trains its cyber warriors, who work through US Cyber Command, to hack some of the most widely used communications equipment in the world. The army has sent soldiers to courses that teach students how Cisco networking devices are built and used.

This isn't so they can maintain the equipment but so they can break in to it and defend it from others trying to do the same.

Under the SIGINT Enabling Project, the NSA also pays phone and Internet companies to build their networks in such a way that the agency can tap into them — or, to use the more opaque language of a classified budget document, "provide for continued partnerships with major telecommunications carriers to shape the global network to benefit other collection accesses."

All this clandestine work underscores the degree to which the NSA is dependent on corporations that build software and hardware and that own and operate portions of the Internet. The agency would find itself generally out of the surveillance and cyber warfare business without the cooperation of these companies. But its efforts to dominate the "fifth domain" of warfare extend beyond deals struck with individual corporations.

For the past ten years the NSA has led an effort in conjunction with its British counterpart, the Government Communications Headquarters, to defeat the widespread use of encryption technology by inserting hidden vulnerabilities into widely used encryption standards. Encryption is simply the process of turning a communication — say, an e-mail — into a jumble of meaningless numbers and digits, which can only be deciphered using a key possessed by the e-mail's recipient. The NSA once fought a public battle to gain access to encryption keys, so that it could decipher messages at will, but it lost that fight. The agency then turned its attention toward weakening the encryption algorithms that are used to encode communications in the first place.

The NSA is home to the world's best code makers, who are regularly consulted by public organizations, including government agencies, on how to make encryption algorithms stronger. That's what happened in 2006 — a year after Alexander arrived — when the NSA helped developed an encryption standard that was eventually adopted by the National Institute of Standards and Technology, the US government agency that has the last word on weights and measures used for calibrating all manner of tools, industrial equipment, and scientific instruments. NIST's endorsement of an encryption standard is a kind of Good Housekeeping Seal of approval. It encourages companies, advocacy groups, individuals, and government agencies around the world to use the standard. NIST works through an open, transparent process, which allows experts to review the standard and submit comments. That's one reason its endorsement carries such weight. NIST is so trusted that it must approve any encryption algorithms that are used in commercial products sold to the US government.

But behind the scenes of this otherwise open process, the NSA was strong-arming the development of an algorithm called a random-number generator, a key component of all encryption. Classified documents show that the NSA claimed it merely wanted to "finesse" some points in the algorithm's design, but in reality it became the "sole editor" of it and took over the process in secret. Compromising the number generator, in a way that only the NSA knew, would undermine the entire encryption standard. It gave the NSA a backdoor that it could use to decode information or gain access to sensitive computer systems.

The NSA's collaboration on the algorithm was not a secret. Indeed, the agency's involvement lent some credibility to the process. But less than a year after the standard was adopted, security researchers discovered an apparent weakness in the algorithm and speculated publicly that it could have been put there by the spy agency. The noted computer security expert Bruce Schneier zeroed in on one of four techniques for randomly generating numbers that NIST had approved. One of them, he wrote in 2007, "is not like the others."

For starters, it worked three times more slowly than the others, Schneier observed. It was also "championed by the NSA, which first proposed it years ago in a related standardization project at the American National Standards Institute."

Schneier was alarmed that NIST would encourage people to use an inferior algorithm that had been enthusiastically embraced by an agency whose mission is to break codes. But there was no proof that the NSA was up to no good. And the flaw in the number generator didn't render it useless. As Schneier noted, there was a workaround, though it was unlikely anyone would bother to use it. Still, the flaw set cryptologists on edge. The NSA was surely aware of their unease, as well as the growing body of work that pointed to its secret intervention, because it leaned on an international standards body that represents 163 countries to adopt the new algorithm. The NSA wanted it out in the world, and so widely used that people would find it hard to abandon.

Schneier, for one, was confused as to why the NSA would choose as a backdoor such an obvious and now public flaw. (The weakness had first been pointed out a year earlier by employees at Microsoft.) Part of the answer may lie in a deal that the NSA reportedly struck with one of the world's leading computer security vendors, RSA, a pioneer in the industry. According to a 2013 report by Reuters, the company adopted the NSA-built algorithm "even before NIST approved it. The NSA then cited the early use ... inside the government to argue successfully for NIST approval." The algorithm became "the default option for producing random numbers" in an RSA security product called the bSafe toolkit, Reuters reported. "No alarms were raised, former employees said, because the deal was handled by business leaders rather than pure technologists." For its compliance and willingness to adopt the flawed algorithm, RSA was paid $10 million, Reuters reported.

It didn't matter that the NSA had built an obvious backdoor. The algorithm was being sold by one of the world's top security companies, and it had been adopted by an international standards body as well as NIST. The NSA's campaign to weaken global security for its own advantage was working perfectly.

When news of the NSA's efforts broke in 2013, in documents released by Edward Snowden, RSA and NIST both distanced themselves from the spy agency — but neither claimed that the backdoor hadn't been installed.

In a statement following the Reuters report, RSA denied that it had entered into a "secret contract" with the NSA, and asserted that "we have never entered into any contract or engaged in any project with the intention of weakening RSA's products, or introducing potential 'backdoors' into our products for anyone's use." But it didn't deny that the backdoor existed, or may have existed. Indeed, RSA said that years earlier, when it decided to start using the flawed number-generator algorithm, "the NSA had a trusted role in the community-wide effort to strengthen, not weaken, encryption." Not so much anymore. When documents leaked by Snowden confirmed the NSA's work, RSA encouraged people to stop using the number generator — as did NIST.

The standards body issued its own statement following the Snowden revelations. It was a model of carefully calibrated language. "NIST would not deliberately weaken a cryptographic standard," the organization said in a public statement, clearly leaving open the possibility — without confirming it — that the NSA had secretly installed the vulnerability or done so against NIST's wishes. "NIST has a long history of extensive collaboration with the world's cryptography experts to support robust encryption. The [NSA] participates in the NIST cryptography development process because of its recognized expertise. NIST is also required by statute to consult with the NSA."

The standards body was effectively telling the world that it had no way to stop the NSA. Even if it wanted to shut the agency out of the standards process, by law it couldn't. A senior NSA official later seemed to support that contention. In an interview with the national security blog *Lawfare* in December 2013, Anne Neuberger, who manages the NSA's relationships with technology companies, was asked about reports that the agency had secretly handicapped the algorithm during the development process. She neither confirmed nor denied the accusation. Neuberger called NIST "an incredibly respected close partner on many things." But, she noted, it "is not a member of the intelligence community.

"All the work they do is . . . pure white hat," Neuberger continued, meaning not malicious and intended solely to defend encryption and promote security. "Their only responsibility is to set standards" and "to make them as strong as they can possibly be."

That is not the NSA's job. Neuberger seemed to be giving the NIST a get-out-of-jail-free card, exempting it from any responsibility for inserting the flaw.

The 2006 effort to weaken the number generator wasn't an isolated incident. It was part of a broader, longer campaign by the NSA to weaken the basic standards that people and organizations around the world use to protect their information. Documents suggest that the NSA has been working with NIST since the early 1990s to hobble encryption standards before they're adopted. The NSA dominated the process of developing the Digital Signature Standard, a method of verifying the identity of the sender of an electronic communication and the authenticity of the information in it. "NIST publicly proposed the [standard] in August 1991 and initially made no mention of any NSA role in developing the standard, which was intended for use in unclassified, civilian communications systems," according to the Electronic Privacy Information Center, which obtained documents about the development process under the Freedom of Information Act. Following a lawsuit by a group of computer security experts, NIST conceded that the NSA had developed the standard, which "was widely criticized within the computer industry for its perceived weak security and inferiority to an existing authentication technology," the privacy center reported. "Many observers have speculated that the [existing] technique was disfavored by NSA because it was, in fact, more secure than the NSA-proposed algorithm."

From NSA's perspective, its efforts to defeat encryption are hardly controversial. It is, after all, a code-breaking agency. This is precisely the kind of work it is authorized, and expected, to do. If the agency developed flaws in encryption algorithms that only it knew about, what would be the harm?

But the flaws weren't secret. By 2007, the backdoor in the number generator was being written about on prominent websites and by leading security experts. It would be difficult to exploit the weakness — that is, to figure out the key that opened NSA's backdoor. But this wasn't impossible. A foreign government could figure out how to break the encryption and then use it to spy on its own citizens, or on American companies and agencies using the algorithm. Criminals could exploit the weakness to steal personal and financial information. Anywhere the algorithm was used — including in the products of one of the world's leading security companies — it was vulnerable.

The NSA might comfort itself by reasoning that code-breaking agencies in other countries were surely trying to undermine encryption, including the algorithms that NSA was manipulating. And surely they were. But that didn't answer the question, why knowingly undermine not just an algorithm but the entire process by which encryption standards are created? The NSA's clandestine efforts damaged the credibility of NIST and shredded the NSA's long-held reputation as a trusted, valued participant in creating some of the most fundamental technologies on the Internet, the very devices by which people keep their data, and by extension themselves, safe. Imagine if the NSA had been in the business of building door locks, and encouraged every homebuilder in America to install its preferred, and secretly flawed, model. No one would stand for it. At the very least, consumer groups would file lawsuits and calls would go up for the organization's leaders to resign.

But the reaction to the NSA's anti-encryption campaign was relatively subdued. In part, that's because many experts, cryptologists among them, had long presumed that the agency was up to this kind of work in the shadows. The revelations were informative but not exactly surprising. But there was also a strong sense among lawmakers and US officials that this is what the NSA does. It breaks codes in order to steal information. NIST sets standards through an open, transparent process. That's anathema to the NSA's secretive nature. From the NSA's perspective, the standards-setting body threatens to propagate hard-to-break algorithms and encryption technologies that would do a very good job protecting information — all things that run counter to the NSA's mission. For years lawmakers who approved the NSA's budget, and administration officials who oversaw its work, sided with the agency. To the extent that they had any misgivings, they could take some solace that as long as the NSA's handiwork stayed secret, the damage to Internet security and the United States' reputation might be minimal. The revelations of 2013 upended those calculations.

Of all the NSA's dark arts, perhaps none has put the security of the Internet and the people using it more at risk than its secretive quest to build cyber weapons.

For the past two decades, NSA analysts have been scouring the world's software, hardware, and networking equipment looking for vulnerabilities for which it can craft computer attack methods known as zero day exploits, so called because they take advantage of previously unknown flaws for which no defense has been built. (The target has had "zero days" to prepare for the attack.)

A zero day is the most effective cyber weapon. It provides the element of surprise, which is the ultimate advantage in battle. The zero day exploit is bespoke, tailor-made to use against a specific vulnerability. And because that defenseless point in a system is likely to be patched as soon as the target realizes he's been hit with a zero day, it may be used only once.

Zero day attacks are especially hard to design because unknown vulnerabilities are hard to find. But the NSA has been stockpiling them for years. In 1997, according to a recently declassified NSA newsletter, at least eighteen organizations in the agency were secretly collecting vulnerability data on technology used by people, businesses, and governments around the world. Today the NSA is widely believed by security experts and government officials to be the single largest procurer of zero day exploits, many of which it buys in a shadowy online bazaar of freelance hackers and corporate middlemen.

This gray market is not precisely illegal, but it operates on the fringes of the Internet. It works like this: security researchers — another term for hackers — find vulnerabilities. (Many of these researchers are based in Europe, where local and national laws against computer hacking are weaker than in the United States.) The researchers then design exploits, or methods for attacking the vulnerability, that only they know about at this point. Next, they sell the exploits to middlemen, which are mostly large defense contractors. Raytheon and Harris Corporation are two major players in the zero day market. They also design traditional weapons systems for the military and are two of the best-established and largest Pentagon contractors. Their ties to the military and to the NSA are deep and long-standing. Also collecting and selling zero days are smaller boutique firms, a number of which are run by former military officers or intelligence officials.

Once the middlemen have the zero days, they sell them to their customer — the NSA. But the supply chain begins with the hacker. To be a good zero day hunter, a hacker has to put himself in the original programmer's shoes and find the flaws in his design. Automated technology can help. "Fuzzing," for instance, is a technique that throws unexpected or random data into the inputs of a computer program, hoping to make it crash. Then the hacker looks for the flaw in the system that caused it to fail.

But to find the deepest cracks, a hacker has to devise novel and more clever techniques that force the computer to show him where it's weak. For instance, in 2005 a PhD student at UCLA discovered that by measuring the "small, microscopic deviations" in the internal clocks of computers, he could uniquely identify one computer out of a network of thousands. The technique would be especially useful, he later wrote in a research paper, to "adversaries thousands of miles" away from the targeted machine who wanted to overcome software meant to hide the machine's physical location — software such as Tor, the anonymizing router system that the NSA was so keen to disrupt. A year after the paper was published, a researcher at Cambridge University discovered that one could, in fact, find which server in a network was actually running Tor's anonymizing software, thus defeating its all-important feature. He did this by sending an anonymous Tor server an especially intensive request for information that literally forced the machine to heat up because it was working so hard. The heat changed the rate at which electrons in the computer moved, which in turn affected the accuracy of the clock. He still didn't know where the anonymous server was located, but he took the unique "clock skew" and queried computers on the public Internet to see if he could find a match. He did. The clock skew gave away the location of the supposedly hidden Tor server. The classified NSA document, "Tor Stinks," which shows how the NSA tried to defeat the network, indicates that the agency studied both these clock-skew techniques in an attempt to find routers on a network.

The ingenious ability to suss out such an obscure, barely discernible flaw is what separates good hackers from great ones and leads to the discovery of zero days. Hackers charge a high price for zero day exploits. If they come in "weaponized" form, that is, ready to use against a system, exploits start at around $50,000 and run to more than $100,000 apiece, according to experts. But some exploits command a higher price because their targets are more valuable or harder to penetrate. The going rate on an exploit for Apple's iOS operating system, used on the iPhone and the company's other mobile devices, is half a million dollars, says one expert. And more complicated exploits, such as those that rely on flaws in the internal mechanics of a piece of hardware, can cost millions. Those exploits are so expensive because they target the engineering of the machine itself, which cannot be patched in the way software can, with new lines of code. The only organizations with the means and the motive to buy such a weapon are organized criminal groups and governments.

Serious buyers of zero days, such as the NSA, don't procure them in one-off fashion. They make stockpiles to use in future attacks. The NSA has stored more than two thousand zero day exploits for potential use against Chinese systems alone, according to a former high-ranking government official who was told about the cache in a classified meeting with NSA officials. That is an astonishingly large number of exploits. The Stuxnet computer worm, which the United States built in conjunction with Israel to disable the Iranian nuclear facility, contained four zero day exploits, which is itself a lot for one attack. A collection of two thousand zero day exploits is the cyber equivalent of a nuclear arsenal.

It also puts people around the world at risk. If the NSA is hoarding those vulnerabilities, rather than telling the makers of technology products that they have found flaws in their hardware and software, then the agency is arguably covering up valuable information that could be used to defend against malicious hackers. To be sure, the NSA does use knowledge of zero day exploits to plug holes in technology that it's using or that might be deployed within the military or intelligence community. But it doesn't warn the wider world — that would render the zero day exploit less effective, possibly even useless. One of the agency's eventual targets in China or Iran might be tipped off if the NSA alerted technology companies to flaws in their technology.

But in the shadowy zero day market, there are no guarantees that the NSA is always buying exclusive knowledge about zero days. One controversial vendor, the French company Vupen, sells the same zero day vulnerability information and exploits to attack them to multiple clients, including government agencies in different countries. The NSA is a Vupen client — publicly disclosed documents show the agency has purchased zero day vulnerability information under a subscription plan, through which the agency would have received a minimum number of zero days during the contract period. (Armed with that information, the NSA can build its own weapons.) Vupen also maintains a catalog of sophisticated, ready-to-launch zero day attacks, which cost more than the information available through its subscription plan.

The NSA knows that Vupen doesn't always make exclusive contracts, so it has to keep buying up more and more zero days, figuring that at least some percentage of them will be rendered useless once another country — or company, or criminal group — uses them. Critics have faulted Vupen for perpetuating a "cyber arms race," pitting government intelligence agencies and national militaries against one another. Vupen clients know that if they pass on a chance to buy a zero day, the company will find a willing customer someplace else. The vulnerabilities Vupen discovers aren't unique to one country. Many of them are found in widely sold technology products that are installed around the world. Countries have an incentive, therefore, to buy up as many zero days as they can, both to defend themselves and to attack their adversaries.

Vupen says that it only sells zero day information to "trusted organizations," which it defines as "security vendors providing defensive solutions," government organizations in "approved countries," and "worldwide corporations," to include those ranked among the top 1,000 by *Fortune* magazine. This is a long list of potential customers, and Vupen admits that it has no way of ensuring that those who buy its zero day subscription plan or choose a weapon from its catalog won't turn around and give it to people Vupen might never sell to directly. Executives give vague assurances that they have an internal process for making sure the dangerous products and knowledge they sell aren't handed off by governments to freelance hackers or mercenaries. This has been a particular concern in North Africa and the Middle East, where repressive regimes trying to crack down on democracy activists have enlisted hackers to unleash commercially available malware to spy on or track down protestors — malware purchased from companies that, like Vupen, say they'd never sell their products for such unsavory purposes. Yet those products show up on the computers and cell phones of activists, some of whom have been rounded up and treated harshly by the authorities and others acting on their behalf.

In any market — gray or otherwise — the biggest buyers have an outsized ability to set terms and conditions. As the reputedly single largest purchaser of zero day vulnerabilities and exploits, the NSA could turn the market on its head if it bought up zero days for the express purpose of disclosing them. The agency has billions of dollars to spend on cyber security. Why not devote some portion of that to alerting the world to the presence of fixable flaws? What responsibility does the agency have to warn the owners and operators of vulnerable technology that the capability of an attack against them exists? That's an ethical dilemma that the agency hasn't had to address. But if there is ever a cyber attack on the United States that results in significant physical damage, or causes widespread panic — or deaths — the agency will be called to account for its failure to prevent that disaster. There's a good chance that some future NSA director, sitting at a witness table before members of Congress and television cameras, will have to explain having known about the vulnerability America's enemies had exploited, but deciding to keep quiet, because the NSA wanted to use it one day.

The targets that are most vulnerable to a devastating zero day attack are the same ones that the NSA is trying to protect: electrical power plants, nuclear facilities, natural gas pipelines, and other critical infrastructures, including banks and financial services companies. Not all of these companies have a system for easily sharing information about vulnerabilities and exploits that have been discovered and publicly disclosed, often by more defensive-minded hackers who see their job as warning technology manufacturers about problems with their products, rather than trying to profit from them. When companies find out about a risk in their system, it's up to them to apply patches and defensive fixes, and their technological fluency varies. Some may be prepared to patch systems quickly, others may not even realize they're using a vulnerable piece of software. They, quite literally, may not have received the memo from the vendor warning that they need to install an update or change the security settings on a product in order to make it safer. Even if a company is using software that receives regular updates over the Internet, the company's systems administrators have to consistently download those fixes, make sure they're applied across the company, and stay on watch for more updates. Some find doing that for hundreds or thousands of computers in a single facility a daunting task.

By buying so many zero day exploits, the NSA is helping to prop up a cyber arms market that puts American businesses and critical facilities at risk. The chances are good that if another country or a terrorist group knocks out the lights in a US city, it will use an exploit purchased from a company that also sells them to the NSA. The sellers of zero day exploits also bear at least some notional responsibility for making the Internet less safe. But they tend to blame software manufacturers for building programs that can be penetrated in the first place. "We don't sell weapons, we sell information," the founders of exploit seller Re-Vuln told a reporter for Reuters, when he asked whether the company would be troubled if some of their programs were used in attacks that destroyed systems or caused people to die. "This question would be worth asking to vendors leaving security holes in their products."

This line of defense is a bit like blaming a locksmith for a burglary. Yes, the locksmith is supposed to make a product that keeps intruders from getting into someone's home. But if a burglar manages to break in and steal a television or, worse, attack the homeowners, we don't prosecute the locksmith. Companies such as ReVuln aren't burglars, but they are selling the equivalent of lock picks. Surely they bear some measure of responsibility, as well, for crimes that are committed — if not a legal responsibility, then a moral one.

And what about the NSA? In the world of burglary, there's no equivalent for what the agency is doing. No one is out there buying up lock picks. But the NSA also wants to be a kind of security guard for the Internet. What would happen if the guard hired to watch over a neighborhood discovered an open window but didn't tell the owner? More to the point, what if he discovered a design flaw in the brand of window that everyone in the neighborhood used that allowed an intruder to open the window from the outside? If the security guard didn't alert the homeowners, they'd fire him — and probably try to have him arrested. They wouldn't accept as a defense that the security guard was keeping the windows' flaw a secret in order to protect the homeowners. And the police surely wouldn't accept that he'd kept that information to himself so that he could go out and rob houses.

The analogy isn't perfect. The NSA isn't a law enforcement agency, it's a military and intelligence organization. It operates by a different set of laws and with a different mission. But as the agency drums up talk of cyber war and positions itself as the best equipped to help defend the nation from intruders and attacks, it should act more like a security guard than a burglar.

In 2013 the NSA had a budget of more than $25 million to procure zero day exploits, referred to as "covert purchases of software vulnerabilities" in an internal budget document. But the NSA is not entirely dependent on a shadowy, unregulated market to obtain its cyber weapons. For the most part, the agency builds its own. And why not? It has an in-house production line comprising some of the country's best hackers, many of whom have come up through the ranks of military service and are put through graduate-level computer security courses on the government's dime. Those personnel represent an expensive, long-term investment. The United States relies on their skills and knowledge in a cyber struggle against China, which will probably always have an edge in terms of sheer numbers of hackers.

The problem for the NSA is that its top-flight cyber warriors don't always stay in government service. They can easily triple their salaries in the private sector, and these days, the work they're doing there is in as high demand as it is in the government.

Charlie Miller, a former NSA employee famous for finding hard-to-detect bugs in Apple products, including the MacBook Air and the iPhone, went to work for Twitter in 2012. Miller is what's known in hacker circles as a "white hat." He tries to break in to systems in order to fix them, before a "black hat" can exploit the flaw and do damage. As the social networking company has grown, it has naturally become a bigger target for spies and criminals. Miller is using his NSA-developed skills, and his innate talent, to protect Twitter — which went public in 2013 — and its hundreds of millions of users.

Justin Schuh followed a similar path. He started his career in the mid-1990s as an intelligence analyst, software engineer, and systems administrator in the Marine Corps. In 2001, Schuh joined the NSA, where he enrolled in the agency's System and Network Interdisciplinary Program (SNIP), which is essentially cyber warrior training. "Graduates of the program become invaluable to [the agency] as the solution to universal [computer network operations] problems," says an NSA brochure, using the technical term for cyber offense. After less than two years Schuh joined the CIA, where he worked in the agency's technical operations unit, which helps the NSA place surveillance equipment in hard-to-reach places. But soon he was off to the private sector, eventually winding up at Google, where he works as an information security engineer.

Google has set up a team, which includes Schuh, devoted to finding security weaknesses and zero day exploits that could be used against Google's customers and its products, such as its e-mail system and web browser. The company itself has been the target of sophisticated hacking campaigns, most notably one by a Chinese group in 2010, which broke in to a database of proprietary software code. The hackers stole the code for a password system that allowed users to sign in to many Google applications at once. It was described by researchers as among the "crown jewels" of the company's intellectual property. The theft triggered panic at the highest ranks of Google, a company that prides itself on protecting its users' security and personal data and has built its reputation on that promise.

Google now has its own team of sleuths, several of whom worked for the NSA and other intelligence agencies, looking for threats to the company. "Here's a little secret. Having a huge index of suspected and confirmed malware is really handy for protecting hundreds of millions of users," Schuh wrote on Twitter in 2012, after Google bought a small company that scans e-mails and websites for viruses. Today Google scans its customers' Gmail for threats and will even alert them with a message, displayed on an arresting red banner, if the system thinks a virus may have been sent by hackers working for a government. The alert doesn't say China, but that's the obvious implication.

Google doesn't have enough employees to find all the zero day vulnerabilities and exploits that might threaten the company and its hundreds of millions of customers around the world. So, it also pays bounties to independent hackers, the same ones selling their discoveries to defense contractors. Google employees say their biggest competition on the zero day gray market is the NSA. It's buying up zero days faster than anyone else, and paying top dollar.

The company also employs middlemen of its own to procure zero days. According to two sources with knowledge of Google's security programs, it uses a boutique firm called Endgame, based just outside Washington, DC, to buy up vulnerability information and known exploits. It is not known precisely what Google intends to do with what it has acquired, but this much is certain: first, having a stockpile of zero day exploits would allow the company to start a private cyber war; and second, that would be illegal. Only the United States government is allowed to conduct offensive cyber operations that result in damage to computer systems.

But governments are not the exclusive targets of hackers — as the United States well knows. Indeed, it was the massive espionage campaign against defense companies that helped prompt US officials to start building up a cyber army. But today, US businesses are starting to realize that this army will never be big enough and strong enough to protect all of them. They have to defend themselves. And one of the first places they look for protection is that same shadowy network of hackers, selling their skills and weapons to the highest bidder.

SIX

The Mercenaries

BRIGHT-FACED twenty- and thirty-somethings clad in polo shirts and jeans perch on red Herman Miller chairs in front of silver Apple laptops and sleek, flat-screen monitors. They might be munching on catered lunch — brought in once a week — or scrounging the fully stocked kitchen for snacks, or making plans for the company softball game later that night. Their office is faux loft industrial chic: open floor plan, high ceilings, strategically exposed ductwork and plumbing. To all outward appearances, Endgame, Inc. looks like the typical young tech startup.

It is anything but. Endgame is one of the leading players in the global cyber arms business. Among other things, it compiles and sells zero day information to governments and corporations, and judging by the prices Endgame has charged, business has been good. Marketing documents show that Endgame has charged up to $2.5 million for a zero day subscription package, which promises twenty-five exploits per year. For $1.5 million, customers have access to a database that shows the physical location and Internet addresses of hundreds of millions of vulnerable computers around the world. Armed with this intelligence, an Endgame customer could see where its own systems are vulnerable to attack and set up defenses. But it could also find computers to exploit. Those machines could be mined for data — such as government documents or corporate trade secrets — or attacked using malware. Endgame can decide whom it wants to do business with, but it doesn't dictate how its customers use the information it sells, nor can it stop them from using it for illegal purposes, any more than Smith & Wesson can stop a gun buyer from using a firearm to commit a crime.

The heart of Endgame's business is the ability to ingest huge amounts of data about vulnerable computers and weaknesses in a network and display that information graphically. To do that, Endgame has used a proprietary software tool, internally known as Bonesaw, which the company has described as a "cyber targeting application."

"Bonesaw is the ability to map basically every device connected to the Internet and what hardware and software it is," an Endgame employee told a reporter in 2013. The software shows which systems are infected with viruses that make them vulnerable to attack.

According to security researchers and former government officials, one of Endgame's biggest customers is the NSA. The company is also known to sell to the CIA, Cyber Command, the British intelligence services, and major US corporations. Endgame has four offices, including one in the fashionable Clarendon section of Arlington, Virginia, a ten-minute drive or four Metro stops away from the Pentagon.

For its clients, Endgame has drawn up lists of computers owned and operated by some of the United States' biggest strategic adversaries. In 2010, Endgame compiled a chart showing eighteen Venezuelan government agencies and large state-owned companies running attackable computers, including a water utility, a bank, the Ministry of Defense, the Ministry of Foreign Affairs, and the Office of the Presidency. The chart, which the company noted was "not an inclusive list," showed the Internet address of each infected system, the city where it was located, and the compromised application it was running. At the end of the chart was a column labeled "EGS Vuln," apparently indicating whether the applications were vulnerable to attack. The word *yes* appeared next to nearly all of the infected machines.

Endgame has also scouted targets in Russia. Internal documents show that the company found computers open to attack in the Ministry of Finance, as well as an oil refinery, a bank, and a nuclear power plant. And the company has identified target packages in China, Latin America, and the Middle East.

This kind of intelligence used to be the near-exclusive domain of government intelligence agencies. They alone had the access and the know-how to sniff out vulnerable computers with such precision, as well as the motive and the means to acquire cyber weapons to attack those systems. Not anymore.

Endgame is one of a small but growing number of boutique cyber mercenaries that specialize in what security professionals euphemistically call "active defense." It's a somewhat misleading term, since this kind of defense doesn't entail just erecting firewalls or installing antivirus software. It can also mean launching a preemptive or retaliatory strike. Endgame doesn't conduct the attack, but the intelligence it provides can give clients the information they need to carry out their own strikes. It's illegal for a company to launch a cyber attack, but not for a government agency. According to three sources familiar with Endgame's business, nearly all of its customers are US government agencies. But since 2013, executives have sought to grow the company's commercial business and have struck deals with marquee technology companies and banks.

Endgame was founded in 2008 by Chris Rouland, a top-notch hacker who first came on the Defense Department's radar in 1990 — after he hacked into a Pentagon computer. Reportedly the United States declined to prosecute him in exchange for his working for the government. He started Endgame with a group of fellow hackers who worked as white-hat researchers for a company called Internet Security Systems, which was bought by IBM in 2006 for $1.3 billion. Technically, they were supposed to be defending their customers' computers and networks. But the skills they learned and developed were interchangeable for offense.

Rouland, described by former colleagues as domineering and hot-tempered, has become a vocal proponent for letting companies launch counterattacks on individuals, groups, or even countries that attack them. "Eventually we need to enable corporations in this country to be able to fight back," Rouland said during a panel discussion at a conference on ethics and international affairs in New York in September 2013. "They're losing millions of dollars, and it's so challenging for governments to help them, I think we have to enable them to do it themselves." Rouland was voicing a frustration of many corporate executives who'd been the target of cyber spies and organized criminals. The Pentagon had chosen to provide special protection to defense contractors and seemed more worried about attacks on critical infrastructure like the power grid than on companies that were less vital to the US economy.

Fighting back could take a number of forms. A company could unleash a torrent of traffic on a malicious computer and knock it offline. It could break in to the hard drive of a Chinese cyber spy, find the stolen proprietary documents, and then delete them. Of course, once inside the spy's computer, the company could delete everything else on it, too, and unleash a virus on its network. A single act of self-defense could quickly escalate into a full-fledged conflict. And to the extent that Chinese cyber spies are supported by the Chinese military, an American firm could end up launching a private cyber war against a sovereign government.

It's illegal for a company or an individual to hack back against a cyber aggressor. But it's not against the law to offer the products and services that Endgame does. Endgame has raised more than $50 million from top-flight venture capital firms, including Bessemer Venture Partners, Kleiner Perkins Caufield & Byers, and Paladin Capital. That's an extraordinary amount of money for a cyber security startup, particularly one specializing in such a controversial field.

Rouland stepped down as the CEO of Endgame in 2012, following embarrassing disclosures of the company's internal marketing documents by the hacker group Anonymous. Endgame had tried to stay quiet and keep its name out of the press, and went so far as to take down its website. But Rouland provocatively resurfaced at the conference and, while emphasizing that he was speaking in his personal capacity, said American companies would never be free from cyber attack unless they retaliated. "There is no concept of deterrence today in cyber. It's a global free-fire zone." One of Rouland's fellow panelists seemed to agree. Robert Clark, a professor of law at the Naval Academy Center of Cyber Security Studies, told the audience that it would be illegal for a company that had been hacked to break in to the thief's computer and delete its own purloined information. "This is the most asinine thing I can think of," Clark said. "It's my data, it's here, I should be able to delete it."

A few months after Rouland's appearance in New York, Endgame appointed a new CEO. Nathaniel Fick was a thirty-five-year-old former Marine Corps captain who'd served in Iraq and Afghanistan and later got his MBA from Harvard Business School and helped run a prominent Washington think tank. Fick wrote a memoir of his combat experience and was profiled in another book, *Generation Kill,* which was made into a miniseries for HBO.

According to two individuals who know Fick and are familiar with Endgame's business strategy, the new CEO was eager to wean the company off its intelligence contracts and to get out of the zero day business, which he saw as too controversial and ultimately not lucrative enough to justify the hundreds of thousands of dollars it takes to buy a single exploit. The margins for cyber arms were apparently too thin.

But getting out of the business won't be easy. Endgame's investors were drawn to its government clients, who had deep pockets and planned to spend billions of dollars over the coming years on cyber defense and offense. Endgame's board of advisers have historic ties to that lucrative customer base. They include a retired senior Pentagon official who served in several influential technology management posts, as well as the former chief information officer for the CIA. Endgame's chairman is the CEO of In-Q-Tel, the venture capital arm of the CIA, and a member of the board is a former director of the National Security Agency.

But as Fick noted in an interview shortly after his appointment in 2012, the post-9/11 bonanza of military spending is coming to end as the United States has wound down the wars in Iraq and Afghanistan and braced for a period of fiscal austerity amid calls in Congress for balanced budgets and smaller government. "The defense budget is going to be under pressure, and it should be," Fick said. "In many cases, the rampant excesses of the last decade are completely unsustainable." But, he added, "I think there are areas that will continue to grow."

That growth is the private sector. The two people who know Fick say that Google has become one of the biggest buyers of Endgame's zero day packages. Google would be breaking the law if it retaliated against those trying to steal its intellectual property. But Google has been among the most vocal corporations — and certainly the most influential — urging Congress and the Obama administration to call out China for its cyber espionage and take diplomatic action if the country fails to rein in its hackers. Google began sharing information about attacks on its networks with the NSA after the company was hit in a massive Chinese spying campaign, which saw some of its intellectual property stolen.

Rouland isn't the only Endgamer who has claimed that companies have a right to defend themselves when the government can't or won't. After Anonymous revealed an Endgame presentation showing how customers could use clusters of infected computers, known as botnets, to launch attacks on websites or steal passwords and other sensitive information, a partner at one of Endgame's major investors defended the idea. "If you believe that wars are going to be fought in the world of cyber in the future, wouldn't you want to believe you would have a cyber army at your disposal?" Ted Schlein, who sits on Endgame's board, told Reuters. "Why wouldn't you want to launch a cyber army if needed?"

Most private cyber security companies are at pains to stress that they don't conduct "hack-backs," that is, breaking in to the intruder's computer, which is illegal in the United States. But companies will spy on intruders once they're inside clients' networks. One prominent player in that business, CrowdStrike, baits the spies with honeypots. The company may lure hackers into what appears to be a client's network but is actually a kind of sterile zone walled off from any real or important computers. The idea is to buy time to watch intruders, to see what they're most interested in — technical diagrams, say, or negotiating points — and then force them to show what tools and techniques they're using to steal that information. The company might protect a document with an especially long password, hoping that the hacker will deploy a novel technique for cracking it. Once the client has seen what's in an intruder's toolkit, CrowdStrike can predict how the intruder will try to break in to other systems in the future. If the client wants to throw the intruder off the trail, it might plant misleading or untrue information in those documents that purport to be about business strategy or plans for a new product launch.

CrowdStrike will also compare an intruder's various victims to see if a particular industry or type of technology is being targeted. Then the company builds a dossier, even giving the hacker a name in some cases. For more than a year CrowdStrike analysts tracked one "adversary," which it named Anchor Panda, as it spied on companies involved in the maritime satellite business, aerospace, and defense contracting and targeted foreign governments with active space-exploration programs. Armed with such specific intelligence about what a hacker is after and what methods the hacker is using to break in — his "signatures"— CrowdStrike's clients can theoretically take more precise defensive actions. It's like sending out an all-points bulletin about a fugitive, complete with a physical description and modus operandi, rather than warning the public to be generally on the lookout for suspicious people.

That sounds a lot like the work of a law enforcement agency. And no surprise, since two of CrowdStrike's top executives are former FBI officials. Shawn Henry, CEO of CrowdStrike Services, the part of the company that tracks and identifies intruders, spent twenty-four years in the bureau, retiring in 2012 as the senior official in charge of all cyber programs and investigations worldwide. (The former deputy head of cyber for the FBI is the company's general counsel.) CrowdStrike is different from other cyber security companies, Henry says, because "when we respond to an incident, we actually hunt for the adversary." He says the company employs network forensics and reverse engineering of malware to understand the hackers' tactics, techniques, and motivations. He is careful to avoid any suggestion that the company breaks in to their adversaries' computers — the former G-man spent years prosecuting people for violating anti-hacking laws. But the word *hunt* reveals a more aggressive form of analysis than many other firms in the business will admit to. CrowdStrike deploys sensors on its clients' networks and uses crowdsourcing to collect more information on hacks as they're happening, rather than wait for a client to be hit and collect evidence after the fact. It uses intelligence to attribute, as closely as possible, the hacker to a particular country or group. This is one of the hardest things to do in cyber forensics, because skilled hackers conceal their physical location, often by launching their attacks from compromised computers in other countries. CrowdStrike promises to tell clients not just how they're being attacked but why, and by whom. The company focuses particularly on spies and hackers operating on behalf of foreign governments, including China, Iran, and Russia. (A group of analysts in the "strategic intelligence group" reads Chinese, Farsi, and Russian.) In its marketing materials, CrowdStrike repeatedly states that it uses its intelligence-gathering methods to identify intruders and hand over specific, useful information about them to its clients.

This, too, is a technique drawn from the FBI's playbook. The bureau has rounded up hackers, most famously some members of the collective Anonymous, by watching them steal data from companies and individuals. That information becomes the basis for a criminal indictment. But CrowdStrike and its clients aren't always looking to press charges. And here the company's business model gets aggressive.

The other feature that separates CrowdStrike from the competition, Henry says, is its "strike capability."

"We're not talking about hacking back at the hackers," Henry says, batting away any notion that the company has crossed a legal line. "What we're talking about is providing the client certain capabilities to make and create a hostile work environment on their network." CrowdStrike executives know that one way some companies create such a hostile environment is to implant malware in honeypots they scatter throughout their networks. When the intruder brings a document or a file back onto his own computer and tries to open it, a virus is unleashed. It could destroy data on his hard drive, or implant spyware or a backdoor for ongoing access by his victim. CrowdStrike says it doesn't engage in that kind of infection via subterfuge. But in an interview in 2013, Dmitri Alperovitch, CrowdStrike's cofounder, said he approved of similar actions by the government of Georgia, which tricked a Russian hacker into downloading spyware that turned on his webcam and let officials take his picture. They published his photograph in an official report. "The private sector needs to be empowered to take that kind of action," Alperovitch said.

In February 2014, after Target reported that hackers had stolen more than 100 million customers' credit and debit card numbers, CrowdStrike publicized an online seminar that teaches business how to combat cybercrime. "Retail(iate): Don't Be a Target," said an advertisement that the company e-mailed to prospective clients. The course promised to teach companies "how to take a proactive approach to defending your network" and to show them "how threat intelligence can be used to get ahead of the game." CrowdStrike may not be hacking back. But the alerts the company sends to its clients, as well as the services it advertises, suggest that customers could end up learning the skills they need if they choose to retaliate on their own.

Finding an adversary is a big step beyond watching his movements — technically and legally. But here, too, there is a market, in which cyber mercenaries are building and selling spyware and hacking tools as sophisticated as any the US government was producing a few years ago. As the power of distributed computing platforms such as cloud services allows smaller groups of people to conduct ever more complicated feats of programming, small companies soon will be building big, powerful cyber weapons that, so far, have remained the exclusive domain of governments. Already the mercenaries have made their mark helping officials intimidate and suppress activists and dissidents. The devices they've built are among the most feared and menacing in cyberspace.

The firm Gamma, based in the United Kingdom, sells a spyware program called FinFisher that hides inside "fake software updates for popular software," according to the company's marketing documents. The spyware, which can take over a computer, copy its files, and record every word a user types, can be disguised as an update to the popular iTunes app. Users click on the update, thinking they're getting the latest version of the music software, but actually they're installing Fin-

Fisher on their computers. Egyptian democracy activists have accused the company of providing spyware to the regime of President Hosni Mubarak, an allegation it denies. Mubarak ordered a brutal crackdown on Egyptian citizens in 2011 before he was ultimately driven from power. Security researchers also claim to have found copies of FinFisher in e-mails sent to democracy activists in Bahrain.

Cyber spies and hackers-for-hire openly market their services to law enforcement and intelligence agencies. An Italian company called Hacking Team, based in Milan, promises "total control over your targets" using "invisible" techniques that are "stealth and untraceable."

"Defeat encryption," says one presentation on the company's home page, parroting the language of the NSA. "Thousands of encrypted communications per day. Get them." In 2011 the company opened an office in Annapolis, Maryland, to sell to US clients.

Hacking Team is upfront about the business it's in. "Sometimes relevant data are bound inside the device, never transmitted and kept well protected . . . unless you are right on that device," says a brochure for one of the company's spyware tools, Remote Control System.

> Question is, is there an easy way to hack into that device? . . . What you need is a way to bypass encryption, collect relevant data out of any device, and keep monitoring your targets wherever they are, even outside your monitoring domain. Remote Control System does exactly that. Take control of your targets and monitor them regardless of encryption and mobility. . . . Hack into your targets with the most advanced infection vectors available. Enter his wireless network and tackle tactical operations with ad-hoc equipment designed to operate while on the move. Keep an eye on all your targets and manage them remotely, all from a single screen.

Reportedly, the product can turn on a laptop computer's camera and microphone, making it an eavesdropping device.

Only at the end of the brochure does Hacking Team mention that its product is intended solely for "governmental interception." (The company was founded by a pair of hackers who had built a spyware product purchased by local Italian police.) Hacking Team claims that it sells only to governmental law enforcement and intelligence agencies, and that it will not sell to "countries blacklisted" by the United States, the European Union and NATO, or members of the ASEAN group of Southeast Asian countries. It also promises to review all potential customers to ensure that the technology won't "be used to facilitate human rights violations."

But in October 2012, researchers with Citizen Lab at the University of Toronto reported that Hacking Team's Remote Control System was used to infect the computer of a prominent pro-democracy activist in the United Arab Emirates named Ahmed Mansoor, a forty-four-year-old electrical engineer who had once been imprisoned for signing an online petition calling for open elections in a country ruled by hereditary monarchs. Mansoor had inadvertently downloaded the spyware, which was hidden inside a seemingly legitimate e-mail. The spyware burrowed deep into his personal computer, inspecting files and recording what Mansoor typed. He noticed that his computer was running slowly, and after seeing reports about FinFisher's use against activists in Bahrain, he contacted a security researcher, who confirmed that he had been hacked. The spyware was so strong that even when he changed his e-mail password the unseen intruder was still able to read his messages. The intruder was fully in control of the computer, able to track all of Mansoor's communications and his network of fellow activists. The intrusion was traced to an Internet address in the United Arab Emirates.

A month after Mansoor and the researcher managed to cleanse his computer of the infection, Mansoor was attacked on the street. The assailant knew Mansoor's name, and Mansoor suspected he was able to track him via his cell phone. He was slightly injured in the scuffle. Less than a week later another man attacked him and repeatedly punched him in the head. He survived the attack.

Mansoor isn't the only activist whom researchers have linked to Hacking Team's spyware. It was part of a larger trend of commercial spyware being used against activists across North Africa and the Middle East during the tumultuous period. There is no evidence that

Hacking Team had any knowledge or involvement in the attacks on Mansoor, and it called the documented evidence that its product had been used in a way it claims to forbid "largely circumstantial."

The company's enforcement regime is entirely of its own design. And in that regard it's not unique. There is no international body or treaty for ensuring that spyware and hacking tools are sold only for legal purposes and to governments that don't suppress civil rights and activism. There is also no regime for controlling the proliferation of cyber weapons such as Stuxnet. Foreign policy officials in the United States, Russia, China, and elsewhere have publicly broached the idea of a cyber arms treaty in recent years, but no country is yet prepared to commit to an agreement that might preemptively bind it from building the next generation of weapons. There is also no obvious way to enforce a cyber arms agreement. Nuclear enrichment facilities can be inspected. Tanks, ships, and aircraft can be seen from a distance. A cyber weapon can be built on a computer. It is practically invisible until it's launched.

The Arab Spring wasn't the first time cyber security companies were accused of being bagmen for governments. In the fall of 2010, just as the website WikiLeaks was preparing to release potentially embarrassing information on Bank of America, including internal records and documents, Justice Department officials contacted the bank's lawyers and encouraged them to get in touch with Hunton & Williams, a Washington law firm. It had put together a trio of small tech companies to run a kind of cyber propaganda operation against opponents of the US Chamber of Commerce, the leading business lobbyist in Washington. The group planned to scour websites and social media with data-mining technology and build dossiers on the Chamber's opponents. Hunton & Williams asked the trio, which operated under the name Team Themis, if they could do the same job for supporters of WikiLeaks, and also if they could locate where the organization was storing classified information it got from its anonymous sources.

"Apparently, if they can show that WikiLeaks is hosting data in certain countries, it will make prosecution easier," a member of the trio wrote in an e-mail to his colleagues. Justice Department officials were looking for information they could use to indict WikiLeaks' founder, Julian Assange, who had posted classified military intelligence reports and State Department cables. Now the feds wanted to outsource part of their investigation, by putting Bank of America in touch with Team Themis, which drew its name from the mythological Greek Titan who represented "divine law," as opposed to the law of men.

Team Themis included Palantir Technologies, a Silicon Valley startup that had been making fast friends with such national security heavyweights as Richard Perle, former chairman of the Defense Policy Board and an influential Republican operative, as well as George Tenet, former director of the CIA, who had gone to work for Herb Allen, a Palantir investor and head of the enigmatic investment bank Allen & Company, which hosts the annual Sun Valley Conference, bringing together celebrity journalists, athletes, and business leaders. Palantir had also had early backing from the CIA's venture capital group, In-Q-Tel, whose current chief is chairman of the board of Endgame.

Rounding out Team Themis were two cyber security firms, HBGary Federal, whose CEO had desperately been trying to make inroads with the NSA, to little avail, and Berico Technologies, which employed an Iraq War veteran who had in-the-field experience with cyber weapons. Themis planned to set up an analysis cell that would feed the law firm information about "adversarial entities and networks of interest," according to a proposal the team created. The CEO of HBGary, Aaron Barr, said the team should collect information about WikiLeaks' "global following and volunteer staff," along with the group's donors, in order to intimidate them. "Need to get people to understand that if they support the organization we will come after them," Barr wrote in an e-mail. He suggested submitting fake documents to WikiLeaks in hopes that the site would publish them and then be discredited. Barr also urged targeting "people like Glenn Greenwald," the blogger and vocal WikiLeaks supporter, and he said he wanted to launch "cyberattacks" on a server WikiLeaks was using in Sweden, in order to "get data" about WikiLeaks' anonymous sources and expose them.

Team Themis never had the chance to launch its espionage and propaganda campaign. In February 2011, Barr was quoted in an article in the *Financial Times* bragging that he could penetrate the inner ranks of Anonymous. The group retaliated, breaking in to Barr's e-mail account and publishing years' worth of his correspondence, including the Team Themis proposals and communications. Barr left the company, telling reporters, "I need to focus on taking care of my family and rebuilding my reputation." Berico is still in business, selling data-mining and geo-location software to government agencies. Palantir is one of the fastest-growing technology companies in the national security field and counts among its customers the CIA, Special Operations Command, and the US Marine Corps, which have all used its software to track down terrorists, as well as the Defense Intelligence Agency, the National Counterterrorism Center, the Homeland Security Department, and the FBI. Keith Alexander, former director of the National Security Agency, has said that Palantir could help the agency "see" hackers and spies in cyberspace, and that the NSA has evaluated the company's product. The Los Angeles Police Department is another Palantir customer, as is the New York Police Department, which runs an intelligence and counterterrorism unit that many experts believe is more sophisticated than the FBI's or the CIA's.

Though Team Themis failed, the US government has turned to other private cyber sleuths to go after WikiLeaks and help with other investigations. Tiversa, a Pittsburgh-based company, grabbed headlines in 2011 when it accused WikiLeaks of using peer-to-peer file-sharing systems, like those used to swap music downloads, to obtain classified US military documents. WikiLeaks, which claims only to publish documents that it receives from whistleblowers, called the allegations "completely false." Tiversa gave its findings to government investigators, who had been trying to build a case against Assange. Tiversa's board of advisers includes prominent security experts and former US officials, such as General Wesley Clark, former Supreme Allied Commander of NATO forces in Europe and onetime Democratic presidential candidate, and Howard Schmidt, who was Barack Obama's cyber security adviser in the White House.

Tiversa has revealed an array of classified and sensitive documents floating around file-sharing networks, and arguably, that does some good. Companies and government agencies embarrassed by a data breach have an incentive to shore up their security and work harder to protect sensitive information. Tiversa claims its analysts have found blueprints for the presidential helicopter, *Marine One,* on a computer in Iran. A defense contractor employee in Bethesda, Maryland, may have been running a file-sharing system and ended up giving an Iranian computer user access to his hard drive. In 2009, Tiversa told a congressional committee that its investigations had discovered a document giving the location of a Secret Service safe house used to protect the First Lady during a national emergency; spreadsheets containing personal identifying information of thousands of US military service members; documents pointing to the location of nuclear facilities; and personal medical information on thousands of individuals, including insurance and billing information as well as diagnosis codes.

But when pointing out weak security, Tiversa has courted controversy. In 2013, LabMD, an Atlanta company that performs cancer diagnoses, filed a complaint accusing Tiversa of stealing patient information from it and other health care companies through peer-to-peer networks. LabMD had been under investigation by the Federal Trade Commission after a data breach allegedly exposed patient information. The company claimed that the government had hired Tiversa to take the documents without LabMD's knowledge or consent. According to court documents, Tiversa found LabMD patient information on a peer-to-peer network and then allegedly made repeated phone calls and sent e-mails to the health care company trying to sell Tiversa's cyber security services. LabMD's lawsuits were subsequently withdrawn or dismissed, and Tiversa has sued LabMD for defamation.

Cyberspace has no clear borders. But geography has a lot to do with how far a cyber mercenary will go to solve clients' problems. Some companies in Europe have less compunction about hacking back because anti-hacking laws there are either loose or nonexistent. Romania is one hotbed of hackers and online scam artists willing to launch malware for a fee. And the gray market where zero day attacks are sold is another place to find hackers-for-hire. Until federal officials shut it down in 2013, the online market Silk Road, which was accessible via the Tor anonymous router system, included hack-back vendors.

To date, no American company has been willing to say that it engages in offensive cyber operations designed to steal information or destroy an adversary's system. But former intelligence officials say hack-backs are occurring, even if they're not advertised. "It is illegal. It is going on," says a former senior NSA official, now a corporate consultant. "It's happening with very good legal advice. But I would not advise a client to try it."

A former military intelligence officer said the most active hack-backs are coming from the banking industry. In the past several years banks have lost billions of dollars to cybercriminals, primarily those based in Eastern Europe and Russia who use sophisticated malware to steal usernames and passwords from customers and then clean out their accounts.

In June 2013, Microsoft joined forces with some of the world's biggest financial institutions, including Bank of America, American Express, JPMorgan Chase, Citigroup, Wells Fargo, Credit Suisse, HSBC, the Royal Bank of Canada, and PayPal, to disable a huge cluster of hijacked computers being used for online crime. Their target was a notorious outfit called Citadel, which had infected thousands of machines around the world and, without their owners' knowledge, conscripted them into armies of "botnets," which the criminals used to steal account credentials, and thus money, from millions of people. In a counterstrike that Microsoft code-named Operation b54, the company's Digital Crimes Unit severed the lines of communication between Citadel's more than fourteen hundred botnets and an estimated five million personal computers that Citadel had infected with malware. Microsoft also took over servers that Citadel was using to conduct its operations.

Microsoft hacked Citadel. That would have been illegal had the company not obtained a civil court order blessing the operation. Effectively now in control of Citadel's victims — who had no idea that their machines had ever been infected — Microsoft could alert them to install patches to their vulnerable software. In effect, Microsoft had hacked the users in order to save them. (And to save itself, since the machines had been infected in the first place owing to flaws in Microsoft's products, which are probably the most frequently exploited in the world.)

It was the first time that Microsoft had teamed up with the FBI. But it was the seventh time it had knocked down botnets since 2010. The company's lawyers had used novel legal arguments, such as accusing criminals who had attacked Microsoft products of violating its trademark. This was a new legal frontier. Even Microsoft's lawyers, who included a former US attorney, acknowledged that they'd never considered using alleged violations of common law to obtain permission for a cyber attack. For Operation b54, Microsoft and the banks had spied on Citadel for six months before talking to the FBI. The sleuths from Microsoft's counter-hacking group eventually went to two Internet hosting facilities, in Pennsylvania and New Jersey, where, accompanied by US marshals, they gathered forensic evidence to attack Citadel's network of botnets. The military would call that collecting targeting data. And in many respects, Operation b54 looked like a military cyber strike. Technically speaking, it was not so different from the attack that US cyber forces launched on the Obelisk network used by al-Qaeda in Iraq.

Microsoft also worked with law enforcement agencies in eighty countries to strike at Citadel. The head of cybercrime investigations for Europol, the European Union's law enforcement organization, declared that Operation b54 had succeeded in wiping out Citadel from nearly all its infected hosts. And a lawyer with Microsoft's Digital Crimes Unit declared, "The bad guys will feel the punch in the gut."

Microsoft has continued to attack botnets, and its success has encouraged government officials and company executives, who see partnerships between cops and corporate hackers as a viable way to fight cybercriminals. But coordinated counterstrikes like the one against Citadel take time to plan, and teams of lawyers to approve them. What happens when a company doesn't want to wait six months to hack back, or would just as soon not have federal law enforcement officers looking over its shoulder?

The former military intelligence officer worries that the relative technical ease of hack-backs will inspire banks in particular to forgo partnerships with companies like Microsoft and hack back on their own — without asking a court for permission. "Banks have an appetite now to strike back because they're sick of taking it in the shorts," he says. "It gets to the point where an industry won't accept that kind of risk. And if the government can't act, or won't, it's only logical they'll do it themselves." And hack-backs won't be exclusive to big corporations, he says. "If you're a celebrity, would you pay someone to find the source of some dirty pictures of you about to be released online? Hell yes!"

Undoubtedly, they'll find a ready supply of talent willing and able to do the job. A survey of 181 attendees at the 2012 Black Hat USA conference in Las Vegas found that 36 percent of "information security professionals" said they'd engaged in retaliatory hack-backs. That's still a minority of the profession, though one presumes that some of the respondents weren't being honest. But even those security companies that won't engage in hack-backs have the skills and the know-how to launch a private cyber war.

A former NSA official says that in his estimation, the best private security firms today are run by former "siginters," and are using not just electronic intelligence but also human sources. From their NSA days, they learned to follow trends and conversations in Internet chat channels frequented by hackers, and how to pose as would-be criminals looking to buy malicious software.

One private security executive says some of the best intelligence on new kinds of malware, hacking techniques, and targets comes, not surprisingly, from the biggest source of spying and theft against the United States — China. Rick Howard, who before he became a private cyber sleuth ran the army's Computer Emergency Response Team, says he stayed in regular contact with hackers and cyber weapons dealers in China when he was in charge of intelligence for iDefense, a private security firm. His sources told iDefense what was the latest malware on the street — as in the United States, it was sold through gray markets — who the major players were, and what targets were on the hackers' lists. Hacking is a human business, after all.

Until 2013, Howard was the chief information security officer for TASC, a large security firm that runs its own "cybersecurity operations center." TASC is located on a sprawling office campus in Chantilly, Virginia, near the corridor of tech companies that has made Washington one of the richest metropolitan areas in the United States. TASC's offices, spread out over three buildings, resemble an NSA installation. The halls are lined with doors marked "Classified," and the entrances are protected by keypad locks and card scanners. Stepping inside those secure rooms, you would find it hard to know for sure if you were in Chantilly or Fort Meade.

Many former NSA hackers aren't afraid to talk about their time in the government. In fact, they publicize it. Brendan Conlon, who worked in the elite TAO group, founded a cyber security company called Vahna, according to his LinkedIn profile, "after 10 years of Offensive Computer Network Operations with the National Security Agency." Conlon began his career developing software implants, then moved on to TAO, where he was chief of the Hawaii unit. He also worked in the NSA's hunting division, which is devoted to tracking Chinese hackers. A graduate of the Naval Academy, he served with the NSA three times in Afghanistan and worked on hacking missions with the CIA. Vahna touts its employees' "years of experience inside the intelligence and defense cyber communities" and claims to have "unparalleled capabilities to assess vulnerability in your information security, mitigate risk across your technology footprint, and provide tactical incident response to security breaches." In other words, all the things that Conlon was trained to do for the NSA, he can now do for corporations.

Over the past several years, large defense contractors have been gobbling up smaller technology firms and boutique cyber security outfits, acquiring their personnel, their proprietary software, and their contracts with intelligence agencies, the military, and corporations. In 2010, Raytheon, one of the largest US defense contractors, agreed to pay $490 million for Applied Signal Technology, a cyber security firm with military and government clients. The price tag, while objectively large, was a relative pittance for Raytheon, which had sales the prior year totaling $25 billion. In 2013 the network-equipment giant Cisco agreed to buy Sourcefire for $2.7 billion in cash, in a transaction that reflected what the *New York Times* called "the growing fervor" for companies that defend other companies from cyber attacks and espionage.

After the acquisition was announced, a former military intelligence officer said he was astounded that Cisco had paid so much money for a company whose flagship product is built on an open-source intrusion detection system called Snort, which anyone can use. It was a sign of just how valuable cyber security expertise had become — either that or a massive bubble in the market, the former officer said.

But the companies are betting on a sure thing — government spending on cyber security. The Pentagon cyber security budget for 2014 is $4.7 billion, a $1 billion increase over the previous year. The military is no longer buying expensive missile systems. With the advent of drone aircraft, many executives believe the current generation of fighter aircraft will be the last ones built to be flown by humans. Spending has plummeted on the big-ticket weapons systems that kept Beltway contractors flush throughout the Cold War, so they're pivoting to the booming cyber market.

SEVEN

Cops Become Spies

THE SPYWARE WAS a triumph of engineering and cunning. It sat unnoticed on its victim's computer and recorded everything he typed. E-mails. Documents. But what it was really after was a password. One in particular — the phrase or series of letters and numbers that the victim used to start an encryption program called Pretty Good Privacy. As encryption programs went, PGP was easy for a layperson to use. It could be downloaded from the Internet, and it afforded a level of security that had previously been available only to government agents and spies. Now, with a few clicks and a password, anyone could turn one's own communications into indecipherable gobbledygook that could be unscrambled only by the intended recipient. The spyware, though, captured that password and sent it back to its master, who could then decode the encrypted messages that the victim believed were private. The designers chose an apt name for their creation, which shined a light into a previously dark space — Magic Lantern.

The creators of this malware weren't Chinese hackers. They weren't identity thieves in Russia. They were employees of the US Federal Bureau of Investigation. And they worked for one of the most secretive and technologically sophisticated operations in the entire bureau, one that, today, is the National Security Agency's indispensable partner in cyber spying and warfare.

It's called the Data Intercept Technology Unit, but insiders refer to it as the DITU (pronounced "DIH-too.") It's the FBI's equivalent of the NSA, a signals intelligence operation that has barely been covered in the press and mentioned in congressional testimony only a few times in the past fifteen years. The DITU is located on a large compound at the Marine Corps base in Quantico, Virginia, which is also home to the FBI's training academy. The DITU intercepts telephone calls and e-mails of terrorists and spies from inside the United States. When the NSA wants to gather mounds of information from Google, Facebook, Yahoo, and other technology giants, DITU is sent to retrieve it. The unit maintains the technological infrastructure for the agency's Prism program, which collects personal information from the large tech companies. In fact, it's the DITU's job to make sure that all American companies are building their networks and software applications in a way that complies with US surveillance law, so they can be easily tapped by the government. And if they're not, the DITU will construct a bespoke surveillance device and do it for them.

The NSA couldn't do its job without the DITU. The unit works closely with the biggest American telecommunications companies — AT&T, Verizon, and Sprint. "The DITU is the main interface with providers on the national security side," says a technology industry representative who has worked with the unit on many occasions. It ensures that telephone and Internet communications can easily be siphoned off the massive network of fiber-optic cables those companies run. In recent years, it has helped construct a data-filtering software program that the FBI wants installed on phone and Internet networks, so that the government can collect even larger volumes of data than in the past, including routing information for e-mails, data on traffic flow, Internet addresses, and port numbers, which handle incoming and outgoing communications and can detect what applications and operating system a computer is running.

Magic Lantern was one of the unit's early triumphs. Developed in the late 1990s, it was a companion to the better-known e-mail-mining program Carnivore, which stripped the header information — the "to," "from," and date lines — out of an e-mail so that investigators could piece together members of a criminal network by their communications patterns. Both devices, along with other spying programs with names such as CoolMiner, Packeteer, and Phiple Troenix, were developed to help the bureau snare drug dealers, terrorists, and child-porn peddlers. But when Carnivore was revealed in news reports, it became synonymous with Big Brother–style government surveillance, and civil liberties groups said the FBI's efforts would undermine encryption for legitimate purposes, such as protecting financial data and patient privacy. The same arguments echoed more than a decade later, when the NSA was revealed to be secretly handicapping encryption algorithms.

The FBI's cyber spying programs began years before the 9/11 attacks and any attempts by the NSA to broaden its surveillance nets to cover the United States. FBI agents have been in the domestic cyber spying business for longer than their friends at Fort Meade. And today they are physically joined in those efforts. A fiber-optic connection runs between Quantico and NSA headquarters, so that the information the DITU collects from companies can be instantly transferred. FBI agents and lawyers from the Justice Department review the NSA's requests to gather e-mails from Google or monitor Facebook posts. They represent the agency before the secret Foreign Intelligence Surveillance Court, which also reviews requests to spy on Americans. It was the FBI that petitioned the court to order telephone companies to give the NSA records of all calls placed in the United States. When journalists and lawmakers say that the NSA "spies on Americans," what they really mean is that the FBI helps them do it, providing a technical and legal infrastructure for domestic intelligence operations. Having the DITU act as a conduit also gives technology companies the ability to say publicly that they do not provide any information about their customers directly to the NSA. And that's true. They give it to the DITU, which then passes it to the NSA.

The NSA is the biggest user of the DITU. But the unit is no mere errand boy. Along with other FBI cyber and surveillance groups, it conducts some of the government's most sophisticated intelligence programs. At the FBI Academy in Quantico, the DITU shares space with the bureau's Operational Technology Division, which is responsible for all FBI technical intelligence collection, processing, and reporting. Its motto is "Vigilance Through Technology." Among the division's publicly disclosed capabilities are surveillance of landline, wireless, and computer network communications technologies, including e-mail applications, switches, and routers; collecting audio files, video, images, and other digital evidence to use in investigations; and counter-encryption. It also specializes in black-bag jobs to install surveillance equipment and computer viruses. The DITU has negotiated with major US technology companies to get privileged access to their systems. For instance, on behalf of the NSA, it worked with Microsoft to ensure that a new feature in Outlook that allowed users to create e-mail aliases would not pose an obstacle to surveillance. The arrangement helped the government circumvent Microsoft's encryption and ensure that Outlook messages could be read by government analysts.

The FBI has been in the cyber hunting business since long before it became a national security priority. The first instances of FBI hacking were conducted under a program called Cyber Knight — that's when the bureau built the Magic Lantern spyware. FBI technologists built "beacons," or programs that can be implanted in an e-mail and used to locate a computer's Internet address. The first beacons were deployed to help find abducted children. When a kidnapper contacted the parents of a child — usually the kidnapper's own ex-spouse or partner — an FBI agent would write back. And when the kidnapper opened that e-mail, the beacon went off. It might not lead agents straight to the kidnapper's doorstep, but it would tell them, at least, where the kidnapper was when the message was sent. That was a golden lead. (These beacons were an early form of the technology used to map out the networks of the Natanz nuclear facility.)

The FBI also used beacons to track child pornographers. And it planted viruses and other spyware on their computers and tagged photos of children so they could be tracked from person to person. The agents were collecting evidence for a criminal prosecution, but they were also trying to learn how child-porn peddlers shared photos. In that respect, it was an intelligence-gathering operation.

Under US law, the FBI is in charge of investigating all cybercrime, espionage, and attacks inside the United States. The bureau runs the National Cyber Investigative Joint Task Force, which was set up by presidential directive and whose members include the Secret Service, the CIA, and the NSA. In addition to cyber spies and infrastructure probes, the task force has monitored financial crime and online scams, so-called hacktivist groups that target businesses and government agencies in protest campaigns, as well as insider threats, such as government employees who leak to journalists.

Normally, it's the FBI's job to collect evidence for use in criminal prosecutions. But when it comes to cyber security, the FBI has moved away from that law enforcement mission and is acting more like an intelligence agency. It's less concerned with taking hackers to court than in forecasting and deterring future attacks.

"The bureau tends to be focused on collecting intelligence and passing it on to the NSA, the intelligence community, and the Defense Department," says a senior law enforcement official who works on cyber investigations involving domestic and international crimes, including bank fraud and child pornography. "The FBI is not driving toward prosecution, generally speaking." The official says that in recent years, the FBI has shifted many of its personnel who were working on counterterrorism cases toward cyber security, which it now lists as a top "national investigative priority," ahead of white collar crime, public corruption, and civil rights enforcement. (The number of counterterrorism and counterintelligence employees — which the bureau groups together — was already high: nearly thirteen thousand in 2013. The number of counterterrorism agents doubled between 2001 and 2009. The rise coincided with a sharp decline in the number of criminal prosecutions for non-terrorism cases, particularly white collar and financial crime. The FBI was faulted for not doing enough to investigate mortgage and securities fraud in the run-up to the financial crisis of 2008.)

In 2012 the bureau was spending $296 million on its various cyber-related operations. The following year officials asked Congress for $86 million more as part of the FBI's Next Generation Cyber Initiative, which would expand the bureau's monitoring capabilities by hiring more personnel and creating a new system for analyzing malware and intrusions. The bureau wanted to hire 152 new employees — on top of the existing 1,232 — the majority of whom were not FBI agents but computer scientists, engineers, forensic examiners, and intelligence analysts. Cyber programs constitute the fastest-growing parts of the FBI's budget. Before he retired, FBI director Robert Mueller — who took the job one week before the 9/11 attacks — told Congress that "the cyber threat will equal or surpass the threat from counter terrorism in the foreseeable future."

Chasing criminal hackers and foreign cyber warriors is the FBI's future. And the agency is looking a lot more like the CIA or the NSA. Most of the new staff are intelligence analysts and hackers, not law enforcement officers. And the official says that the FBI is using the Foreign Intelligence Surveillance Act more often to gather information during cyber investigations because it's easier to obtain surveillance authorizations under that law than using criminal statutes, which require law enforcement to show probable cause that a crime is being committed.

"When information comes from FISA, it's not being used in a criminal prosecution. So, why are we collecting it? I scratch my head at that," the senior law enforcement official says. "At some point, we're no longer driving an investigation. We're just collecting intelligence." Put another way, the FBI is spying.

This is a historic shift in policy for the United States' top law enforcement agency. When the FBI collects information to use in a trial, it follows stricter procedures for control of evidence and narrows its investigations. When it makes intelligence its primary mission, it casts a wider net and puts more emphasis on providing targets for the NSA and military cyber warriors than on bringing criminals to justice.

Some of the FBI's most important intelligence targets today are Chinese cyber spies stealing intellectual property. "We do a lot of collection on China's victimizing US companies," says a former senior FBI official who managed cyber cases. The bureau has broken in to the computers of Chinese hackers and stolen the lists of specific companies they're targeting. "We identify and notify those companies: 'This is a computer on your network taken over by China. This is how we know.'"

FBI cyber operators have also obtained the e-mail addresses of employees whom Chinese hackers intend to spear phish, sending them legitimate-looking e-mails that actually contain spyware. "We knew what luring words and phrases the e-mails used before they were sent," the former official says. "We told companies what to be on the lookout for. What e-mails not to open. We could tell them 'You're next on the list.'"

Among the most worrisome people on those lists were employees of American oil and natural gas companies. These businesses own and operate major refineries and pipelines that are run by SCADA (supervisory control and data acquisition) systems, the same kinds of devices that the NSA attacked in the Iranian nuclear facility to make centrifuges break down. Chinese attempts to penetrate oil and natural gas companies "were never-ending," the former official says. The campaign reached a fever pitch in the spring of 2012, when hackers penetrated the computer networks of twenty companies that own and operate natural gas pipelines. FBI and Homeland Security Department officials swooped in and gave classified briefings to executives and security personnel. They watched the hackers move on the networks in order to get a better sense of how they got in, and what damage they might cause. There's no evidence that they gained access to the critical SCADA systems that actually control the pipelines — the spies could also have been looking for strategy documents or information about US energy supplies. But the penetrations were so rampant, and so alarming, that the Homeland Security Department issued a broad alert to the energy industry about the threat and what steps they could take to protect their systems.

The former official says the FBI has also infiltrated Russian and Eastern European criminal organizations that specialize in stealing money out of companies' bank accounts — to the tune of several billions of dollars a year. The FBI discovered the crooks' targets, then warned those people and companies that an attack was coming. And the bureau infiltrated the computers of the hacker collective Anonymous, found its target lists, and warned the people on them.

Does any of this intelligence actually stop attacks from happening? "I definitely saw prevention," the former official says, in the form of software patches applied, particular IP addresses blocked from connecting to corporate computer networks, or improvements in basic security practices such as using longer or harder-to-guess passwords, which even sophisticated companies sometimes fail to do. But success is hard to quantify. Companies don't acknowledge individual cases where assistance from the government paid off, because they don't want to admit that they were at risk in the first place.

The FBI spends most of its cyber budget and its investigative time tracking Chinese intrusions into US computer networks and trying to prevent a major attack on critical infrastructure, current and former officials say. This is an undoubtedly important mission, but it's not law enforcement, which is the FBI's mandate. The bureau doesn't decide which cases to prosecute — that's up to the Justice Department, federal prosecutors, and ultimately the attorney general. But to date the United States has never brought a case against any Chinese hacker for intellectual-property theft or violating US anti-hacking laws.

"What's happened in national security cases is the US government has prioritized counterintelligence, in the hopes that it will result in some strategy to stop China from doing what they're doing," says the former official. Rather than resort to courts, the Obama administration has decided to publicly call out Chinese hackers and lean on their government to rein them in. Evidence collected by the FBI — and the NSA — helps them do that. (To be sure, the Chinese government would almost certainly not cooperate with a US criminal case against one of its own citizens. Chinese leaders barely acknowledge that their country is the source of so much spying on the United States, and they accuse American hackers — with some cause — of spying on them.)

While officials look for a diplomatic solution to rampant espionage, the information that the FBI gives to corporations is supposed to help them fend off future attacks. Much like the NSA providing intelligence to defense contractors, the FBI is giving it to owners and operators of critical infrastructure and to banks and financial services companies — which officials have deemed vital to US economic security and the basic functions of daily life.

The FBI doesn't always warn companies that they've been hacked. Sometimes it uses them as bait, and the consequences can be disastrous.

In early December 2011, George Friedman, CEO of the private intelligence company Stratfor, got a call from Fred Burton, his senior vice president for intelligence and a former counterterrorism specialist with the State Department. Burton told Friedman that the company's website had been hacked, and that credit card information for subscribers to its various reports about world affairs and international relations had been stolen. Those numbers had not been encrypted, a basic security measure the company had failed to take. The next morning, according to an account Friedman later wrote, he met with an agent from the FBI, "who made clear that there was an ongoing investigation and asked for our cooperation."

The ongoing operation was an FBI sting against members of the hacker group Anonymous, who had targeted Stratfor because of its perceived connections to the US government and intelligence community. (One of the hackers later accused the company of "spying on the world," as well as on Anonymous itself.) Stratfor employs former government personnel, but it's a private company that generates reports and analysis not unlike many consulting firms or even news organizations. Its daily summaries of world events are read by government employees, including those within the military and the intelligence agencies, but they're not produced solely for them.

Six months before Stratfor learned that it had been infiltrated, the FBI had arrested the prominent hacker Hector Xavier Monsegur, who went by the name Sabu, and turned him into an informant. Monsegur was a leader in another hacker group, LulzSec, which had also targeted corporations and government agencies, including the CIA, whose website it once claimed to take offline. FBI officials would later say that Monsegur helped them charge hackers in Britain, Ireland, and the

United States, and that the information he helped generate prevented intrusions against three hundred government agencies and companies. But Stratfor wasn't one of them.

The FBI learned that Anonymous had gone after Stratfor in December 2011, when Jeremy Hammond, the accused leader of the operation, contacted Monsegur and informed him that he'd broken in to the company's networks and was decrypting confidential information. But rather than alert Stratfor, the FBI baited a trap.

The bureau told Monsegur to persuade Hammond and his fellow hackers that they should transfer information from Stratfor to another computer, which was secretly under the FBI's control. According to a criminal complaint, the hackers moved "multiple gigabytes of confidential data," including sixty thousand credit card numbers and records about Stratfor's clients, as well as employee e-mails. But during the two-week operation, the FBI also watched as the hackers stole innocent subscribers' financial information and deleted Stratfor's proprietary documents. The hackers also sent five million Stratfor e-mails to WikiLeaks. (The FBI later claimed it was powerless to stop the hackers because they'd stored the e-mails on their own computers.)

The FBI told Friedman not to inform his customers about the breach and not to go public with the news that Stratfor had been hacked. They wanted him to wait as the FBI followed the hackers' moves. But then, early on the afternoon of December 24, Friedman was informed that the Stratfor website had been hacked again. This time the hackers posted a "triumphant note" on the homepage announcing that they'd stolen credit card numbers and a large amount of e-mail, and that four Stratfor servers had been "effectively destroyed along with data and backups," Friedman wrote.

This was a crippling blow to the company's infrastructure. Those servers stored years' worth of reports and analysis that Stratfor had produced and sold to subscribers. It was the essence of Stratfor's business. The e-mails were private and confidential, and in some cases contained embarrassing correspondence among Stratfor employees, such as Burton, who used various racial epithets to refer to Arabs.

Hammond later said that destroying servers was common practice. "First you deface, then you take the information, then you destroy the server, for the Lulz [fun of it], and so they can't rebuild the system. We don't want them to rebuild. And to destroy forensic information that could be used to find out who did it and how it was done."

Deleting Stratfor's archives and exposing private communications materially damaged the company's business and its reputation. The FBI could have warned Stratfor to take emergency precautions to protect its information. It could have tried to apprehend the hackers earlier. But officials decided it was more important to get Hammond and his colleagues to move information onto an FBI computer, so it could be used to build a criminal case. Stratfor was caught in the crossfire of the FBI's hunt for Anonymous.

So were its clients. In the days after the break-in, hackers released credit card numbers of subscribers, which were reportedly used to make $700,000 in fraudulent purchases. Those transactions, some of which took the form of charitable donations, could be reversed by credit card companies. But the hackers also disclosed subscribers' e-mail addresses, which were later used for malware attacks. Some of Stratfor's subscribers were retired intelligence officers. Many others worked in academia, international relations, or corporate security. Notable subscribers have included former secretary of state Henry Kissinger, former national security adviser John Poindexter, and former vice president Dan Quayle.

Stratfor estimated that the hack cost the company $2 million in lost revenue and cleanup expenses. It also settled a class-action lawsuit brought by a former subscriber, which reportedly cost the company at least another $2 million in free subscriptions it agreed to give to current and former customers, as well as attorney fees and credit-monitoring services for customers who requested it.

Stratfor's case is a chilling indication of the harm a company can suffer at the hands of hackers under FBI surveillance. To be sure, the bureau has to acquire evidence of a crime if it's going to arrest hackers. Officials later claimed that Monsegur helped them effectively topple the LulzSec group, which was blamed for a string of website defacements and intrusions. And many companies have been warned by the bureau about threats to their business. But the Stratfor operation exposed an ugly truth about the FBI's counter-hacking strategy. If the purpose is gathering intelligence, namely, about Chinese and Russian groups, then the FBI will help to preempt attacks and prevent damage. But if the bureau is operating in its traditional mode — catching bad guys and bringing them to justice — it's willing to sacrifice the victims.

Monsegur has proved to be a productive ally for the FBI. In 2013 the Justice Department requested that a judge delay sentencing him in light of the assistance he continued to provide with other undisclosed investigations. "Since literally the day he was arrested, the defendant has been cooperating with the government proactively," a federal prosecutor wrote to a judge in New York. "He has been staying up sometimes all night engaging in conversations with co-conspirators that are helping the government to build cases against those co-conspirators." If given the maximum sentence, Monsegur could have spent the rest of his life in prison.

Jeffrey Hammond alleges that Monsegur's work for the government went well beyond targeting groups such as Anonymous. "What many do not know is that Sabu was also used by his handlers to facilitate the hacking of targets of the government's choosing — including numerous websites belonging to foreign governments. What the United States could not accomplish legally, it used Sabu, and by extension, me and my co-defendants, to accomplish illegally." Hammond, who was later sentenced to ten years in prison for the Stratfor hack, offered no evidence for his claims, and the FBI has never acknowledged enlisting hackers to penetrate foreign targets.

Sometimes the government and the companies they're ostensibly trying to protect seem to be working against each other. But as contentious as the relationship can be, there's an alliance forming between government and business in cyberspace. It's born of a mutual understanding that US national security and economic well-being are fundamentally threatened by rampant cyber espionage and potential attacks on vital infrastructure. The government views protecting whole industries as the best way to protect cyberspace writ large. But it can't do it alone. About 85 percent of the computer networks in the United States are owned and operated by private groups and individuals, and any one of them could be the weak link in the cyber security chain. They're the big telecom companies that run the Internet backbone. They're tech titans such as Google, which is responsible for a huge portion of Internet traffic and is beginning to lay its own cables in some American cities to provide Internet and television service. They're the financial institutions whose proprietary data networks reconcile trillions of dollars in transactions every day and move money seamlessly between accounts around the world. And they're the defense contractors, the traditional allies of government, whose networks are chock-full of top-secret weapons plans and classified intelligence. The government has decided that protecting cyberspace is a top national priority. But the companies have a voice in how that job gets done. That's the alliance at the heart of the military-Internet complex, and it will define the nature of cyberspace, and how we all work and live there, in the twenty-first century.

PART II

EIGHT

"Another Manhattan Project"

May 2007
The Oval Office

I T HAD TAKEN Mike McConnell just fifteen minutes to persuade George W. Bush to authorize a cyber war in Iraq. McConnell had asked for an hour with the president and his top national security advisers, figuring it'd take at least that long to convince them that such a risky undertaking was worth considering. What was he to do with the remaining forty-five minutes?

"Is there anything else?" Bush asked.

"Well, as a matter of fact, there is," McConnell replied.

Ever since he'd returned to government service in February, McConnell had been looking for an opportunity to talk with Bush about one of his biggest unaddressed concerns for national security: that the United States was vulnerable to a devastating cyber attack on a national scale. McConnell feared that the country's communications systems, like those in Iraq, could be penetrated by outsiders and disrupted or destroyed. And he was especially worried that the financial sector hadn't taken sufficient precautions to guard account information and records of stock transactions and funds transfers, or to stop criminals from stealing billions of dollars from personal and corporate bank accounts.

But physical infrastructure was also at risk. Two months earlier, the Homeland Security Department had asked the Idaho National Laboratory, which conducts nuclear and energy research for the federal government, to test whether hackers could gain remote access to an electrical power plant and cause a generator to spin out of control. The results were startling. A videotape of the test, which was later leaked to the press, showed a hulking green generator shaking as if in an earthquake, until steam and black smoke billowed out. The effect was almost cartoonish, but it was real, and the test revealed a critical weakness at the heart of America's electrical grid. Officials feared that hackers could disable electrical power equipment and cause blackouts that might last for weeks or even months while the equipment was replaced.

The cyber threat was no longer theoretical. Defense Department officials had by now begun to notice intrusions into contractors' computer networks. Among the secret plans and designs for weapons systems that the spies either had stolen or would eventually steal were those for the Joint Strike Fighter; Black Hawk helicopters; the Global Hawk long-range surveillance drone, as well as information on drone video systems and the data links used to remotely fly the unmanned aircraft; the Patriot missile system; a line of General Electric jet engines; the Aegis missile defense system; mine reconnaissance technology; sonar used for undersea mapping; the navy's littoral combat ship; schematics for lightweight torpedoes; designs for Marine Corps combat vehicles; information on the army's plans to equip soldiers with advanced surveillance and reconnaissance equipment; designs for the behemoth cargo plane, the C-17 Globemaster, as well as information on the army's global automated freight-management system; and systems designs for the RC-135 reconnaissance aircraft, signals intercept technology, and antenna mechanisms used by the navy. Every branch of the US Armed Forces had been compromised, along with the technology and weapons that the United States used to fight in every domain — land, air, sea, and space.

But how to convey this urgency to Bush? McConnell knew the president was no technologist. This was the man who had once said he used "the Google" only occasionally, to look at satellite images of his ranch in Texas. It would be difficult to explain in technical terms how someone sitting at a keyboard could wreak havoc from thousands of miles away, using a machine with which the president was largely unfamiliar. So McConnell appealed to the idea that had most captivated Bush's attention during most of his presidency: terrorism.

McConnell asked Bush to consider a hypothetical scenario: if instead of hijacking commercial airliners and flying them into buildings on September 11, 2001, al-Qaeda terrorists had broken into the databases of a major financial institution and erased its contents, the gears of the global financial system could grind to a halt. Transactions couldn't be processed. Trades wouldn't clear. The trillions of dollars that sloshed around the world every day did so through computer networks. The "money" was really just data. It was balances in accounts. A distributed network of electronic ledgers that kept track of who bought and sold what, who moved money where, and to whom. Corrupt just a portion of that information, or destroy it, and mass panic would ensue, McConnell said. Whole economies could collapse just for lack of confidence, to say nothing of whether all banks and financial institutions would ever be able to recover the data they lost.

Bush seemed incredulous. How could an intruder armed with only a computer penetrate the inner sanctums of the US financial system? Surely those companies would have taken precautions to protect such precious assets. What else was vulnerable? Bush wanted to know. Was the White House at risk? Bush pointed to the secure phone on his desk that he used to talk to cabinet officials and foreign leaders. "Could someone get into that?" he asked.

A silence fell over the Oval Office. Some of Bush's senior national security aides looked nervously at one another. McConnell realized that until this moment, the president had never been told just how weak the government's own electronic defenses were, or the country's.

"Mr. President," McConnell said, "if the capability to exploit a communications device exists, we have to assume that our enemies either have it or are trying to develop it."

And this after McConnell had been telling Bush about all the ways that the United States could exploit Iraq's communications systems. It was starting to dawn on the president: what he could do to others, they could do to him.

Returning to the hypothetical cyber attack on the financial system, McConnell drew another comparison to terrorism.

"The economic effects of this attack would be far worse than those of the physical attacks of 9/11," McConnell told Bush, who knew that the strike on the Twin Towers and the Pentagon had plunged the United States even deeper into a recession.

Bush looked stunned. He turned to his Treasury secretary, Henry Paulson, whose last job was CEO of Goldman Sachs. "Hank, is what Mike is saying true?"

Paulson replied, "Not only is it true, Mr. President, but when I was in charge of Goldman, this is the scenario that kept me up at night."

Bush stood up. "The Internet is our competitive advantage," he told his aides and cabinet officials. "We have to do what's necessary to protect it. We'll do another Manhattan Project if we have to," Bush said, alluding to the secret World War II program that built the first atom bomb.

McConnell had never imagined such a muscular response. For more than a decade he'd been hoping the president — any president — would hone in on the dangers that he believed were lurking right beneath the surface of daily life.

Bush turned to McConnell. "Mike, you brought this problem in here. You've got thirty days to fix it."

No one could "fix" this problem in thirty days — if it could truly be solved at all. But President Bush had just asked for a comprehensive, national plan to shore up the nation's cyber defenses, invoking one of the greatest scientific challenges in American history. McConnell saw a rare opportunity, and he seized it. But he couldn't do the work alone. So, the spymaster turned to the source of technical wizardry that he knew best.

From the beginning, the government's cyber defense plan was run by the NSA. It was treated as a military and intelligence program and, as such, kept in strict secrecy. It was officially codified in a presidential directive that Bush signed in January 2008. The administration proposed to spend $40 billion on the effort in its first five years — a huge sum of money for a single initiative. Like McConnell, Keith Alexander had been waiting for a moment when a president put his full weight and influence behind a national effort to push back against the invisible enemies that Alexander believed posed a near-existential threat to the United States. Alexander also thought that malicious hackers, probably acting on behalf of enemy nations or terrorist groups, would eventually target Wall Street financial institutions, the power grid, and other vital infrastructure.

The first stage of the national counteroffensive was to give the enemy fewer targets to hit. The Defense Department pared down its own network connections to the public Internet to a mere eighteen points, called gateways. That in itself was an extraordinary feat, considering that Internet access had been distributed to every far-flung corner of the armed forces, down to most company headquarters in war zones. (That was what made the insurgent-hunting machine in Iraq work so smoothly.) The Defense Department did a better job than any other government agency fending off intrusions to its networks, but occasionally adversaries got through. In June 2007, hackers broke in to the unclassified e-mail system that Secretary of Defense Robert Gates and hundreds of other department officials used. It was an urgent reminder that the time had come to pull up the virtual drawbridges, tightly restricting access to the outside world.

Meanwhile, the NSA began to intensely monitor those gateways for signs of malicious activity. This was the active side of computer defense, what a senior Pentagon official would later describe as "part sensor, part sentry, part sharpshooter." If the hackers or their botnets touched a Defense Department network, the military could block an Internet address to prevent the computer from sending malicious traffic, and then send out the alert to military and intelligence organizations that they should watch for dangerous traffic coming from that location. The idea was to better protect the Defense Department's own networks using the NSA's intelligence-gathering skills, but also to provide a kind of early-warning system to companies by watching for any passing malware that might indicate a campaign targeting critical industries, and then pass along the intelligence to them. Energy and financial services companies were at the top of the list to receive warnings.

But these were piecemeal measures that didn't amount to a broad plan for protecting the nation. Trying to spot malware across the Internet through a handful of access points was like trying to find a fly on a wall while looking through a soda straw. (There is no evidence that the NSA ever helped avert a major cyber attack as part of this strategy of monitoring its own networks.) Alexander said that to thoroughly defend the country, the NSA needed more pathways into the networks of US companies. It had some through a secret counterintelligence program called Operation Byzantine Foothold, in which NSA hackers traced Chinese and other foreign spies who had penetrated military contractors. The NSA followed the trail of spear-phishing e-mails loaded with malware back to their source, and the intelligence they gleaned about hacker tactics helped fortify the companies' defenses. But only a few dozen companies were cooperating with the Pentagon, sharing information from their own networks and letting the NSA get a glimpse inside. Alexander wanted the government to expand the plan to companies beyond the Defense Industrial Base. But that would take time and a level of political will that Bush might not have at this late point in his presidency. McConnell, for one, thought it'd be politically disastrous if the NSA's hands-on role in domestic cyber defense were revealed. It had been less than two years since a front-page article in the *New York Times* exposed the NSA's program of warrantless phone and e-mail surveillance inside the United States. The agency's role in cyber defense marked an expansion of those activities, and a blending of intelligence gathering and warfare — to the extent that the agency fought back against the hackers. Some members of Congress wanted to rein in the NSA's surveillance efforts, which were a requisite piece of its cyber defense mission. McConnell thought that for now the agency needed to keep a low profile and stay focused on the least controversial part of defense, scanning the department's networks and those of its contractors.

Meanwhile, McConnell got the ball rolling on the civilian side of government. The Homeland Security Department, which had the legal authority for securing the .gov Internet domain used by most government departments (excluding the military and the intelligence agencies), oversaw an initiative to trim the number of civilian Internet gateways from more than a thousand down to fifty. It was a bigger and more diffuse challenge than the Defense Department's—these civilian networks weren't centrally managed, and there were many more of them. The project was guaranteed to outlast the remainder of Bush's time in office, and therefore McConnell's.

But Alexander wasn't under a term limit. He'd only been in office since 2005, and while tradition suggested that his tour would probably last four or five years, there was no reason that a future president or secretary of defense couldn't extend it. Indeed, Alexander's predecessor had served for six years, longer than anyone at that point in the agency's fifty-six-year history. As the NSA's influence over intelligence operations grew, particularly in counterterrorism, its directors became essential, and harder to replace. Alexander understood that the agency's future dominance in the intelligence hierarchy depended on cementing its role as the leader in cyber defense and offense. This was the next big problem to which the whole of government would focus its national security priorities. In a crude calculus, counterterrorism was out, cyber security was in. Alexander just had to wait for the moment when more of the country's leaders saw that, and would turn to him for help. He needed a crisis.

NINE

Buckshot Yankee

FRIDAY, OCTOBER 24, 2008, had already been an unusually busy day at NSA headquarters. President Bush came up to Fort Meade that afternoon to meet with senior agency leaders, his last scheduled visit before leaving office in January. At 4:30 p.m., when most NSA employees were getting ready to head home for the weekend, Richard Schaeffer, the top official in charge of computer security, walked into Keith Alexander's office with an urgent message.

A young analyst in one of the NSA's hunt teams that look for malicious intrusions had spotted a rogue program running on a military network. It was sending out a beacon, a signal to a host computer somewhere on the Internet, asking for instructions on what to do next — perhaps copy files or erase data. That itself wasn't so alarming. But the beacon was emanating from inside a classified network used by US Central Command, which ran the wars in Iraq and Afghanistan. And that was supposed to be impossible, because the network wasn't connected to the Internet.

No classified, air-gapped military network had ever been breached. Those networks were kept disconnected from the public Internet because they contained some of the military's most important secret communications, including war plans and orders to troops in the field. Analysts had been working feverishly for the past few days to determine how the malicious program had made its way onto the network, and they speculated that it must have piggybacked on an infected USB drive, probably inserted by an unwitting soldier in Afghanistan, where the majority of infections seemed to have occurred. And that was the other problem — there were infections, plural. The malware was replicating itself and spreading to different computers on the network via USB drives. And it appeared to have shown up on two other classified networks as well.

NSA officials immediately suspected the work of a hostile intelligence service trying to steal classified military information. Analysts speculated that an infected USB could have been dropped in a parking lot, waiting for an unsuspecting human — "patient zero" — to pick it up and insert it into a secure computer inside a Centcom facility or at a military base. The malicious program couldn't connect to the Internet to retrieve its orders. But a spy could be communicating with the malware from a few miles away via radio waves — the NSA used equipment to do that when it injected spyware behind an air gap. And there were indications that the worm was spreading to unclassified systems, too, which were connected to the outside world and could give foreign spies an entry point into the Pentagon.

The breach was unprecedented in military and intelligence history. Alexander said it was time to sound the alarm.

Air force general Michael Basla was working in the Pentagon Friday night when an emergency call came in from Fort Meade. Basla was then the vice director of command, control, communications, and computer systems for the Joint Chiefs. He quickly grasped the urgency of what the NSA official on the line was telling him. "In so many words," Basla later recalled, "it was, 'Houston, we've got a problem.'"

The gears of the national military command structure started spinning. That night Basla, along with NSA officials, briefed Admiral Mike Mullen, chairman of the Joint Chiefs and President Bush's top military adviser. The agency also informed the deputy secretary of defense, Gordon England, who'd been instrumental in setting up the Defense Industrial Base Initiative, as well as the leaders of Congress.

No one was sure when, or if, the malware would attempt to execute its mission — whatever it might be. But the members of the NSA hunt team who discovered the worm thought they had a way to neutralize it. It was sending out a message for orders from a host server. So why not give the worm what it wanted? The hunt team wanted to build an impostor command-and-control server that would make contact with the worm and then tell it, in effect, to go to sleep and take no further actions. The plan wasn't without risk. If the team disrupted or disabled legitimate programs running on the classified network, such as those that controlled communications among battlefield commanders, then they could harm military operations in Afghanistan and Iraq. The classified network still had to function.

The Pentagon told the NSA to move forward with its plan, which was given the code name Buckshot Yankee. The hunt team worked all Friday night to fine-tune the details, drinking soda to stay awake and bingeing on pizza. On Saturday they put a computer server onto a truck and drove to the nearby Defense Information Systems Agency, which runs the Defense Department's global telecommunications systems. They allowed the server to become infected with the malware, then activated the impostor controller that told the worm to stand down. It worked.

Now the NSA had a way to deactivate the worm. But first it had to find it — and all of the copies it had made of itself that had spread across Defense Department networks. The NSA called in its best hackers, the elite Tailored Access Operations group. They looked for worm infections on the military's computers. But then they went farther out, looking for its traces on nonmilitary computers, including those on civilian US government networks and in other countries. They found that the worm had spread widely.

That was not surprising. As it turned out, the worm was not so new. It had been discovered by a Finnish security researcher and, in June 2008, had shown up on the military computers of a NATO member country. The researcher dubbed it Agent.btz, *agent* being a generic name for a newly discovered piece of malware, and the *.btz* an internal reference marker. There was no evidence that any infection of Agent .btz on a US computer had resulted in stolen or destroyed data. In fact, the worm didn't appear to be that sophisticated, which raised the question of why a foreign intelligence service would go to the trouble of building a worm that burrowed into computers around the world and didn't steal anything.

But military leaders still treated the breach as a dire threat to national security. The week after the NSA alerted the Pentagon, Mullen briefed President Bush and Secretary of Defense Gates. The NSA took on the mission of hunting down every infection of Agent.btz and using the impostor controller to turn it off. In November, US Strategic Command, which at that time had overall responsibility for cyber warfare, sent out a decree: the use of thumb drives was henceforth banned on all Defense Department and military computers worldwide. It was an overreaction, and underscored the degree to which senior military leaders felt threatened.

Alexander was not so alarmed. In the panic he saw the chance to make the NSA the military's new leader in cyberspace. It was his hunt team that discovered the worm, he argued. His experts who devised a clever way to kill it. His elite hackers who used their spying skills to track the worm in its hiding places. Pentagon officials wondered if they should launch an offensive cyber strike to eradicate the worm, rather than just tricking it into talking to their impostor. (The process of getting rid of the infections ultimately took fourteen months.)

At the time, the responsibility for carrying out a coordinated military strike—a true cyber war—lay principally with the Joint Functional Component Command for Network Warfare, a subordinate to Strategic Command. But it was small in comparison with the NSA, and it didn't have the NSA's expertise in computer defense and espionage. Officials decided that an offensive strike, particularly on computers in other countries, was a step too far for countering Agent.btz—which after all hadn't done any damage. But the Buckshot Yankee operation showed them that in the event of a real national crisis—a cyber attack on a power grid or a bank—the military needed all its sharpest shooters under one roof.

"It became clear that we needed to bring together the offense and defense capabilities," Alexander told a congressional committee in 2010, after the Pentagon declassified certain details of the operation. It was what he had wanted all along.

The Buckshot Yankee operation became the catalyst for establishing US Cyber Command, a single entity that oversaw all of the military's efforts to defend against virtual attacks on their systems, and to initiate their own. This was the idea that national intelligence director Mike McConnell had backed and that eventually won the support of Bob Gates. Senior military leaders realized that they'd been caught flatfooted, and that many of them had overestimated their ability to respond quickly to an incursion into the Pentagon's computers. "It opened all our eyes," Basla says.

The quick thinking of Alexander and his team of cyber warriors convinced the Pentagon brass, Gates, and the White House that the NSA was best positioned to marshal the military's cyber forces, and therefore should take the lead. Alexander would run the new Cyber Command from Fort Meade. He would get more personnel and a budget. But the warriors and the infrastructure would come mostly from the NSA.

The NSA also still had to completely eradicate the Agent.btz infections. That process lasted more than a year, and the agency used it to expand its newfound power. Whenever a new infection was found, the NSA restricted all information to those with a "need to know" what had occurred. Each instance became a kind of classified sub-project of the larger operation. According to a former Defense Department intelligence analyst who was cleared to know about Buckshot Yankee, this made it more difficult for agencies other than the NSA to respond to the breach and to gather information about what had happened — which is apparently just what Alexander wanted. A veil of secrecy fell over nearly every aspect of the NSA's new cyber mission. The former Defense Department analyst describes the NSA's response to Buckshot Yankee as "a power grab."

The need for secrecy would be understandable if the Agent.btz infection really was part of an intelligence campaign by Russia, China, or a hostile nation. But Pentagon officials never claimed that the breach caused a loss of secrets or any other vital information. And it was never settled whether the infected USB drive that analysts thought was the initial vector was deliberately planted near a military facility or if some careless soldier or contractor had just picked up the Agent.btz worm on the outside, maybe when connecting a laptop at an Internet café, and then brought the worm behind the air gap. It's possible that patient zero simply happened upon the worm, and that it wasn't the handiwork of a foreign government at all. In fact, Agent.btz turned out to be a variant of a three-year-old, mostly harmless worm. Some officials who worked on Buckshot Yankee doubted that foreign spies were to blame. If they were going to break in to the inner sanctum of military cyberspace, wouldn't they be craftier? And wouldn't they actually steal something? Then again, perhaps they were testing the Americans' defenses, seeing how they'd respond to an incursion in order to learn how they'd designed their security.

Had lawmakers and Bush administration officials understood that the Agent.btz infection was relatively benign, they might have thought twice about giving the NSA so much authority to control cyber defense and offense. Perhaps Alexander and his lieutenants were eager to keep the details of the incursion a secret so as not to undercut their own case for putting NSA in charge of Cyber Command. That would be in keeping with Alexander's pattern of trying to frighten government officials about the cyber threat, and then assure them he was the one who could keep the bogeymen at bay. "Alexander created this aura, like the Wizard of Oz, of this incredible capability behind the curtain at Fort Meade," says a former Obama administration official who worked closely with the general on cyber security issues. "He used classification to ensure that no one could pull back that veil."

Secrecy was — and still is — a great source of the NSA's power. But the agency was also aided by a low-grade paranoia that took root among senior Defense Department officials after Buckshot Yankee. To ward off the risk of future infections, senior leaders banned the use of thumb drives across the entire department and in all branches of the armed forces, a decree met with outrage by service members in the field who relied on the portable storage devices to carry documents and maps between computers. The ban persisted for years after Buckshot Yankee. "If you pulled out a USB and put it in my computer, in a few minutes someone will knock on my door and confiscate the computer," Mark Maybury, chief scientist of the air force, said during an interview in his Pentagon office in 2012.

Bush administration officials were swept up in a wave of cyber anxiety. It washed over them, and onto the next president.

TEN

The Secret Sauce

ROM THE MOMENT he took the oath of office, Barack Obama
was bombarded with bad news about the state of America's cyber
defenses. He'd already had his classified national security briefing
with Mike McConnell in Chicago, where the intelligence director told
him a version of the dire story he'd laid out for Bush in 2007. During the campaign, Obama staffers' e-mail accounts had been hacked
by spies in China, as had those of his opponent, Senator John McCain. Now, as the forty-fourth president settled into the Oval Office,
the Center for Strategic and International Studies, a respected Washington think tank, had just issued a comprehensive and discouraging
analysis of US cyber security. The report's authors, who had conducted
at least sixteen closed-door sessions with senior government and military officials, listed a number of hair-raising intrusions that had been
declassified. Among them were the hacking of Secretary of Defense
Robert Gates's e-mail; a spyware infection at the Commerce Department, which was attributed by several outside experts to a program
that Chinese hackers had installed on the laptop computer of Secretary
of Commerce Carlos Gutierrez during an official visit to Beijing; and
computer break-ins at the State Department that caused the loss of

"terabytes" of information. But these and other incursions enumerated in the final document were only about 10 percent of all the breaches the authors had identified, according to a staff member who worked on the report. The rest were too sensitive, and perhaps too alarming, to discuss publicly.

The panel members — which included senior officials from the National Security Agency, executives at some of the country's biggest technology and defense companies, members of Congress, and cyber security experts who would go on to serve in the new administration — praised the Manhattan Project–style initiative that Bush had launched. But they said it didn't go far enough. The Obama administration should build on those efforts and enact regulations requiring certain industries and critical infrastructure to fortify and maintain their cyber security. "This is a strategic issue on par with weapons of mass destruction and global jihad, where the federal government bears primary responsibility," the panel members wrote. "America's failure to protect cyberspace is one of the most urgent national security problems facing the new administration. . . . It is a battle we are losing."

Foreign spies worked relentlessly to get access to the communications, speeches, and position papers of senior members of the new president's administration. During Obama's first year in office, Chinese hackers launched a campaign targeting State Department officials, including Secretary of State Hillary Clinton. In a particularly clever play, five State Department employees who were negotiating with Chinese officials on reducing greenhouse-gas emissions received spear-phishing e-mails bearing the name and contact information of a prominent Washington journalist, Bruce Stokes. Stokes was well known at the State Department because he covered global trade and climate change issues. He was also married to Ambassador Wendy Sherman, who'd been Bill Clinton's top policy adviser on North Korea and would later go on to the number three position at State, leading US negotiations with Iran over its nuclear program in 2013. The US climate change envoy to China, Todd Stern, was also an old friend of Stokes's. The subject line of the e-mail read, "China and Climate Change," which seemed innocuous enough to pass for a reporter's inquiry. And the body of the message included comments related to the recipients' jobs and what they were working on at the time. Whoever sent the message had studied Stokes and knew his network of friends and sources well enough to pose as him in an e-mail. It's still unclear whether any of the recipients ever opened the messages, which came loaded with a virus that could have siphoned documents off the officials' computers and tracked their communications.

Also in 2009 a senior member of Hillary Clinton's staff received an e-mail that appeared to come from a colleague in the office next door. The e-mail contained an attachment that the author claimed was related to a recent meeting. The recipient couldn't recall the meeting and wasn't sure it had ever occurred. He walked over to his colleague's office and asked about the e-mail he'd just sent.

"What e-mail?" his colleague asked.

Thanks to a young staffer's suspicions, the State Department blocked spies from potentially installing surveillance equipment on the computers in Clinton's office. It was a reminder of how sophisticated the spies had become, and clear evidence that they were mapping out the relationships of administration employees, most of whose names rarely or never appeared in the press. Chinese spies honed this technique over the coming years, and they still use it today. Charlie Croom, a retired air force general who ran the Defense Information Systems Agency and is now vice president for cyber security at Lockheed Martin, says cyber spies will scour the company's website looking for names of employees in press releases, lists of public appearances by executives, and other tiny nuggets of information that might help them refine their approach to a potential target. A generation ago, spies had to rifle through people's garbage and trail them on the street to get those details.

In the face of warnings about American defenses and a foreign intelligence campaign against his own staff, Obama signaled early on that he intended to make cyber security one of the top priorities. In a speech from the East Room of the White House in May 2009 he said, "We know that cyber intruders have probed our electrical grid and that in other countries cyber attacks have plunged entire cities into darkness." Obama didn't say where, but intelligence and military officials had concluded that two blackouts in Brazil, in 2005 and 2007, had been triggered by hackers who gained access to the SCADA systems that controlled electrical equipment there.

Until Obama's speech, US officials had, for the most part, only hinted that electrical grids had been breached, and they rarely agreed to be quoted by name. Owners and operators of electrical facilities denounced rumors of hacker-caused outages, including some in the United States, as speculative nonsense, and cited official investigations that usually attributed the outages to natural phenomena, like fallen trees or soot on power lines. But now the president was acknowledging that the American electrical grid was vulnerable and that the nightmare of a cyber blackout had come true in another country.

"My administration will pursue a new comprehensive approach to securing America's digital infrastructure," Obama announced. "This new approach starts at the top, with this commitment from me: From now on, our digital infrastructure — the networks and computers we depend on every day — will be treated as they should be: as a strategic national asset. Protecting this infrastructure will be a national security priority. We will ensure that these networks are secure, trustworthy and resilient. We will deter, prevent, detect, and defend against attacks and recover quickly from any disruptions or damage."

Protecting cyberspace, Obama declared, was the government's job.

Keith Alexander agreed. For him, the only question was, who in the government should take on such a herculean task?

Not long after he became NSA director, in 2005, Alexander paid a visit to the headquarters of the Homeland Security Department, a complex of buildings in the prosperous Washington neighborhood of Cathedral Heights where navy cryptologists had helped to break the Nazi Enigma code in World War II. He was carrying a rolled-up sheet of paper to share with Michael Chertoff, a former federal prosecutor and judge who had been confirmed as the new secretary of homeland security earlier that year. By law, the department was supposed to co-ordinate cyber security policy across the government, protect civilian agencies' computer networks, and work with companies to protect critical infrastructure. It was a huge and ill-defined portfolio of responsibilities, and one of myriad tasks delegated to the two-year-old department, including patrolling US borders, screening airline passengers and cargo, fixing the nation's broken immigration system, and ensuring that terrorists didn't launch another surprise attack in the United States.

In an eavesdropping-proof room, Alexander rolled the paper out over the length of a conference table. It was a huge diagram, showing all the malicious activity on the Internet that NSA knew of at that time. Alexander's message could be interpreted two ways. He was there to help the fledgling department fulfill its cyber defense mission. Or he was not so subtly conveying that the department would be lost without the NSA's help, and that Homeland Security should step aside and let the experts take over. The truth was, Homeland Security couldn't produce a diagram like the one Alexander had just presented. It lacked the trained personnel, the huge budgets, the global architecture of surveillance, and the bureaucratic and political clout in Washington to perform at the NSA's level.

As Alexander and his lieutenants saw things, it would be irresponsible bordering on negligent not to assist the department however they could. But that didn't mean surrendering NSA's role as the center of gravity in cyber security. The agency was part of the Department of Defense, and its writ extended to protecting the nation from foreign attacks, whether on land, in the air, at sea, or on a computer network.

Chertoff and Alexander got along well, according to former officials who worked with both of them, and the secretary seemed happy to let the cyber warriors at Fort Meade take the lead. Alexander spent the next four years building up NSA's cyber forces, culminating in the successful Buckshot Yankee operation and the establishment of Cyber Command. In 2009, Obama named former Arizona governor Janet Napolitano as his homeland security secretary. Alexander told his staff to give Napolitano and her team whatever help and advice they needed. But he had no intention of ceding the battlefield. Not when he was about to launch his biggest campaign yet.

Alexander had seen how the Defense Industrial Base Initiative was able to give the government access to information from corporate computer networks. The companies had become digital scouts in cyberspace, and the information they reported back helped to feed NSA's catalog of threat signatures — the lists of known malware, hacker techniques, and suspect Internet addresses that could be used to fortify defenses. Alexander liked to call it "the secret sauce." The DIB had started with just twenty companies. Now he wanted to use the DIB model in new industries, including the energy and financial sector, and to bring as many as five hundred companies into the fold.

At NSA the plan became known as Tranche 2. Operators of "critical infrastructure"—which could be broadly defined to include electrical companies, nuclear power plant operators, banks, software manufacturers, transportation and logistics companies, even hospitals and medical device suppliers, whose equipment could be hacked remotely — would be required by law or regulation to submit the traffic to and from their networks for scanning by an Internet service provider. The provider would use the signatures supplied by the NSA to look for malware or signs of a cyber campaign by a foreign government. It was a version of Alexander's original plan to make the NSA the central clearinghouse for cyber threat intelligence. The NSA wouldn't do the scanning, but it would give all the requisite threat signatures to the scanner. That helped the NSA avoid the impression that it was horning its way into private computer networks, even though it was actually in control of the whole operation. Once the scanners detected a threat, NSA analysts would move in and assess it. They would decide whether to let the traffic pass or to block it, or, if need be, to strike back at the source.

The agency had already developed a scanning system called Tutelage that could isolate e-mails containing viruses and put them in a kind of digital petri dish, so that analysts could examine them without infecting any computers. This was the "sensor, sentry, and sharpshooter" that the NSA had used to monitor its Internet gateways back in 2009. Now Alexander wanted to bring that capability to bear as part of Tranche 2, effectively turning hundreds of companies and critical-infrastructure operators into a new front in the cyber wars.

This made some Obama administration officials nervous. The president had clearly stated his intentions to protect cyberspace as a critical national asset. But he had always been conflicted about how long a leash to give the NSA. Obama had never warmed to the agency or Alexander. And although he appreciated and embraced the powerful capabilities that the NSA had to offer, the culture of espionage seemed alien to him.

In the summer 2009, Pentagon officials drafted an "execute order" that would allow the military to launch a counterstrike on computers sending malicious traffic not just to a military system but also against privately owned critical-infrastructure facilities, such as electrical power stations. That was an extraordinary step. Heretofore, the government had only given assistance to companies in the form of intelligence about hackers and malware, which they could use to bolster their own defenses. Now the NSA wanted authority to launch a defensive strike against anyone attacking key American businesses in such a way that loss of life might occur — a blackout, say, or an attack on the air traffic control system — or if the US economy or national security would be jeopardized. That latter set of criteria was arguably broad and open to interpretation. Would a massive denial of service attack against American banks, for instance, which didn't shut them down or steal funds but disrupted their operations, count as a hostile act that jeopardized the US economy?

Obama administration officials pared back the order — but only slightly. Obama didn't push the NSA out of the business of retaliatory strikes. He just required it to get authorization from him or his secretary of defense.

Perhaps sensing that he couldn't always count on Obama's unconditional support, Alexander took his plans for Tranche 2 to Capitol Hill and the lawmakers who controlled his agency's multibillion-dollar budget. Alexander told them and their staff that he supported legally requiring companies to share their data with government-appointed traffic scanners. But that was not a proposal the administration supported, at least not in its current form. White House aides had to admonish Alexander several times during 2011 and 2012, when a cyber bill was moving through Congress, not to speak on the president's behalf and make promises that the administration wasn't sure it could keep.

"They're pretty mad at me downtown," Alexander said sheepishly in one meeting with congressional staffers. But that didn't stop him from pushing harder. Alexander was an awkward public speaker, but in small groups he could be charming and compelling. He formed alliances with the Democratic and Republican chairs of the House and Senate Intelligence Committees. Lawmakers gave him the money he wanted and appropriated new funds for cyber security. Congressional oversight of NSA's activities was minimal and nonintrusive. Alexander was winning the war on Capitol Hill. But inside the administration, he had enemies.

By the time she arrived at the Homeland Security Department as the new deputy secretary in early 2009, Jane Holl Lute found that a battle for control of cyber security had already been fought — and Alexander had won. Many of her colleagues had long since concluded that the NSA was the only game in town, because it was the only agency with an extensive catalog of threat signatures, including malware, hacker techniques, and suspect Internet addresses. They knew that information had been gleaned from classified, expensive intelligence-gathering operations, which gave it a certain cachet and credibility. They also knew that Homeland Security had no comparable store of information, and scarcely a cyber security staff to speak of. The department employed twenty-four computer scientists in 2009, while the Defense Department employed more than seven thousand, most of whom worked at the NSA. Homeland Security's computer-emergency watch center also couldn't monitor network traffic in real time, making it practically useless as an early-warning system for cyber attacks. The best Homeland Security could hope to do was play a public relations role, encouraging companies to adopt good "cyber hygiene," better monitor their own networks, and share information with the government. But these were gestures, not actions.

The first time Lute met the official in charge of the department's budding cyber defense mission was when he handed her his letter of resignation. In March, Rod Beckstrom quit in protest over what he described as the NSA's interference in policies that, by law, were Homeland Security's responsibility. "NSA effectively controls DHS cyber efforts," Beckstrom wrote in a scathing rebuke. The NSA had stationed its employees in the department's headquarters and installed its own proprietary technology. And recently NSA leaders had proposed relocating Beckstrom and his staff—all five of them—to the agency's headquarters at Fort Meade.

"During my term as director, we have been unwilling to subjugate the [center] underneath the NSA," Beckstrom wrote. He warned Lute, Napolitano, and the president's top national security advisers, including Secretary of Defense Robert Gates, that if the NSA were given the reins, it would run roughshod over privacy and civil liberties and subsume the department into a culture of secrecy.

Lute was no cyber expert. A former army officer, she last served managing peacekeeping operations for the United Nations. But as the de facto chief operating offer of the department, she'd been charged with making sense of its muddied cyber policies. Clearly, that was going to entail battle with the NSA. (Napolitano didn't want the job, and was arguably unqualified for it. Practically a technophobe, she had no personal online accounts, and even at work she didn't use e-mail.)

Lute had been around intelligence officials long enough to conclude that they gained much of their power from secrecy, and by cultivating an appearance of omniscience. She didn't adhere to the conventional wisdom that only the NSA had the know-how to defend cyberspace. "Pretend the Manhattan phone book is the universe of malware," she once told colleagues. "NSA only has about one page of that book." Lute thought that many companies already had the most important threat signatures, because they were collecting them from the hackers and foreign governments who tried to break in to their networks every day. Private security companies, antivirus researchers, even journalists were collecting and analyzing malware and other threat signatures, and either selling the information or publishing it as a public service. Software companies sent out automatic patches to fix known holes in their programs. The NSA tracked all this information. Why should anyone presume their intelligence didn't incorporate what was already widely known? The spy agency's information might be helpful, but companies didn't require it to defend themselves, Lute said. They needed to share what they knew with one another, like an Internet version of a neighborhood watch.

Lute wasn't alone in thinking that Alexander had oversold his "secret sauce."

"There's a presumption that if something is classified, it must be true, which is not remotely the case," says a senior law enforcement official who sparred with NSA officials in several meetings about whether it should take the leading role in defending companies' computer networks. "We can lay out information to a policymaker that's 'law enforcement sensitive' [a lower level of classification than top secret], and they'll say, 'No, we've got this top-secret report, it must be true.' And that's hard to refute, because the NSA doesn't bring the facts to the table about how it got that information or whether it's unique. Policymakers and the public are not getting an accurate picture of the threat."

Even when Alexander met with senior executives from the world's biggest technology firms, including Google, who knew plenty about cyber spies and attackers and had a financial interest in stopping them, he tried to persuade them that the NSA's intelligence was superior. "His attitude was, 'If only you knew what we knew, you'd be very afraid. I'm the only one that can help you,'" says a former senior security official.

"Alexander convinced many lawmakers and policymakers that the NSA had a monopoly on this and it was all at Fort Meade," says the former administration official who worked on cyber security issues. "And he'd use that phrase, 'secret sauce.' I've been behind the curtain up there; there is no secret sauce. It's complete bullshit."

A low-grade tension persisted for the first two years of Lute's tenure at Homeland Security. In February of 2011, it erupted into a public turf war. At a defense industry conference in Colorado Springs, the home of the US Air Force Academy, Alexander declared that the NSA should take a leading role in protecting cyberspace, the fifth domain of warfare. He called for new powers to defend against potentially crippling attacks on the United States. "I do not have the authority to stop an attack against Wall Street or industry, and that's a gap I need to fix," he said. Alexander had thrown down the gauntlet, effectively declaring US cyberspace a militarized zone.

Alexander was scheduled to give a version of the same talk eight days later at one of the biggest annual computer security conferences, in San Francisco. Major newspapers and technology trade press would be there. Lute cut him off at the pass. On February 14, three days ahead of his speech, she and another senior Homeland Security official published an online op-ed for *Wired*, the influential technology magazine. "These days, some observers are pounding out a persistent and mounting drumbeat of war, calling for preparing the battlefield, even saying that the United States is already fully into a 'cyberwar,' that it is, in fact, losing," Lute wrote. "We disagree. Cyberspace is not a war zone."

It was a direct shot at Alexander. "Conflict and exploitation are present there, to be sure, but cyberspace is fundamentally a civilian space," Lute wrote, "a neighborhood, a library, a marketplace, a school yard, a workshop — and a new, exciting age in human experience, exploration and development. Portions of it are part of America's defense infrastructure, and these are properly protected by soldiers. But the vast majority of cyberspace is civilian space."

Alexander was undeterred. He gave his speech as scheduled and repeated the same themes. And a few days later he fired back at Lute. "There's a lot of folks that say we'd like the technical capabilities of NSA ... but we don't want NSA in there" protecting networks, Alexander said at a conference in Washington about domestic security, which was the Homeland Security Department's domain. He bristled at the suggestion that his agency should lean back and only help defend when asked, rather than rush to the front lines. Alexander even invoked the Maginot Line, the long stretch of concrete fortifications France built along its border with Germany in the 1930s, suggesting that the United States risked being overrun if it focused its defense purely on strategy and underestimated the cunning of their enemies. (The Nazis overcame the line by going around it, a move the French hadn't planned for, and ultimately conquered the country in six weeks.)

The turf war was getting hot. The White House ultimately nixed Alexander's Tranche 2 plan, not because Obama thought the NSA wasn't up to the job of defending cyberspace but because it looked too much like a big government-surveillance program. The administration didn't abandon Alexander's core idea. It opted instead to use the existing DIB program, which was itself a big government-surveillance program, to test whether Internet service providers could monitor traffic using classified government intelligence — that NSA secret sauce. It was a compromise. The NSA wouldn't get access to companies' networks, but it would funnel intelligence to them through the Internet service providers.

In the spring of 2011, seventeen defense companies volunteered for the test. The NSA still gave threat signatures to three service providers — CenturyLink, AT&T, and Verizon. The latter two were intimately familiar with NSA surveillance, having been a part of the agency's bulk collection of Americans' phone records since shortly after the 9/11 terrorist attacks. And all three companies were accustomed to handing over e-mails and online data about their customers at the request of the FBI and NSA.

The test focused on two specific countermeasures: quarantining incoming e-mails infected with malware and preventing outbound traffic from contacting malicious Internet addresses, a process known as sinkholing. Most organizations only monitored traffic coming into their networks and ignored data that was being sent from inside their systems. Hackers took advantage of that ignorance and frequently disguised a company's own documents as legitimate outbound traffic, before sending it on to a server under the hackers' control.

The test was a qualified success. An independent review by Carnegie Mellon University, one of the top technology research institutions in the country, found that the Internet service providers were able to receive the classified threat signatures and keep them secret. But there was some bad news for the vaunted cyber warriors at Fort Meade: practically none of the signatures told the companies anything they didn't already know, a finding that supported Lute and others who doubted the power of Alexander's secret sauce.

Most of NSA's intelligence was out of date by the time it was received. Of fifty-two cases of malicious activity that were detected during the test, only two were the result of NSA threat signatures. The rest the companies found on their own, because they'd spent the last few years building their own network-monitoring capabilities and beefing up their defenses.

The NSA could take some pride in knowing that those companies got so much better at defense because of their early participation in the DIB program, back in 2007, when they'd been essentially required to hand over threat information and take the government's help if they wanted to keep doing business with the military. But the pilot undercut Alexander's argument that his agency was uniquely qualified to protect the nation.

Not that the companies needed a university study to tell them that. As early as 2010, corporate executives began to question whether the NSA was as sophisticated as Alexander claimed. During a meeting with CEOs at Homeland Security Department headquarters, Alexander gave a presentation on the NSA's threat signature catalog. According to one participant, Google CEO Eric Schmidt leaned over to the person sitting next to him and whispered, "You mean to tell me they spent all this money and this is what they came up with? We've all moved beyond this now." Google, like many other large companies that were frequent targets of hackers, had its own sources of threat intelligence from private security companies — such as Endgame, which sells zero day information — and had begun its own intelligence-gathering operations on hackers in China. But the company was also using other tactics, such as implementing stronger encryption for its users, and moving toward a "secure sockets layer" service that would set end-to-end encryption by default for everyone logged in to their Google account. Threat signatures alone "don't work anymore," Schmidt said. "The threats don't just come where the NSA points its sensors." Hackers were constantly changing their techniques and looking for new points of entry. They knew that the government was monitoring them — that's why they changed up their tactics.

For Google, like other large companies, there was no one secret sauce but a stew of techniques whose recipe was constantly changing. Broadly speaking, companies were taking security more seriously, investing money in protecting their information at its source and hiring outside expertise to make up for what they lacked.

Still, Alexander persisted. In 2011 he traveled to New York and met with executives from some of the country's biggest financial institutions. Sitting in a conference room in Manhattan, he'd have been forgiven for thinking he was back in that secure room at the Pentagon in 2007, about to tell titans of industry what a big problem they had on their hands.

The NSA had already been sharing some threat signatures with the banks through a nonprofit group the banks themselves had set up, called an information sharing and analysis center. It wasn't a real-time system, but it helped the banks stay abreast of security trends and in some cases get early warning about types of malware and intrusion techniques. Other industries had set up similar centers as a way of pooling their collective knowledge, but the banks were generally thought to be the best at it, because they had so much to lose (billions of dollars a year to cyber theft) and because their businesses ran on data networks.

Alexander told the executives that he wanted to expand the DIB information-sharing program to the banking sector, but this time with a twist. It would be much easier to protect the companies, Alexander explained, if they let the NSA install surveillance equipment on their networks. Cut out the middleman. Let the analysts at Fort Meade have a direct line into Wall Street.

A silence fell over the room. The executives looked at one another, incredulous. *Is this guy serious?*

"They thought he was an idiot," says a senior financial services executive who was at the meeting and who had met Alexander on previous occasions. "These are all private networks he was talking about. The attacks we've seen in the industry have generally been on Internet interfaces with customers — websites for online banking, or the website for Nasdaq." Those websites had been hit in recent years with so-called denial-of-service attacks, which flood servers with requests for information and cause them to crash but don't do any damage to the account data inside a bank's computers. And much of that information, the executive says, moves over networks that are air-gapped, or have very few connections to the public Internet. "Just to say that the banks are open to Internet attacks is not true. And the Federal Reserve, the Treasury Department, the securities brokers, the settlement systems — they all have a really good handle on the whole financial services infrastructure and how it works. Alexander didn't understand it at all."

The financial services companies weren't indifferent to the cyber threat. Two-thirds of US banks reported that they'd been affected by denial-of-service attacks, according to one study. But Alexander was asking the companies to take on inordinate risk. He was trying to embed his spies in their computers. The political ramifications were enormous if the operations ever became known. Furthermore, the companies could be held liable for illegal surveillance if the agency installed equipment without a warrant or some legal order approved by a court.

Even if the banks had let the NSA in, it's debatable how much the spy agency could have told them that they didn't already know from their own sources. Many large US banks have set up their own security divisions to monitor credit card fraud and account theft. Estimates vary as to the amount of money financial institutions lose to cybercrime each year, but they range from hundreds of millions of dollars to billions depending on the type and scale of the crime. The FBI investigates hacker rings that try to infiltrate bank networks and steal funds or process fraudulent credit card transactions, and it has tried to share what it knows with financial institutions. But frequently the G-men find that their corporate security counterparts are already ahead of them.

In 2009 about thirty law enforcement and intelligence officials met with security personnel from the leading US banks at FBI headquarters in Washington. "Halfway through the meeting, we asked, 'How is information sharing going between the financial services sector and the government?'" says Steve Chabinsky, who was the FBI's deputy assistant director for cyber issues and now works for the private security firm CrowdStrike. "Everyone took a deep breath."

"You want us to be honest?" asked a representative from the banks' information-sharing council, which they'd set up to communicate with one another and the authorities. "It's not going very well. We give you all our information voluntarily, and we get nothing back."

The FBI countered that it had just given the banks a list of threat signatures, including suspicious Internet addresses linked to cyber-criminals. The report had taken a lot of effort to produce. Some of the information was considered "law enforcement sensitive" and even classified.

"Well," the bank representative replied, "if that's the best you can do, we're in trouble. Because we knew all that information already."

The banks were sharing information with one other, and they were buying information from private intelligence firms. Government officials began to realize that they didn't have a monopoly on intelligence gathering. The FBI decided to share with the banks the rundown of cases it was tracking, so the banks could see for themselves the breadth of the bureau's knowledge, Chabinsky says. It turned out that the banks had been tracking every case on the list, except one. Hackers had targeted the automated clearinghouse network, an electronic system that processes bulk transactions, including direct deposits, credit and debit card purchases, and electronic funds transfers between accounts. After stealing username and password credentials of people using the network, the thieves were able to move money out of various accounts, to the tune of $400 million. The banks were aware that hackers had gone after the clearinghouse network before, but not on this scale, and not using the particular techniques the FBI had detected for stealing log-in credentials. The banks were grateful for the intelligence and were able to shore up a weakness in their security systems. But it was a rare instance in which the FBI knew something that the banks didn't.

Prosecuting cybercriminals is rarely an option, particularly when the crooks are based in countries with weak cybercrime laws and a policy of not extraditing suspects to the United States. "The Russians will alert hackers that we're tracking them and tell them to change their names, so they're harder for us to find," says a senior law enforcement official who works on cybercrime cases. That leaves banks in the unenviable position of having to mostly fend for themselves against a wave of criminal activity that is growing in size, scope, and ambition, and that law enforcement has proven generally powerless to hold back.

The financial executives resisted Alexander's plan to install surveillance equipment on their networks. But they didn't stop his bigger campaign. Back in Washington, he lobbied to put the NSA in charge of defending other critical industries. High on the list was the electric power sector, followed by water utilities. "He wanted to create a wall around other sensitive institutions in America . . . and to install equipment to monitor their networks," says the former administration official. Tranche 2 was dead, and the DIB pilot had undermined NSA's preeminent standing, but Alexander pressed on. And largely with the administration's backing. The pilot program was not greeted as a total failure. Some administration officials — including at the Homeland Security Department — said it showed that a government-appointed third party could channel classified information to industry. That they could work in an alliance — however uneasy — to defend cyberspace. Even though the NSA data detected only two unique threats, that was better than nothing, they reasoned.

Homeland Security took over nominal control of an expanded DIB program and made membership available to non-defense companies that were deemed essential to US national and economic security. The government was picking and choosing which kinds of companies would get special protection. And the threat signatures and most of the technical analysis of malware and intrusions were still coming from the NSA, often working with teams at the FBI, which now had an even bigger stake in cyber security as it shifted its focus — and its budgets — from counterterrorism cases. As of 2013, the NSA employed more than one thousand mathematicians, the largest number working for a single organization in the United States; more than nine hundred PhDs; and more than four thousand computer scientists. The brains and the muscle for government cyber defense continue to come from the NSA, and probably always will.

There'd been a bureaucratic brawl, but in the end the government was still taking control of protecting cyberspace and treating the Internet as a strategic national asset, just as Obama had promised he would in his White House speech in May 2009. Alexander knew that his agency couldn't follow every threat on the Internet; it still needed intelligence from the companies. So he ratcheted up the public pressure. In speeches and congressional testimony, he warned that the hackers were getting better, that cybercrime was on the rise, and that companies were ill equipped to defend themselves. He pressed for more regulation, to force companies to raise their security standards and to provide legal immunity for those that handed over information about their customers' communications without a warrant or a court order, so that the NSA could study it. Alexander called cybercrime and espionage "the greatest transfer of wealth in history" and warned that unless American businesses shored up their digital defenses, the nation faced the prospect of a "Cyber Pearl Harbor."

"What we see is an increasing level of activity on the networks," Alexander warned at a security conference in Canada in 2013, two years after his meeting with financial executives. "I am concerned that this is going to break a threshold where the private sector can no longer handle it and the government is going to have to step in."

Some companies were getting the message. But not in the way Alexander thought. They knew that threats were lining up against them. They saw them rooting around in their networks and stealing data every day. But they'd concluded that despite the NSA's big talk, the government couldn't protect everyone. The companies had to defend themselves.

ELEVEN

The Corporate Counterstrike

I N MID-DECEMBER 2009, engineers at Google's headquarters in Mountain View, California, began to suspect that hackers in China had obtained access to private Gmail accounts, including those used by Chinese human rights activists opposed to the government in Beijing. Like a lot of large, well-known Internet companies, Google and its users were frequently targeted by cyber spies and criminals. But when the engineers looked more closely, they discovered that this was no ordinary hacking campaign.

In what Google would later describe as "a highly sophisticated and targeted attack on our corporate infrastructure originating from China," the thieves were able to get access to the password system that allowed Google's users to sign in to many Google applications at once. This was some of the company's most important intellectual property, considered among the "crown jewels" of its source code by its engineers. Google wanted concrete evidence of the break-in that it could share with US law enforcement and intelligence authorities. So they traced the intrusion back to what they believed was its source — a server in Taiwan where data was sent after it was siphoned off Google's systems, and that was presumably under the control of hackers in mainland China.

"Google broke in to the server," says a former senior intelligence official who's familiar with the company's response. The decision wasn't without legal risk, according to the official. Was this a case of hacking back? Just as there's no law against a homeowner following a robber back to where he lives, Google didn't violate any laws by tracing the source of the intrusion into its systems. It's still unclear how the company's investigators gained access to the server, but once inside, if they had removed or deleted data, that would cross a legal line. But Google didn't destroy what it found. In fact, the company did something unexpected and unprecedented — it shared the information.

Google uncovered evidence of one of the most extensive and far-reaching campaigns of cyber espionage in US history. Evidence suggested that Chinese hackers had penetrated the systems of nearly three dozen other companies, including technology mainstays such as Symantec, Yahoo, and Adobe, the defense contractor Northrop Grumman, and the equipment maker Juniper Networks. The breadth of the campaign made it hard to discern a single motive. Was this industrial espionage? Spying on human rights activists? Was China trying to gain espionage footholds in key sectors of the US economy or, worse, implant malware in equipment used to regulate critical infrastructure? The only things Google seemed certain of was that the campaign was massive and persistent, and that China was behind it. And not just individual hackers, but the Chinese government, which had the means and the motive to launch such a broad assault.

Google shared what it found with the other targeted companies, as well as US law enforcement and intelligence agencies. For the past four years, corporate executives had been quietly pressing government officials to go public with information about Chinese spying, to shame the country into stopping its campaign. But for President Obama or Secretary of State Hillary Clinton to give a speech pointing the finger at China, they needed indisputable evidence that attributed the attacks to sources in China. And looking at what Google had provided it, government analysts were not sure they had it. American officials decided the relationship between the two economic superpowers was too fragile and the risk of conflict too high to go public with what Google knew.

Google disagreed.

Deputy Secretary of State James Steinberg was at a cocktail party in Washington when an aide delivered an urgent message: Google was going to issue a public statement about the Chinese spying campaign. Steinberg, the second-highest-ranking official in US foreign policy, immediately grasped the significance of the company's decision. Up to that moment, American corporations had been unwilling to publicly accuse the Chinese of spying on their networks or stealing their intellectual property. The companies feared losing the confidence of investors and customers, inviting other hackers to target their obviously weak defenses, and igniting the fury of Chinese government officials, who could easily revoke access to one of the biggest and fastest-growing markets for US goods and services. For any company to come out against China would be momentous. But for Google, the most influential company of the Internet age, it was historic.

The next day, January 12, 2010, Google's chief legal officer, David Drummond, posted a lengthy statement to the company's blog, accusing hackers in China of attacking Google's infrastructure and criticizing the government for censoring Internet content and suppressing human rights activists. "We have taken the unusual step of sharing information about these attacks with a broad audience not just because of the security and human rights implications of what we have unearthed, but also because this information goes to the heart of a much bigger global debate about freedom of speech," said Drummond.

Back at the State Department, officials saw a rare opportunity to put pressure on China for spying. That night Hillary Clinton issued her own statement. "We have been briefed by Google on these allegations, which raise very serious concerns and questions. We look to the Chinese government for an explanation," she said. "The ability to operate with confidence in cyberspace is critical in a modern society and economy."

As diplomatic maneuvers go, this was pivotal. Google had just given the Obama administration an opening to accuse China of espionage without having to make the case itself. Officials could simply point to what Google had discovered as a result of its own investigation. "It gave us an opportunity to discuss the issues without having to rely on classified sources or sensitive methods" of intelligence gathering, Steinberg says. The administration had had little warning about Google's decision, and it was at odds with some officials' reluctance to take the espionage debate public. But now that it was, no one complained. "It was their decision. I certainly had no objection," Steinberg says.

The Obama administration began to take a harsher tone with China, starting with a major address Clinton gave about her Internet Freedom initiative nine days later. She called on China to stop censoring Internet searches and blocking access to websites that printed criticism about the country's leaders. Clinton likened such virtual barriers to the Berlin Wall.

For its part, Google said it would stop filtering search results for words and subjects banned by government censors. And if Beijing objected, Google was prepared to pull up stakes and leave the Chinese market entirely, losing out on billions of dollars in potential revenues. That put other US technology companies in the hot seat. Were they willing to put up with government interference and suppression of free speech in order to keep doing business in China?

After Google's declaration, it was easier for other companies to admit they'd been infiltrated by hackers. After all, if it happened to Google, it could happen to anyone. Being spied on by the Chinese might even be a mark of distinction, insofar as it showed that a company was important enough to merit the close attention of a superpower. With one blog post, Google had changed the global conversation about cyber defense.

The company had also shown that it knew a lot about Chinese spies. The NSA wanted to know how much.

Google had also alerted the NSA and the FBI that its networks were breached by hackers in China. As a law enforcement agency, the FBI could investigate the intrusion as a criminal matter. But the NSA needed Google's permission to come in and help assess the breach.

On the day that Google's lawyer wrote the blog post, the NSA's general counsel began drafting a "cooperative research and development agreement," a legal pact that was originally devised under a 1980 law to speed up the commercial development of new technologies that are of mutual interest to companies and the government. The agreement's purpose is to build something — a device or a technique, for instance. The participating company isn't paid, but it can rely on the government to front the research and development costs, and it can use government personnel and facilities for the research. Each side gets to keep the products of the collaboration private until they choose to disclose them. In the end, the company has the exclusive patent rights to build whatever was designed, and the government can use any information that was generated during the collaboration.

It's not clear what the NSA and Google built after the China hack. But a spokeswoman at the agency gave hints at the time the agreement was written. "As a general matter, as part of its information-assurance mission, NSA works with a broad range of commercial partners and research associates to ensure the availability of secure tailored solutions for Department of Defense and national security systems customers," she said. It was the phrase "tailored solutions" that was so intriguing. That implied something custom built for the agency, so that it could perform its intelligence-gathering mission. According to officials who were privy to the details of Google's arrangements with the NSA, the company agreed to provide information about traffic on its networks in exchange for intelligence from the NSA about what it knew of foreign hackers. It was a quid pro quo, information for information. And from the NSA's perspective, information in exchange for protection.

The cooperative agreement and reference to a "tailored solution" strongly suggest that Google and the NSA built a device or a technique for monitoring intrusions into the company's networks. That would give the NSA valuable information for its so-called active defense system, which uses a combination of automated sensors and algorithms to detect malware or signs of an imminent attack and take action against them. One system, called Turmoil, detects traffic that might pose a threat. Then, another automated system called Turbine decides whether to allow the traffic to pass or to block it. Turbine can also select from a number of offensive software programs and hacking techniques that a human operator can use to disable the source of the malicious traffic. He might reset the source's Internet connection or redirect the traffic to a server under the NSA's control. There the source can be injected with a virus or spyware, so the NSA can continue to monitor it.

For Turbine and Turmoil to work, the NSA needs information, particularly about the data flowing over a network. With its millions of customers around the world, Google is effectively a directory of people using the Internet. It has their e-mail addresses. It knows where they're physically located when they log in. It knows what they search for on the web. The government could command the company to turn over that information, and it does as part of the NSA's Prism program, which Google had been participating in for a year by the time it signed the cooperative agreement with the NSA. But that tool is used for investigating people whom the government suspects of terrorism or espionage. The NSA's cyber defense mission takes a broader view across networks for potential threats, sometimes before it knows who those threats are. Under Google's terms of service, the company advises its users that it may share their "personal information" with outside organizations, including government agencies, in order to "detect, prevent, or otherwise address fraud, security or technical issues" and to "protect against harm to the rights, property or safety of Google." According to people familiar with the NSA and Google's arrangement, it does not give the government permission to read Google users' e-mails. They can do that under Prism. Rather, it lets the NSA evaluate Google hardware and software for vulnerabilities that hackers might exploit. Considering that the NSA is the single biggest collector of zero day vulnerabilities, that information would help make Google more secure than others that don't get access to such prized secrets. The agreement also lets the agency analyze intrusions that have already occurred, so it can help trace them back to their source.

Google took a risk forming an alliance with the NSA. The company's corporate motto, "Don't be evil," would seem at odds with the work of a covert surveillance and cyber warfare agency. But Google got useful

information in return for its cooperation. Shortly after the China revelation, the government gave Sergey Brin, Google's cofounder, a temporary security clearance that allowed him to attend a classified briefing
about the campaign against his company. Government analysts had
concluded that the intrusion was directed by a unit of the People's Liberation Army. This was the most specific information Google could
obtain about the source of the intrusion. It could help Google fortify
its systems, block traffic from certain Internet addresses, and make a
more informed decision about whether it wanted to do business in
China at all. Google's executives might pooh-pooh the NSA's "secret
sauce." But when the company found itself under attack, it turned to
Fort Meade for help.

In its blog post, Google said that more than twenty companies had
been hit by the China hackers, in a campaign that was later dubbed
Aurora after a file name on the attackers' computer. A security research
firm soon put the number of targets at around three dozen. Actually,
the scope of Chinese spying was, and is, much larger.

Security experts in and outside of government have a name for the
hackers behind campaigns such as Aurora and others targeting thousands of other companies in practically every sector of the US economy: the advanced persistent threat. It's an ominous-sounding title,
and a euphemistic one. When government officials mention "APT"
today, what they often mean is China, and more specifically, hackers
working at the direction of Chinese military and intelligence officials
or on their behalf.

The "advanced" part of the description refers in part to the hackers' techniques, which are as effective as any the NSA employs. The
Chinese cyber spies can use an infected computer's own chat and
instant-messenger applications to communicate with a command-
and-control server. They can implant a piece of malware and then remotely customize it, adding new information-harvesting features. The
government apparatus supporting all this espionage is also advanced,
more so than the loose-knit groups of cyber vandals or activists such
as Anonymous that spy on companies for political purposes, or even
the sophisticated Russian criminal groups, who are more interested

in stealing bank account and credit card data. China plays a longer game. Its leaders want the country to become a first-tier economic and industrial power in a single generation, and they are prepared to steal the knowledge they need to do it, US officials say.

That's where the "persistent" part comes into play. Gathering that much information, from so many sources, requires a relentless effort, and the will and financial resources to try many different kinds of intrusion techniques, including expensive zero day exploits. Once the spies find a foothold inside an organization's networks, they don't let go unless they're forced out. And even then they quickly return. The "threat" such spying poses to the US economy takes the form of lost revenue and strategic position. But also the risk that the Chinese military will gain hidden entry points into critical-infrastructure control systems in the United States. US intelligence officials believe that the Chinese military has mapped out infrastructure control networks so that if the two nations ever went to war, the Chinese could hit American targets such as electrical grids or gas pipelines without having to launch a missile or send a fleet of bombers.

Operation Aurora was the first glimpse into the breadth of the ATP's exploits. It was the first time that names of companies had been attached to Chinese espionage. "The scope of this is much larger than anybody has ever conveyed," Kevin Mandia, CEO and president of Mandiant, a computer security and forensics company located outside Washington, said at the time of Operation Aurora. The APT represented hacking on a national, strategic level. "There [are] not 50 companies compromised. There are thousands of companies compromised. Actively, right now," said Mandia, a veteran cyber investigator who began his career as a computer security officer in the air force and worked there on cybercrime cases. Mandiant was becoming a go-to outfit that companies called whenever they discovered spies had penetrated their networks. Shortly after the Google breach, Mandiant disclosed the details of its investigations in a private meeting with Defense Department officials a few days before speaking publicly about it.

The APT is not one body but a collection of hacker groups that include teams working for the People's Liberation Army, as well as so-called patriotic hackers, young, enterprising geeks who are willing to ply their trade in service of their country. Chinese universities are also stocked with computer science students who work for the military after graduation. The APT hackers put a premium on stealth and patience. They use zero days and install backdoors. They take time to identify employees in a targeted organization, and send them carefully crafted spear-phishing e-mails laden with spyware. They burrow into an organization, and they often stay there for months or years before anyone finds them, all the while siphoning off plans and designs, reading e-mails and their attachments, and keeping tabs on the comings and goings of employees — the hackers' future targets. The Chinese spies behave, in other words, like their American counterparts.

No intelligence organization can survive if it doesn't know its enemy. As expansive as the NSA's network of sensors is, it's sometimes easier to get precise intelligence about hacking campaigns from the targets themselves. That's why the NSA partnered with Google. It's why when Mandiant came calling with intelligence on the APT, officials listened to what the private sleuths had to say. Defending cyberspace is too big a job even for the world's elite spy agency. Whether they like it or not, the NSA and corporations must fight this foe together.

Google's Sergey Brin is just one of hundreds of CEOs who have been brought into the NSA's circle of secrecy. Starting in 2008, the agency began offering executives temporary security clearances, some good for only one day, so they could sit in on classified threat briefings. "They indoctrinate someone for a day, and show them lots of juicy intelligence about threats facing businesses in the United States," says a telecommunications company executive who has attended several of the briefings, which are held about three times a year. The CEOs are required to sign an agreement pledging not to disclose anything they learn in the briefings. "They tell them, in so many words, if you violate this agreement, you will be tried, convicted, and spend the rest of your life in prison," says the executive.

Why would anyone agree to such severe terms? "For one day, they get to be special and see things few others do," says the telecom executive, who, thanks to having worked regularly on classified projects, holds high-level clearances and has been given access to some of the

NSA's most sensitive operations, including the warrantless surveillance program that began after the 9/11 attacks. "Alexander became personal friends with many CEOs" through these closed-door sessions, the executive adds. "I've sat through some of these and said, 'General, you tell these guys things that could put our country in danger if they leak out.' And he said, 'I know. But that's the risk we take. And if it does leak out, they know what the consequences will be.'"

But the NSA doesn't have to threaten the executives to get their attention. The agency's revelations about stolen data and hostile intrusions are frightening in their own right, and deliberately so. "We scare the bejeezus out of them," a government official told National Public Radio in 2012. Some of those executives have stepped out of their threat briefings meeting feeling like the defense contractor CEOs who, back in the summer of 2007, left the Pentagon with "white hair." Unsure how to protect themselves, some CEOs will call private security companies such as Mandiant. "I personally know of one CEO for whom [a private NSA threat briefing] was a life-changing experience," Richard Bejtlich, Mandiant's chief security officer, told NPR. "General Alexander sat him down and told him what was going on. This particular CEO, in my opinion, should have known about [threats to his company] but did not, and now it has colored everything about the way he thinks about this problem."

The NSA and private security companies have a symbiotic relationship. The government scares the CEOs and they run for help to experts such as Mandiant. Those companies, in turn, share what they learn during their investigations with the government, as Mandiant did after the Google breach in 2010. The NSA has also used the classified threat briefings to spur companies to strengthen their defenses. In one 2010 session, agency officials said they'd discovered a flaw in personal computer firmware — the onboard memory and codes that tell the machine how to work — that could allow a hacker to turn the computer "into a brick," rendering it useless. The CEOs of computer manufacturers who attended the meeting, and who were previously aware of the design flaw, ordered it fixed.

Private high-level meetings are just one way the NSA has forged alliances with corporations. Several classified programs allow companies to share the designs of their products with the agency so it can inspect them for flaws and, in some instances, install backdoors or other forms of privileged access. The types of companies that have shown the NSA their products include computer, server, and router manufacturers; makers of popular software products, including Microsoft; Internet and e-mail service providers; telecommunications companies; satellite manufacturers; antivirus and Internet security companies; and makers of encryption algorithms.

The NSA helps the companies find weaknesses in their products. But it also pays the companies not to fix some of them. Those weak spots give the agency an entry point for spying or attacking foreign governments that install the products in their intelligence agencies, their militaries, and their critical infrastructure. Microsoft, for instance, shares zero day vulnerabilities in its products with the NSA before releasing a public alert or a software patch, according to the company and US officials. Cisco, one of the world's top network equipment makers, leaves backdoors in its routers so they can be monitored by US agencies, according to a cyber security professional who trains NSA employees in defensive techniques. And McAfee, the Internet security company, provides the NSA, the CIA, and the FBI with network traffic flows, analysis of malware, and information about hacking trends.

Companies that promise to disclose holes in their products only to the spy agencies are paid for their silence, say experts and officials who are familiar with the arrangements. To an extent, these openings for government surveillance are required by law. Telecommunications companies in particular must build their equipment in such a way that it can be tapped by a law enforcement agency presenting a court order, like for a wiretap. But when the NSA is gathering intelligence abroad, it is not bound by the same laws. Indeed, the surveillance it conducts via backdoors and secret flaws in hardware and software would be illegal in most of the countries where it occurs.

Of course, backdoors and unpatched flaws could also be used by hackers. In 2010 a researcher at IBM publicly revealed a flaw in a Cisco operating system that allows a hacker to use a backdoor that was supposed to be available only to law enforcement agencies. The intruder could hijack the Cisco device and use it to spy on all communications passing through it, including the content of e-mails. Leaving products vulnerable to attack, particularly ubiquitous software programs like those produced by Microsoft, puts millions of customers and their private information at risk and jeopardizes the security of electrical power facilities, public utilities, and transportation systems.

Under US law, a company's CEO is required to be notified whenever the government uses its products, services, or facilities for intelligence-gathering purposes. Some of these information-sharing arrangements are brokered by the CEOs themselves and may be reviewed only by a few lawyers. The benefits of such cooperation can be profound. John Chambers, the CEO of Cisco, became friends with George W. Bush when he was in office. In April 2006, Chambers and the president ate lunch together at the White House with Chinese president Hu Jintao, and the next day Bush gave Chambers a lift on *Air Force One* to San Jose, where the president joined the CEO at Cisco headquarters for a panel discussion on American business competitiveness. California governor Arnold Schwarzenegger also joined the conversation. Proximity to political power is its own reward. But preferred companies also sometimes receive early warnings from the government about threats against them.

The Homeland Security Department also conducts meetings with companies through its "cross sector working groups" initiative. These sessions are a chance for representatives from the universe of companies with which the government shares intelligence to meet with one another and hear from US officials. The attendees at these meetings often have security clearances and have undergone background checks and interviews. The department has made the schedule and agendas of some of these meetings public, but it doesn't disclose the names of companies that participated or many details about what they discussed. Between January 2010 and October 2013, the period for which public records are available, the government held at least 168 meetings with companies just in the cross sector working group. There have been hundreds more meetings broken out by specific industry categories, such as energy, telecommunications, and transportation.

A typical meeting may include a "threat briefing" by a US government official, usually from the NSA, the FBI, or the Homeland Security Department; updates on specific initiatives, such as enhancing bank website security, improving information sharing among utility companies, or countering malware; and discussion of security "tools" that have been developed by the government and industry, such as those used to detect intruders on a network. One meeting in April 2012 addressed "use cases for enabling information sharing for active cyber defense," the NSA-pioneered process of disabling cyber threats before they can do damage. The information sharing in this case was not among government agencies but among corporations.

Most meetings have dealt with protecting industrial control systems, the Internet-connected devices that regulate electrical power equipment, nuclear reactors, banks, and other vital facilities. That's the weakness in US cyberspace that most worries intelligence officials. It was the subject that so animated George W. Bush in 2007 and that Barack Obama addressed publicly two years later. The declassified agendas for these meetings offer a glimpse at what companies and the government are building for domestic cyber defense.

On September 23, 2013, the Cross Sector Enduring Security Framework Operations Working Group discussed an update to an initiative described as "Connect Tier 1 and USG Operations Center." "Tier 1" usually refers to a major Internet service provider or network operator. Some of the best-known Tier 1 companies in the United States are AT&T, Verizon, and CenturyLink. "USG" refers to the US government. The initiative likely refers to a physical connection running from an NSA facility to those companies, as part of an expansion of the DIB pilot program. The expansion was authorized by a presidential executive order in February 2013 aimed at increasing security of critical-infrastructure sites around the country. The government, mainly through the NSA, gives threat intelligence to two Internet service providers, AT&T and CenturyLink. They, in turn, can sell "enhanced cybersecurity services," as the program is known, to companies that the government deems vital to national and economic security. The program is nominally run by the Homeland Security Department, but the NSA provides the intelligence and the technical expertise.

Through this exchange of intelligence, the government has created a cyber security business. AT&T and CenturyLink are in effect its private sentries, selling protection to select corporations and industries. AT&T has one of the longest histories of any company participating in government surveillance. It was among the first firms that voluntarily handed over call records of its customers to the NSA following the 9/11 attacks, so the agency could mine them for potential connections to terrorists — a program that continues to this day. Most phone calls in the United States pass through AT&T equipment at some point, regardless of which carrier initiates them. The company's infrastructure is one of the most important and frequently tapped repositories of electronic intelligence for the NSA and US law enforcement agencies.

CenturyLink, which has its headquarters in Monroe, Louisiana, has been a less familiar name in intelligence circles over the years. But in 2011 the company acquired Qwest Communications, a telecommunications firm that is well known to the NSA. Before the 9/11 attacks, NSA officials approached Qwest executives and asked for access to its high-speed fiber-optic networks, in order to monitor them for potential cyber attacks. The company rebuffed the agency's requests because officials hadn't obtained a court order to get access to the company's equipment. After the terrorist attacks, NSA officials again came calling, asking Qwest to hand over its customers' phone records without a court-approved warrant, as AT&T had done. Again, the company refused. It took another ten years and the sale of the company, but Qwest's networks are now a part of the NSA's extended security apparatus.

The potential customer base for government-supplied cyber intelligence, sold through corporations, is as diverse as the US economy itself. To obtain the information, a company must meet the government's definition of a critical infrastructure: "assets, systems, and networks, whether physical or virtual, so vital to the United States that their incapacitation or destruction would have a debilitating effect on security, national economic security, national public health or safety, or any combination thereof." That may seem like a narrow definition, but the categories of critical infrastructure are numerous and vast, encompassing thousands of businesses. Officially, there are sixteen sectors: chemical; commercial facilities, to include shopping centers, sports venues, casinos, and theme parks; communications; critical manufacturing; dams; the defense industrial base; emergency services, such as first responders and search and rescue; energy; financial services; food and agriculture; government facilities; health care and public health; information technology; nuclear reactors, materials, and waste; transportation systems; and water and wastewater systems.

It's inconceivable that every company on such a list could be considered "so vital to the United States" that its damage or loss would harm national security and public safety. And yet, in the years since the 9/11 attacks, the government has cast such a wide protective net that practically any company could claim to be a critical infrastructure. The government doesn't disclose which companies are receiving cyber threat intelligence. And as of now the program is voluntary. But lawmakers and some intelligence officials, including Keith Alexander and others at the NSA, have pressed Congress to regulate the cyber security standards of critical-infrastructure owners and operators. If that were to happen, then the government could require that any company, from Pacific Gas and Electric to Harrah's Hotels and Casinos, take the government's assistance, share information about its customers with the intelligence agencies, and build its cyber defenses according to government specifications.

In a speech in 2013 the Pentagon's chief cyber security adviser, Major General John Davis, announced that Homeland Security and the Defense Department were working together on a plan to expand the original DIB program to more sectors. They would start with energy, transportation, and oil and natural gas, "things that are critical to DOD's mission and the nation's economic and national security that we do not directly control," Davis said. The general called foreign hackers' mapping of these systems and potential attacks "an imminent threat." The government will never be able to manage such an extensive security regime on its own. It can't now, which is why it relies on AT&T and CenturyLink. More companies will flock to this new mission as the government expands the cyber perimeter. The potential market for cyber security services is practically limitless.

TWELVE

Spring Awakening

THE UNITED STATES has never suffered a major cyber attack that disabled critical infrastructure. But in early 2012 some officials worried that the event they'd long feared might be in the offing. In March of that year at least twenty natural gas pipeline companies in the United States alerted the Homeland Security Department to suspicious e-mails sent to their employees. They appeared to come from someone the employees knew or were likely to know because of their jobs — standard spear phishing. Some of the employees — it's still unclear how many — opened the messages and released spyware onto the corporate networks of the pipeline operators. The hackers didn't have access to the control systems of the pipelines themselves, but they were potentially within striking distance. If the pipeline operator had air-gapped the facility's control systems from the public Internet, they were probably safe. Of course, there was always the risk that an unsuspecting employee could carry the malware over the air gap via a USB drive.

Officials at the highest levels of the FBI, Homeland Security, and the NSA were on alert. An intruder who could control the pipeline could conceivably disrupt the flow of natural gas, or perhaps cause internal controls to malfunction, leading to a breakdown or even an explosion. Approximately 200,000 miles of natural gas pipelines crisscross the United States, and natural gas accounts for nearly a third of the nation's energy supply. There'd never been a confirmed cyber attack that destroyed a pipeline. But at the height of the Cold War, the CIA allegedly installed malicious software in equipment used on a Siberian pipeline that exploded in 1982. In theory, it was possible to remotely change the pressure inside the pipeline, a form of attack similar to the one the NSA used on the Iranian nuclear facility.

Once the natural gas companies informed the government that they were being probed, officials sent "fly away" teams to the facilities and gathered information from computer hard drives and network logs. The source of the e-mails was traced to a single campaign that analysts said started as early as December 2011. The alerts from companies about spies on their networks were "never-ending," says a former law enforcement official who worked on the case. But the true intent of the campaign still eluded analysts. Were the intruders trying to gather competitive information about the pipeline companies, such as where they planned to look next for gas or where they'd build their next facility? Or were they trying to disrupt energy flows, or plant malware that could be triggered at some later date to destroy the pipeline?

In order to find out, government investigators decided not to issue a public warning and instead to watch the intruders and see what information they went after. It was a risky move. At any moment the intruders might have launched an aggressive attack on the corporate networks, stealing or erasing valuable information. And there was still the chance, however slim, of an attack on the pipelines themselves, which would have disastrous economic consequences and could kill anyone near an explosion. The authorities met with individual companies and held classified briefings about what they knew so far. They shared "mitigation strategies" with corporate security personnel, including the known e-mail addresses that had sent the spear phishes and certain IP addresses to which the pipeline operators could block outbound access. But the government didn't purge the networks of the spies, nor did it instruct the companies to do so. On March 29 an emergency response team stationed at the Homeland Security Department that works in tandem with the NSA posted an alert to all pipeline companies on a classified government website instructing them to allow the spies to keep rooting around as long as they didn't appear to threaten the operations of the pipelines themselves. In Washington, government officials alerted the trade associations representing oil and gas companies and told them to keep the operation under wraps.

The response to the pipeline intrusions marked a new, heightened level of government influence over cyber defense in the energy sector. The natural gas companies and their lobbyists in Washington followed the government's lead and instructions. Throughout most of the investigation, the government successfully enforced a press and public information blackout among the energy companies. A significant campaign against a vital US infrastructure had been under way for weeks, and barely anyone knew. News reports about the breach first appeared in May, two months after the government surveillance operation began.

The government pushed into other energy sectors as well. That summer, Homeland Security and the Energy Department sponsored a classified cyber threat briefing for the CEOs of electric utilities, offering them the temporary security clearances so they could learn more about threats against their sector. Energy companies were less cognizant of the dangers to their networks than companies in other sectors, particularly financial services, where companies shared information routinely and had set up systems for sharing details about intrusions and hacking trends in a classified setting. The energy companies, by contrast, feared looking weak to their competitors and possibly giving them insights about future strategy if they opened up about their inadequate cyber security.

But government officials had grown impatient. In Congress, advocates of a new law to regulate cyber security standards for utility companies continued to press their case, pointing to the rash of intrusions against natural gas pipelines to bolster their argument. Their efforts would ultimately fail that autumn, paving the way for Obama to implement as many defenses as he could through an executive order. Companies would be encouraged to adopt security standards and practices developed by the National Institute of Standards and Technology, which consulted with a broad range of industry experts and the intelligence agencies. Companies were free to ignore the government's advice. But if their infrastructure were damaged by a preventable cyber attack, they might be held civilly or even criminally liable and then have to explain to a judge why they chose to strike out on their own.

In the wake of the 2012 intrusions into gas pipeline companies, the government has held classified briefings for nearly seven hundred utility company personnel. Homeland Security, the FBI, the Energy Department, and the Transportation Security Administration launched what officials called an "action campaign" to give companies "further context of the threat and to highlight mitigation strategies," according to a Homeland Security bulletin. The campaign began in June 2013 and has featured classified meetings in at least ten American cities, including Washington, New York, Chicago, Dallas, Denver, San Francisco, San Diego, Seattle, Boston, and New Orleans, as well as "numerous others via secure video teleconferences." Energy companies have also begun to train their employees in the basics of cyber defense. Shell, Schlumberger, and other major companies have sent their employees fake spear-phishing e-mails with pictures of cute cats and other enticements. Experts who've trained the companies say that nearly all employees initially fall for the e-mails, but after training, as many as 90 percent learn to avoid clicking on embedded links and attachments, which are the usual triggers to unleash malware.

Inside the NSA, officials have continued to press for greater authority to expand their defense writ. In a rare public appearance in Washington in May 2013, Charles Berlin, director of the NSA's National Security Operations Center, reflected a widely held view among America's spies that it would be "almost immoral" for the agency to focus solely on protecting government computer networks and information. "The mission of the Department of Defense . . . [is] to protect America," said Berlin, who ran the agency's nerve center for signals intelligence and defense of computer networks. "I've been on the ramparts pouring boiling oil on the attackers for years," he said. "At the present time, we're unable to defend America."

• • •

Throughout the anxious spring of 2012, there was little doubt among law enforcement, intelligence, and private security officials where the attackers were coming from. But the question remained: what was their goal?

The former law enforcement official who worked the case says the hackers were based in China and that their campaign was part of a broader Chinese strategy of mapping critical infrastructure in the United States. Whether their precise purpose was espionage or laying the grounds for cyber warfare remains unclear. But the two activities are connected along a spectrum: in order to attack a facility, the intruder needs to map it out and understand its weak spots. And there are warning signs that the Chinese are looking for such vulnerabilities. A few months after the intrusions into the natural gas pipelines were revealed, the Canadian technology company Telvent, which makes industrial control or SCADA systems used in Canada and the United States, said its networks had been infiltrated by hackers the company believes were in China.

But cyber warfare with the United States isn't in China's long-term interest. Economic competition is, however. The country has a pressing need to learn more about where US companies have found sources of energy, and how they plan to extract it. In part, that's to support China's ambitions in the energy sphere. But the country also needs to fuel a rapidly expanding economy, which, though it has slowed in recent years, still saw GDP growth of 7.8 percent from 2009 to 2013.

China is seeking to replace its traditional sources of fossil fuels. The country depends mostly on coal for its energy, and the toxic air quality in many Chinese cities shows it. China is the world's second-largest consumer of coal and accounts for nearly half of all coal consumption. Oil production in China has peaked, forcing the country to look more for deposits offshore and to turn toward cleaner and more abundant sources of fuel.

To secure China's future sources of energy, state-run companies have been looking to extract natural gas, which so far accounts for a tiny fraction of the country's energy consumption — just 4 percent in 2009. But to get that gas, the Chinese need fracking technology and insights into horizontal drilling techniques, which American companies pioneered and have continued to develop. A report in 2013 by the security research firm Critical Intelligence concluded that "Chinese adversaries" have infiltrated the networks of US energy companies in order to steal information about fracking and gas extraction. They noted that Chinese hackers had also targeted companies that make petrochemicals, such as plastics, for which natural gas is a precursor ingredient. The intrusions into the gas pipeline companies in 2011 and 2012 may have been related to this campaign, the research company determined.

Not that China is giving up on its traditional sources of energy. In 2009, American oil companies were hit by a wave of cyber intrusions that stole information on oil deposits the companies had discovered around the world, according to the security firm McAfee. China is the world's second-largest consumer of oil, behind the United States, and since 2009 the second-largest net importer of oil. At least one US energy company that planned to drill in disputed waters that China claims as its territory was infiltrated by Chinese hackers.

China is competing for natural resources at the same time that it tries to build a national energy industry. To that end, Chinese targeting of US energy companies and facilities is rampant. In 2012 the Homeland Security Department publicly reported 198 "attacks" against critical infrastructure, a 52 percent increase from the previous year. Forty percent of the attacks specifically targeted energy companies. If the United States ever went to war with China, its military would undoubtedly attempt to use footholds inside those companies' computer networks to damage or disable vital infrastructures. But for the foreseeable future, China has little interest in wounding the US economy or turning out the lights. China is one of the United States' biggest foreign lenders and its most important trading partner. It has a direct interest in America's overall economic health and the purchasing power of US consumers. And the country has pursued legitimate paths toward finding sources of energy in the United States and learning about American technology, placing more than $17 billion in oil and natural gas deals in the United States and Canada since 2010.

China is playing a double game — investing in American companies at the same time that it steals knowledge from them. It's an unsustainable path. If Chinese theft of American intellectual property makes those companies less competitive in the global market, the US economy could suffer, and so would China. US intelligence officials have concluded that short of intense diplomatic pressure or economic sanctions, the Chinese are unlikely to halt their cyber campaign. So, the government has become more aggressive in its attempts to protect critical infrastructure. That's what helped drive the decision to defend and monitor the natural gas pipelines in 2012. The only comfort for US national security is that, so far, the Chinese have shown no indication that they want to escalate their campaign from espionage to warfare.

But that's not the case for another US adversary.

Beginning in September 2012, banks across the United States found themselves in the cross hairs of what appeared to be a relatively common form of cyber attack. It wasn't the banks' money the hackers were after but their websites, which allow customers to log in to their accounts, check balances, pay bills, and transfer money. The attackers flooded the banks' web servers with traffic sent from other computers that were under their control, overwhelming them and causing the sites to crash. Dozens of bank sites were hit, causing significant disruptions in business for Bank of America, Wells Fargo, Capital One, Citigroup, HSBC, and other marquee and lesser-known institutions.

Banks, like many companies that conduct business on the web, had faced these so-called denial-of-service attacks before. Most security experts saw them as a nuisance, not an existential threat to the company, and usually an affected website was back up and running within a few hours. But this attack was unprecedented in its scale and sophistication. The attackers created huge networks of computers from which to launch their assault, which sent a staggering amount of traffic the banks' way. By one estimate, the flow was several times larger than what Russia had directed at computers in Estonia in 2007, an attack that ground the country's electronic infrastructure to a halt and was generally regarded as among the most devastating on record. The banks' Internet service providers reported more traffic than they'd ever seen directed at a single website. The attackers appeared to have hijacked whole data centers, or clouds, of thousands of computer servers. It was as if rather than launching a few ships against their targets, they had sent an armada.

Analysts were able to track the source of some traffic back to particular Internet addresses. Internet service providers blocked them, but then the flood just came from someplace else. As with the intrusions into the natural gas companies, the highest levels of government went on alert. But this time officials found themselves facing a more formidable adversary. The spies who targeted the gas companies seemed to want information and not to damage pipelines. But the bank attackers wanted to disrupt the companies' operations and sow panic among customers and in the financial industry. Their strategy worked, perhaps better than intended. Bank security personnel were panicked by the amount of traffic being fired at them, according to former US officials who responded to the attacks. "For the first two or three weeks, there were some very late nights" as officials tried to trace the source of the attacks and understand their motive, says Mark Weatherford, then deputy undersecretary for cyber security at the Homeland Security Department, its top cyber security official.

And that was the other troubling feature of this attack—it didn't stop after a single strike. Indeed, the attackers, who called themselves the Izz ad-Din al-Qassam Brigades, kept coming at the banks and adding new targets. And they continued their work into the next year. In 2013 the NSA identified approximately two hundred additional bank website attacks emanating from the same group. The attackers claimed to be a band of anti-American vigilantes carrying out the strikes in retaliation for an amateur online video called *The Innocence of Muslims,* which depicted Mohammed as a bloodthirsty pedophile and sparked protests across the Middle East. But US intelligence officials suspected this was a cover story, and that the attackers were really working on behalf of the government of Iran, possibly exacting revenge for the cyber strike on the Natanz nuclear facility.

For the past few years, American intelligence agencies had been tracking an Iranian buildup of cyber forces. Leaders of the Iranian

Revolutionary Guard Corps, which owned the biggest telecommunications company in Iraq, had spoken openly about their ambitions to build a cyber army to rival that of the United States. Analysts believed the force was growing and comprised a network of intelligence and military units as well as patriotic "hacktivists." Reportedly, the Iranian regime had spent more than $1 billion since 2011 on offense and defensive capabilities, in response to the Stuxnet attack as well as two other computer viruses that infected systems in Iran and were widely presumed to be the work of American and Israeli intelligence services.

Only a nation had the financial and technical resources, as well as the expertise and the motive, to pull off the operation against the banks, US officials concluded. "The scale and sophistication of the attacks was off the charts. It couldn't have been some guy in his basement," Weatherford says.

What had at first seemed like an ordinary denial-of-service attack was now a potential international cyber war of unprecedented proportions. The question arose among senior US officials: could the United States launch a retaliatory cyber strike against Iran? Officials debated whether hitting an Iranian critical infrastructure would compel the attackers to stop, and whether such a strike was even legal. There was no clear answer and no consensus. Banks were a critical infrastructure by the government's own definition. But the attackers were targeting websites, not account information or the systems that handle interbank transactions. This was not the nightmare scenario Mike McConnell had painted for George W. Bush in 2007. Weatherford says that the senior Homeland Security official in charge of the department's cyber emergency response efforts came to him with no good options. "He said, 'We have no playbook for this.'"

Officials grew concerned that a denial-of-service attack of this scale, if directed at other corporate computer networks, could cause physical disruption, not just inconvenience. US officials stayed in daily contact with the banks and their Internet service providers. The attackers announced in online forums when they planned to launch a new round of strikes. Each time the banks and the government braced for incoming. "There was some pretty significant concern by the ISPs and the federal government that we could get overwhelmed," Weatherford says. "And that this could affect other critical infrastructure and the Internet itself."

After al-Qassam announced one of its rounds of strikes, the chief security officer for an ISP confronted Weatherford and, by extension, the entire government. "What are you guys doing about this?" the executive asked him. "An event is about to happen any day now that will cause national-level impact. What is the government going to do?"

Weatherford tried to assure him that the situation was under control, but he knew there was no counteroffensive coming. In fact, Weatherford thought the NSA was taking too long to declassify threat intelligence that could help defend the banks. The agency had to scrub the information off all sources and methods about how it was gathered before passing it to Homeland Security, which made it available to the ISPs. Weatherford says he phoned NSA officials every day and urged them to quickly make more intelligence available to the companies before the next round of strikes. "It took six hours to turn the information around. But the event might last only six hours," he says.

A group of financial executives pressed their case personally in a meeting with NSA officials. They wanted to know why the government didn't just attack the sources of the traffic floods and take them offline, as if firing cruise missiles at an enemy encampment. The NSA officials told the executives they were stockpiling cyber weapons, primarily thousands of zero day exploits, to use during a national emergency or if the country ever went to war. "Once we use one of them, we can never use it again," an official explained, according to a senior financial executive who participated in the meeting. "You really want us to waste these weapons just because your websites are down?"

The executives backed off.

The bank attacks were a test of national will. The NSA and the military would not respond with force unless the attackers threatened the transactional infrastructure of the financial services sector, or corrupted the accounts data so that they were no longer reliable. There'd have to be a crippling cyber attack that caused ripple effects in the broader society before the government would retaliate. Taking down a website, however frightening, wasn't justification for war. Nor was espionage.

For the banks — for all companies that suffered the onslaught of foreign cyber attackers and marauders — it raised the obvious question: if the government wasn't going to rescue them, who would?

THIRTEEN

The Business of Defense

THIRTY MILES FROM downtown Washington, DC, in the suburb of Gaithersburg, Maryland, a low-slung office building sits across a busy highway from a Sam's Club, a truck dealership, and a Toys "R" Us. The pair of security guards at the gated checkpoint are the first clue that this isn't another box store or an ordinary office park. In a mostly windowless 25,000-square-foot wing of the building is a cyber watch center. There a few dozen analysts and malware researchers monitor traffic as it moves across a globally dispersed network of computers and servers that contain some of the most highly classified information in the United States, including designs for military fighter jets, missile control systems, and spy satellites. But this facility, which could pass for a top-secret command post at Fort Meade or the Pentagon, is neither owned nor controlled by the government. The NexGen Cyber Innovation & Technology Center, as it's properly called, is run by Lockheed Martin, the largest federal government contractor. Here, and in centers like it in Denver, Farnborough, England, and Canberra, Australia, a company that made its name building weapons systems is creating a new business in cyber defense.

It's a subject that Lockheed learned about firsthand when it was targeted by Chinese hackers who stole plans for the Joint Strike Fighter in 2006. The company is the largest seller of information technology goods and services to civilian and intelligence agencies and the military, and as such it remains a huge target. It spent the first few years after the 2006 attack closely studying the methods and techniques of hackers trying to break in to its classified systems and steal more of the government's secrets. A young Lockheed analyst named Eric Hutchins heard some pilots use the term "kill chain" to describe all the steps they went through before ever firing a weapon, from identifying a target to geographically fixing its location to tracking it. It occurred to Hutchins that the sophisticated hackers trying to penetrate Lockheed's networks also followed a step-by-step process, scouting out a target, acquiring malware, firing off a spear phish, and ultimately stealing data. Working with two colleagues, he appropriated the military's concept and the "cyber kill chain" became the foundation of Lockheed's defense strategy, one it uses now to protect not only its own networks but those of some of its government customers, as well as banks, pharmaceutical companies, and at least seventeen public utilities that share information with the company and let it scan their traffic for threats.

The cyber kill chain has seven distinct steps, most of them offering an opportunity to block an intrusion or an attack before it occurs. The chain starts with reconnaissance. Lockheed monitors what keywords people are searching on Google and other search engines that lead them to the company's website. Hackers look for names of employees in company press releases and on Lockheed web pages in order to better tailor their spear-phishing e-mails. They identify program managers working on particular government contracts. They even keep track of speeches executives give so they can craft an e-mail that relates to a planned event. The company will alert employees who appear to be potential targets, so they know to be especially careful when opening documents attached to e-mails or clicking on links.

In step two, what Lockheed calls "weaponization," analysts look for telltale forensic evidence of malware; for instance, an infected pdf document attached to an e-mail. Lockheed maintains a database of all the infected Adobe pdf files its analysts have ever seen, and it programs the information into scanners that automatically examine every e-mail that's sent to an employee, and quarantines potential carriers of malware.

The kill chain continues through the process of "delivery" (sending malware via an e-mail or an infected USB drive, for instance), "exploit," in which analysts pay particular attention to finding zero days (they have discovered at least three specifically targeting Adobe products, Hutchins says), "installation" onto a computer, "command-and-control" communication with a host machine, and, finally, "actions on objectives" (stealing files, erasing data, or destroying a piece of physical machinery). At step seven, a hacker poses the greatest threat. If Lockheed analysts detect such an action, they immediately notify the target company's CEO. Hackers spotted earlier in the chain, say at step three, pose less of a threat, because they still have a number of steps to complete before they can cause any damage. If analysts determine that a hacker may try to infect computers using USB drives, a company can program its systems not to allow any USB drives to run computer code. The earlier in the chain that Lockheed or anyone using the kill chain can install a defense, the more secure it will be.

Using the kill chain model, Lockheed has been able to alert its customers to potential intrusions before they occur, according to retired general Charlie Croom, vice president of cyber security solutions. Lockheed doesn't disclose who those customers are, so it's impossible to verify that claim. And the kill chain concept sounds like common sense. But many cyber security experts, including those who work for Lockheed's competitors, say it marked a turning point in the evolution of cyber defense when the company unveiled the concept in 2011. The kill chain broke down intrusions into discrete actions and moments, each of which offered defenders an opportunity to block their adversaries. And those defenders could marshal their resources more efficiently, because not every warning sign had to be treated as an emergency. The kill chain offered a conceptual map for how to build layers of defenses farther away from a target, and to block the intruders before they got too close.

The kill chain was important for another reason: it was developed by a corporation, not a government agency. Hutchins, who at thirty-four is Lockheed's chief intelligence analyst, had never worked for the government, nor did he serve in the armed forces. In fact, he's never worked anywhere but Lockheed, which he joined in 2002 after graduating from the University of Virginia with a degree in computer science. Lockheed is stocked with former government officials and military officers — among them Croom, who ran the Defense Information Systems Agency until he retired in 2008. But Lockheed developed the kill chain as a way of protecting itself, rather than relying on help from the NSA or any other agency. And then it turned that knowledge into a business.

Today Lockheed's cyber analysts monitor traffic on their own network, but they also receive information from about fifty defense companies that also work on sensitive and classified government programs. Lockheed is also the main contractor for the Defense Cyber Crime Center, the largest cyber forensics organization in the government, which handles counterterrorism and counterintelligence cases. And the company manages the Global Information Grid, applying its kill chain methodology to the Defense Department's secure worldwide information technology network. The contract is worth up to $4.6 billion. On just its own networks, Lockheed monitors about two billion individual transactions per day — every e-mail sent and received, every website visited, any action that leaves a digital record or log. All the data is stored for a year, and any information related to malicious activity is kept indefinitely. Lockheed has effectively built a library of hacker history from which it can draw when studying new intrusions. Using older data, analysts have discovered that more recent intrusions are actually part of broader campaigns that began months or years earlier and targeted several companies and organizations. Croom says that when he retired from the military in 2008, the Defense Department had identified and was tracking approximately fifteen campaigns attributed to nation-states. Today Lockheed is tracking about forty campaigns. The Defense Department is tracking some of the same ones — Croom declines to say which — and the company shares its information with the government through the Defense Industrial Base program. Lockheed has also discovered six campaigns that the Defense Department didn't know about, Croom says. The details are now classified.

About the only thing that Lockheed can't do — legally — is to break in to other computer systems to gather intelligence. That's still the NSA's domain. But the company has its eyes on the same foreign adversaries as the government. In the NexGen Center's primary command center, clocks on the wall show the time in all the countries where Lockheed has a cyber monitoring station — and also the time in Beijing. The company has collected seven years' worth of information on advanced persistence threat campaigns, and analysts have access to all of it. A huge monitor on the forward wall shows all the campaigns Lockheed is tracking around the world, mostly gleaned from attempted intrusions into its own networks, which include three million Internet addresses at nearly six hundred locations in sixty countries. The bigger a target a company is, the bigger a source for information it becomes. Selling to the government is still the company's primary business, accounting for more than 80 percent of its $47.2 billion in sales in 2012. But in 2011, Lockheed expanded into the commercial sector, Croom says, focusing on technology services for the top 200 of the Fortune 500, with an emphasis on critical-infrastructure operators. And the company wants to open another cyber center in the Middle East to take advantage of a growing regional appetite for network surveillance and security.

Lockheed is hardly the only company taking cyber defense into its own hands. Since the attacks on bank websites in 2012, US financial institutions have been setting up their own cyber intelligence units. (Some of them are undoubtedly Lockheed's customers.) Their efforts were under way before the terrifying traffic floods caused so much disruption, and they have accelerated. Today most large banks in the United States employ cyber security personnel trained to detect vulnerabilities in software and network configurations, analyze malware to understand how they work and what they're designed to do, and respond to intrusions. Among the main pools of talent for the banks are the US military and intelligence agencies.

The former chief information security officer for Bank of America was previously a senior technology official in the Office of the Director of National Intelligence who began his career as a cryptologic linguist in the air force. The chief information security officer at Wells Fargo served for twenty years in the navy, including stints as an information warfare officer, and later worked for the FBI. The chief information risk officer for JPMorgan Chase never worked in government, but he worked for a year at SAIC, which is largely supported by intelligence agency contracts and is often called "NSA West." And he worked for a year at Booz Allen Hamilton, which is one of the top cyber security contractors for the federal government and where former NSA director Mike McConnell hangs his hat.

"Within a couple of years, all the guys in cyber who've got game will be working for the banks. They'll lock down their networks and only share information among themselves," says a former military intelligence officer who was part of the 2007 cyber offensive in Iraq and later went to work for a large defense contractor.

According to experts, the banks have aggressively hired military and intelligence employees who've been trained in government to the highest standards but who can double or even triple their salaries working in the private sector. Banks are also becoming bigger buyers of zero day vulnerabilities and exploits from private security researchers, which have usually counted the NSA as their biggest customer. A security expert with close ties to sellers of zero day exploits says the banks are amassing cyber weapons in the event that they feel compelled to retaliate against the attackers. If a "private" cyber war ever breaks out, it will probably be launched by a bank.

But financial services companies aren't the only ones setting up their own defense operations. The list of companies that employ a senior-level information security officer, with an executive title such as vice president or chief, includes Johnson & Johnson, T-Mobile USA, Automated Data Processing (the payroll services company), Coca-Cola, Intel, AstraZeneca, eBay, FedEx, and hundreds more. When companies can't provide adequately for their own defense, they hire outside help, and that segment of the security market is growing. In its 2012 annual report to shareholders, Lockheed Martin said it was "facing increased competition, particularly in information technology and cyber security . . . from non-traditional competitors outside of the aerospace and defense industry." It was a veiled reference to upstart security companies such as CrowdStrike, Mandiant, and Endgame, which are building their own sources and methods of intelligence collection and analysis.

Companies find themselves at the dawn of a new era in private cyber security. "We've already got the cyber equivalent of the Pinkerton Guards," says Mark Weatherford, the former top cyber security official at the Homeland Security Department. Like many security experts, Weatherford worries that some firms aren't solely devoted to defense, and that they'll cross the line into hacking back in order to repel spies and attackers. He draws a distinction between hacking back and making it more difficult for an intruder to steal data from a target's network. Planting honeypots, or even tricking intruders into bringing malware-laden documents back onto their own systems, is arguably still on the defensive side of the line. "But actually reaching into that network, attacking it, that's a bridge I don't want to cross," he says.

Within a few years Weatherford expects to see more companies develop the capability to filter traffic on behalf of their customers, effectively becoming cyber sentries. That model is already taking shape through the government's program of passing classified threat signatures to Internet service providers. Part of Obama's 2013 executive order to beef up critical-infrastructure security calls on the government to "provide guidance" to companies on what commercially available products and services they could buy that meet approved standards for defense. It's another example of the government fueling the growth of private cyber security, a trend that's probably unavoidable and maybe even preferable to the government monopolizing this realm.

"The government will never be as responsive as the private sector," Weatherford says. Businesses may be better off fending for themselves.

As companies take up the mantle of national cyber defense, they're influencing the course of US government policy. On February 18, 2013, the computer security firm Mandiant released an unprecedented report about Chinese cyber spying that publicly named the People's Liberation Army as the source of pervasive and relentless espionage against the United States. That was a direct accusation that no government official had been willing to make on record. Mandiant's report was extraordinarily detailed. It gave the physical address where the hackers were located. It even included a photo of their office, a beige twelve-story building in the Pudong New Area of Shanghai. Based on the size of the building — more than 130,000 square feet — as well as public statements from Chinese officials, Mandiant estimated that hundreds and perhaps thousands of people worked there.

Mandiant focused on just one group out of the approximately twenty it had been following for years. The hackers were housed within China's equivalent of the National Security Agency. Dubbed APT1 by Mandiant, the hackers worked in the Second Bureau of the People's Liberation Army General Staff Department's Third Department, more commonly known by a numerical designation, 61398. The General Staff Department is analogous to the US Joint Chiefs of Staff, and the Third Department handles signals intelligence and computer attack and exploitation. Mandiant called APT1 "one of the most persistent of China's cyber threat actors."

Mandiant, a company that had been founded less than ten years earlier by an ex–air force computer-forensics expert, had just set off a bomb in one of the most delicate and thorny areas of US foreign policy. The report was greeted as a revelation. Not just because it named Chinese hackers so specifically — something no investigators, private or governmental, had been willing to do — but also because the information was so precise. The report ran seventy-four pages. It illuminated a vast infrastructure of spying, comprising 937 servers, or "listening applications," hosted on 849 distinct Internet addresses, the majority of them registered to organizations in China but more than 100 in the United States. The investigators found websites that the hackers had set up to look like legitimate news sites, such as CNN.com, but that were actually used in coordination with APT's intrusions. Mandiant named individual hackers, including one who went by the handle Ugly Gorilla, and who had years earlier identified himself in an online chat about Chinese cyber warfare with a leading computer science professor who wrote a seminal book on China's "network warfare." Mandiant used forensic evidence to link certain hackers to one another and was confident that some of them not only knew one another personally but probably worked in the same office. The report even gave lessons in Chinese hacker slang, such as "meat chicken," which meant an infected computer.

Mandiant also concluded that the Chinese cyber force was "directly supported by linguists, open source researchers, malware authors," and "industry experts." There was likely a staff that purchased and maintained computer equipment, as well as people to handle finances, facility management, and logistics and shipping. In other words, it was a highly organized bureaucracy, not unlike a US government agency.

The details in the Mandiant report were of a kind one normally expects to find in a classified government intelligence document. That was another reason it was so significant. The report showed that private investigators could collect and analyze information as effectively as a government spy agency, if not more so. That was partly a testament to Mandiant's technical prowess. But it also revealed something about the nature of cyberspace. In an uncontrolled environment, in which hackers can move about on a collective, networked infrastructure, there really are no secrets. With enough training and the right tools, a private sleuth can track a hacker as well as a government spy or a military operative can. Mandiant's report not only blew the lid off China's cyber spying, it belied the notion that only the government was prepared to do battle in cyberspace.

The effects of Mandiant's report were swift and far-reaching. Chinese officials issued their usual denials, calling allegations of government-directed espionage unfounded. Less than a month later, the US national security adviser, Tom Donilon, put Beijing on notice in a major speech, in which he called Chinese cyber espionage "a growing challenge to our economic relationship with China" and a "key point of concern and discussion with China at all levels of government." There'd been closed-door talks between both sides, in which US officials demanded that China stop its aggressive operations. Now those discussions were out in the open. Donilon's remarks were the first public statement by a White House official directed at Chinese cyber spying. The problem had "moved to the forefront of [the administration's] agenda," Donilon said, calling for action by the Chinese government to address "the urgency and scope of this problem and the risk it poses — to international trade, to the reputation of Chinese industry, and to our overall relations." That was the first time the Americans had demanded China to address cyber espionage. "Beijing should take serious steps to investigate and put a stop to these activities," Donilon said, and "engage with us in a constructive direct dialogue to establish acceptable norms of behavior in cyberspace."

The Obama administration had finally thrown down the gauntlet. And Mandiant helped them do it. As with Google's revelation about Chinese spying after the Aurora operation, senior US officials had an opening to talk about a problem that had been quietly vexing them for years. Mandiant's report provided them with a detailed and, most important, an unclassified document from which to draw specific allegations. The government would never have been so bold as to come out with such a report.

Mandiant's findings landed with a shock. But the report's publication was a carefully crafted event, played for maximum media attention and coordinated with the government. As early as October 2012, after years of collecting information on Chinese spies, Mandiant executives considered writing a public report about its findings. "We decided it was an interesting idea, and we should go forward," says Dan McWhorter, Mandiant's managing director in charge of threat intelligence. But the company initially figured it would write a short brief, nothing like the seventy-four-page indictment it eventually issued. That plan began to change in November, after Mandiant got a call from the *New York Times*. Not from a reporter asking for an expert comment on a story. This was a call for help. The *Times* believed it had been hacked, and it wanted Mandiant to investigate.

Mandiant's forensic analysts found that Chinese spies had overrun the newspaper's networks and were spying on more than sixty employees, including a reporter in China working on an exposé of political corruption and influence at the highest levels of the government. The spies tried to mask their identities by routing traffic through hijacked computers at US universities in North Carolina, New Mexico, Arizona, and Wisconsin, a technique Mandiant had seen in other espionage campaigns it traced to China. The spies gained access to a computer on the *Times*'s network, and they were eventually able to steal passwords and get access to fifty-three employees' personal computers, most of them outside the newsroom. The hackers were part of a group that Mandiant had already been tracking, which the company dubbed APT Number 12. From the *Times,* they apparently wanted more details about a lengthy article the paper was planning to run on Chinese prime minister Wen Jiabao's relatives, and how they used their political connections to make billions of dollars in shadowy business deals. Mandiant had also found evidence that Chinese spies stole information from more than thirty journalists and executives at other Western news outlets, including their e-mails, contact information for sources, and files. What's more, the spies had gone after specific journalists again and again. At the *Times,* it was later revealed, the spies built custom malware to break in to the e-mail account of Jim Yardley, then the paper's South Asia bureau chief, who worked in India and had previously run the Beijing bureau. They also targeted David Barboza, the Shanghai bureau chief, who wrote the article on Prime Minister Wen, for which he later won the Pulitzer Prize. The *Washington Post* and the *Wall Street Journal* had also been penetrated by Chinese cyber spies, subsequent investigations showed.

Mandiant executives decided that a short paper on Chinese spying wouldn't suffice. The company believed that it had plenty of evidence of a broad, persistent campaign going back to 2006, targeting different sectors of the US economy, including defense contractors. Chinese officials' denials had become "comical," McWhorter says. In January 2013 the *Times* wrote about its own experience getting hacked. Chinese officials publicly questioned Mandiant's credibility — the company had assisted in the investigation and was quoted in the *Times* article, which could have been read as an endorsement of Mandiant's investigative work. The company decided it was time to name names. China's attempts to discredit the firm and what it knew "definitely cemented our resolve to make this a very public document," McWhorter says.

Obama administration officials were generally pleased with Mandiant's decision. It wasn't as though the president and his national security team didn't already know what China was up to; but now a credible document, filled with evidence that could be tested and debated by experts, had changed the nature of the conversation about Chinese spying. No more off-the-record accusations. No more using "advanced persistent threat" as a euphemism for China. And the United States wouldn't have to reveal any secret intelligence sources and methods to talk openly about Chinese spying. (At the same time Mandiant was crafting its report, the Justice Department was secretly building a legal case against members of the 61398 hacker group. In May 2014, prosecutors announced indictments against five Chinese military officials, whom they claimed were connected to the group, marking the first time the United States had ever filed criminal hacking charges against nation-state actors.)

On the same day Mandiant released its report, the Homeland Security Department issued a bulletin to a select group of critical infrastructure owners and operators and other information security professionals authorized to see government information. It contained some of the same Internet addresses and websites that appeared in the Mandiant report. But notably the Homeland Security document never mentioned China and didn't tie the cyber spies to any particular location. Nor did the report mention Mandiant. Sharing of the report was restricted to "peers and partner organizations," and it was not to be distributed via publicly accessible channels, the department advised. Mandiant's report was more useful, because it was more detailed and accessible to anyone. But the government report supported its findings. Its timing was also telling. Homeland Security could have released its version first, but it waited for Mandiant to lift the veil on APT1. Mandiant was doing the government a favor. Sources close to the drafting of the report say that the government also gave Mandiant some intelligence it used in the report, but the vast majority of the findings came from its own investigative work, going back seven years.

Practically overnight, Mandiant went from a relatively obscure forensics company known mostly to security experts and other tech startups to a sought-after name in computer security. Mandiant executives became go-to sources for journalists and sat on panels with former intelligence officials and think tank members, opining on how best to defend cyberspace from spies and attackers. Business ticked up. In 2013 the company made more than $100 million in sales, more than half of which came from a proprietary software Mandiant developed to help companies guard against APT hackers. Reportedly, more than a third of Fortune 100 companies have hired Mandiant after their computers were breached. In January 2014, less than a year after Mandiant released the APT1 report, it was bought by another computer security firm, FireEye, for $1 billion. It was the biggest acquisition in the cyber security business in recent years and one of ten in 2013, a twofold increase from 2012.

FireEye was already a darling of Silicon Valley. The company began publicly offering shares on the Nasdaq in September 2013, and by January, the per share price had more than doubled. FireEye's was the most successful IPO for a cyber security company in 2013. Teaming up with Mandiant would make a formidable security operation. Whereas Mandiant specialized in investigating cyber intrusions, FireEye aimed to prevent them. Its technology pulls aside incoming traffic on a network into a virtual cage and examines it for any signs of malware before deciding whether to let it pass. The process was similar to one used by the Homeland Security Department to screen traffic on government networks, yet another sign that officials had no monopoly on cyber defense.

For Mandiant and FireEye, widespread Chinese spying coupled with revelations about the NSA's global intelligence operations helped to create new business and directly led to the merger. "A lot of companies, organizations, and governments said, 'Look how pervasive these superpowers are in monitoring and stealing from these companies,'" said David DeWalt, FireEye's chairman and CEO. His customers decided they needed to protect themselves. "There is an accelerating awareness that just wasn't there a year ago."

If companies needed any more reason to hire a private security company, it arrived in June 2013, when a twenty-nine-year-old NSA contractor named Edward Snowden revealed himself as the source of an enormous cache of stolen classified documents about the agency's global surveillance apparatus. Snowden shared the documents with journalists working for the *Guardian* and the *Washington Post,* and a cascade of press coverage followed, unprecedented in its scope and specificity. Practically every conceivable aspect of how the agency spies was laid bare. The documents showed how the NSA collected vast stores of information from Google, Facebook, Yahoo, and other technology and telecommunications companies. The agency had also been scooping up the phone records of hundreds of millions of Americans and holding on to them for five years. Administration officials tried to reassure anxious citizens that most of the NSA's spying was aimed at foreigners overseas. Technology executives were dumbfounded. As they explained to officials, publicly and in private meetings, many of their customers lived in foreign countries, and were hardly at ease with the NSA spying on them simply because they weren't Americans.

Before the Snowden leaks, the NSA had made a public effort to court support among hackers for its cyber defense mission. In 2012, Keith Alexander had famously appeared at that Def Con, hacker conference in Las Vegas, dressed in blue jeans and a black T-shirt, shedding his army uniform for an outfit he deemed more palatable to his audience of hackers and security researchers. In July 2013, a month after the first NSA stories appeared, Def Con's organizers rescinded their invitation to have Alexander give another speech. Def Con's sister conference, Black Hat, was willing to host the spymaster. But about a half hour into his talk, members of the audience began heckling him. "Freedom!" shouted one of them, a private security consultant. "Exactly, we stand for freedom," Alexander replied.

"Bullshit!" the consultant retorted. The crowd applauded.

Some "white hat hackers," the ones who ply their trade to improve cyber defense and who had been cooperating with the NSA on technical discussions, are now questioning their decision, according to former agency officials who fear that the hackers may now take up arms against the government and try to expose more secrets or even attack government agencies and contractors' systems. Snowden showed that just one person could expose vast swaths of the NSA's surveillance architecture. What damage could an entire movement of highly motivated hackers do?

Snowden himself was a trained hacker. While working as an NSA contractor, he took advanced courses in "ethical hacking" and malware analysis at a private school in India. He was in the country on a secret mission for the government, performing work at the US embassy in New Delhi, according to people familiar with his trip. The exact nature of the job is classified, but by the time he arrived, in September 2010, Snowden had already studied some advanced hacking techniques and was a quick learner in class, according to his instructor. He was taught how to break in to computers and steal information, ostensibly for the purpose of learning how to better fend off malicious hackers. He wouldn't need those skills to steal most of the classified NSA documents, to which he had unfettered access by virtue of his top-secret security clearance. It turned out that the NSA, which wanted to protect computers from Wall Street to the water company, couldn't keep a twenty-nine-year-old contractor from making off with the blueprints to its global surveillance system.

The Snowden revelations were the most politically damaging in the NSA's sixty-one-year history. In July the House of Representatives nearly passed a bill that would have declawed the agency's collection of Americas' phone records, which would have been the first significant rollback of the government's surveillance powers since the 9/11 attacks. Republicans and Democrats found a rare bipartisan alliance in their desire to put the spy agency on a leash. President Obama appointed a panel of intelligence and legal experts to suggest changes to NSA surveillance. They came back with a three-hundred-plus-page report and forty-six recommendations, among them ending the NSA's practice of acquiring zero day exploits, no longer inserting backdoors into encryption products, putting a civilian in charge of the spy agency, and splitting the leadership of NSA and Cyber Command so that they weren't led by the same person. It was a blueprint for diminishing the agency's leading role in cyber security.

And yet the need to defend cyberspace was as urgent as ever. In September 2013 a senior air force official said the service still didn't know how vulnerable to hackers its networks were, because it was only a quarter of the way through a comprehensive vulnerability review. And this more than four years after intruders were able to penetrate the air force's air traffic control system, which could have allowed them to interfere with aircraft flight plans and radar systems. A month after the air force's admission, a Defense Department inspector general issued a report that found that the Pentagon, the Homeland Security Department, and the NSA had no central system for sharing cyber alerts with one another and companies in real time. The government had a system for circulating alerts, and another for sending follow-up instructions on how to respond to cyber threats, but those two systems weren't connected.

News from the critical-infrastructure sectors that the government wanted to protect wasn't any more encouraging. Earlier in the year a pair of engineers had discovered vulnerabilities in communications systems used by power and water utilities across the country that could allow an attacker to cause a widespread power outage or damage water supplies. Homeland Security officials issued alerts, but few utilities had applied a patch to the vulnerable software. And cyber espionage against US companies showed no signs of abating. "There isn't a computer system in this country of consequence that isn't penetrated right now with information going out at the terabyte level," former NSA director McConnell said during a speech in Washington in October, a claim echoed publicly and privately by numerous intelligence, military, and law enforcement officials.

US officials were still reeling over an attack the previous year against the Saudi Arabian state-owned oil company Aramco, which by some measures was the most valuable company in the world, supplying 10 percent of the world's oil. Hackers used a powerful virus to completely erase information on about 75 percent of its computers, thirty thousand machines in all. The virus deleted e-mails, spreadsheets, and documents in an attack that company officials said was aimed at stopping its oil and gas production. The hackers didn't succeed in disrupting Aramco's production facilities, but the attack was a reminder that hackers could severely wound a company by obliterating its stores of corporate information. Some US officials suspected that Iran mounted the attack in retaliation for the Stuxnet worm. If that was so, it marked an escalation in intentional cyber warfare and showed that the United States couldn't expect to launch cyber attacks without reprisals.

Cybercrime was also rampant in the United States. In mid-December 2013, the retail giant Target discovered that hackers had forced their way into the company's systems and stolen debit and credit card information. The crooks installed malware directly onto cash registers in Target stores and siphoned financial data. The company initially estimated that thieves took 40 million customers' financial information. But a month later, it revised that number to between 70 and 110 million. It was a staggering number, making the Target breach one of the biggest cyber thefts in history. Investigators concluded that the hackers were probably based in Eastern Europe or Russia, and that they first penetrated Target's network using stolen network credentials from a Pennsylvania company that maintains refrigeration systems in supermarkets. Target also discovered that the thieves swiped customers' names, phone numbers, and e-mail and mailing addresses. The company faced potentially steep fines for not complying with industry standards to protect credit and debit card information.

Government agencies didn't fare much better in protecting their own networks. In February 2014 a Senate committee report found that with few exceptions, federal civilian agencies hadn't installed available software patches or kept antivirus software up to date. Unlike their military and intelligence agency counterparts, the civilian agencies lacked some of the most fundamental training and awareness about common sense security. Government employees were using flimsy passwords. One popular choice the investigators found: "password." Even the Homeland Security Department hadn't installed software security updates on all of its systems, "the basic security measure just about any American with a computer has performed," the report found.

In the wake of the Snowden revelations, Alexander remained defiant. The bad news about weak cyber defenses only bolstered his own argument that the NSA should take a more forceful role protecting the country. At an October 2013 security conference in Washington, DC, sponsored by the military and cyber security contractor Raytheon, Alexander asked for more powers to defend the financial sector, using some questionable technical arguments. He imagined the NSA having real-time information from the banks so the agency could spot "a cyberpacket that's about to destroy Wall Street" and intercept it like an incoming missile. The term "cyberpacket" had no clear meaning in that context. Presumably Alexander wanted to imply that a sophisticated computer worm or a virus could disrupt financial institutions' computers or the data they house. But the notion that a single packet of data could wipe out Wall Street was absurd. That was like saying a paintball could take out a tank.

The degree to which Alexander was willing to exaggerate the cyber threat and dumb down his own agency's response was a measure of how desperately he wanted public support for his mission, and how threatened he felt. Snowden had helped undermine the case Alexander had been building for years.

FOURTEEN

At the Dawn

O N JANUARY 17, 2014, Barack Obama stood at a lectern in the Great Hall of the Justice Department in Washington to announce his decision on which NSA surveillance and cyber security programs he'd keep and which ones he'd scrap. If America's spies had feared the president would pull them back from the front, they could rest easy after they heard the first words out of his mouth.

Obama began by comparing the employees of the NSA to Paul Revere and the Sons of Liberty, who formed a "secret surveillance committee" to patrol the streets of colonial Boston, "reporting back any signs that the British were preparing raids against America's early patriots." It was the most full-throated defense of the NSA and US signals intelligence that Obama had ever given. The president had just likened them to the heroes of the American Revolution.

Obama then recounted how spies in balloons had tracked the size of the Confederate army during the Civil War, how code breakers during World War II had provided insights into Japanese war plans, and how "when Patton marched across Europe, intercepted communications helped save the lives of his troops." It was in that spirit, and in the early days of a new Cold War, that President Harry Truman had created the

National Security Agency "to give us insights into the Soviet bloc, and provide our leaders with information they needed to confront aggression and avert catastrophe."

By the time Obama took the stage, White House officials had already briefed journalists on his intended changes to NSA surveillance. They were minimal. Obama would make some alterations to the controversial program of collating Americans' phone records, namely, storing them somewhere other than in NSA's databases. But he punted to Congress and the attorney general the hard work of figuring out where that storage should be. Eventually, the administration and lawmakers settled on a plan that kept the records with the phone companies but still allowed the NSA access to them for investigative purposes. Obama also afforded some relatively minor privacy protections to foreigners who came under scrutiny from NSA's digital reconnaissance. But by and large, the agency's surveillance powers were left intact.

Obama either rejected or deferred on every substantive recommendation his advisers had given him for reining in the NSA. He had already overruled the proposal to split the leadership of NSA and Cyber Command. Now he dismissed a call by his appointed review panel to strip the agency of its information assurance mission, the work of defending computer systems from cyber attack and exploitation. Had Obama accepted the change, it would have fundamentally altered the NSA's mission, to the point that the organization would be unrecognizable from its previous form.

Obama also rejected the panel's suggestion that he take away the NSA's authority to conduct or assist in operations inside the United States. And the president further rejected calls to make the NSA director a civilian and to subject his nomination to Senate confirmation. NSA director Keith Alexander could rest easy; much of his empire would remain intact, despite the beating he'd taken personally in the press after the Snowden leaks. The general planned to step down in March. To replace him, Obama chose Vice Admiral Michael Rogers, who had been groomed for the job of NSA director and cyber commander. Rogers ran the navy's signals intelligence and its cyber warfare operations. Like Alexander, he was used to wearing two hats.

As for the panel's recommendation that the NSA stop hoarding zero day exploits and undermining encryption standards, Obama said nothing in his speech. A senior administration official later said the president had asked his aides to look into these recommendations and report back to him. The administration eventually settled on a vague policy that was biased toward disclosing vulnerabilities but keeping secret any information that the government deemed vital to national security. That was a huge exception that could allow the NSA to classify all zero days as essential security tools and keep conducting business as usual. The new policy hardly ended the debate. Effectively, Obama had deferred on this issue as well, and it seemed unlikely that he or his advisers would propose any significant changes.

In practically every way, from operations to personnel, Obama had opted to maintain the status quo. Indeed, his embrace of the historic importance of intelligence to warfare underscored his desire to protect the NSA and keep its mission intact.

The timing of Obama's speech was fitting, if unintentionally so. On January 17, 1961, exactly fifty-three years earlier, President Dwight Eisenhower had warned in his farewell address to the nation of a "military industrial complex," whose "total influence — economic, political, even spiritual — is felt in every city, every state house, every office of the federal government." Eisenhower said the military of the day bore little resemblance to the one in which he served during World War II or that his predecessors in the White House had commanded. "Until the latest of our world conflicts, the United States had no armaments industry," Eisenhower said, admonishing his fellow citizens to "guard against the acquisition of unwarranted influence, whether sought or unsought," by an alliance of government and industry, which he saw as a necessary bulwark against the forces of communist tyranny, and yet one that portended "grave implications" if "the potential for the disastrous rise of misplaced power" was not checked. "This conjunction of an immense military establishment and a large arms industry is new in the American experience," Eisenhower said.

And so is the conjunction of that military establishment with a large Internet technology industry. Until recently, there was no cyber arms industry in the United States. The armed forces didn't view the Internet as a battlefield. Corporations didn't sell protection from spies and hackers. Barack Obama presided over the rise and rapid expansion of an alliance between big military and big business. But unlike Dwight Eisenhower, he sees little cause for dread and foreboding.

Eisenhower died eight years after his prescient speech. He correctly predicted the emergence of the military-industrial complex, but even he might not have imagined a day when the market value of top defense contractors exceeds the gross domestic product of many countries and the US Armed Forces rely on contractors to build their weapons, transport soldiers to battle, and even feed them in the war zone. The military-Internet complex will also dramatically change the nature of war and more broadly of cyberspace itself. What will the next decade look like?

For starters, governments won't be the dominant actors, at least not from day to day. That's a fundamental shift in the balance of power since Eisenhower's time, and suggests that his warning has gone unheeded. National governments will set policies and enact laws and regulate security standards that banks, public utilities, and other critical infrastructure will honor (perhaps in the breach). And they will raise cyber armies that train to fight on networks and will eventually become integrated into the full arsenal of national military might. If China, Iran, or another hostile nation ever launches a major attack on a US electrical plant or a bank, the military will respond, both in cyberspace and offline. An attack that causes widespread panic, disruption, or loss of life will be met with resounding force.

But the day-to-day work of defending critical facilities will be the job of corporations, who will perform the task as well if not better than government. Lockheed Martin and its ilk will create a new business in scanning traffic and applying their proprietary methods for detecting malware and hacker activity — methods that will be based on the real-time intelligence they collect from their own, vast global information networks, as well as those of their customers. It will be a kind of crowdsourcing. Similarly, companies such as CrowdStrike and the newly merged Mandiant and FireEye will promise to protect their customers' networks from prospective threats, the same way we expect security guards to keep intruders out of our homes and office buildings, not just to investigate the invasion after it happens.

The military-Internet complex is like its industrial predecessor insofar as the government has always outsourced national security to some degree. The military doesn't build weapons and defenses, it pays companies to do that, and it has since the founding of the republic. But the government has always had a monopoly on the use of force. And that's where the military-Internet complex takes a screaming turn off the road of history. Corporations' intelligence-gathering capabilities are as good if not better than the government's. They are designing threat signatures and discovering zero days, and they employ them for their own purposes. For all the emerging, menacing power that Eisenhower saw in the military-industrial complex, he didn't predict that corporations would compete with government in the conduct of hostilities.

The market is ripe for sophisticated and reliable cyber security technologies and tactics. With every revelation of a high-profile data breach, particularly those like the Target credit and debit card theft in 2013 that affected nearly a third of the US population and captured headlines for weeks, more companies will become desperate to prevent losses. Federal authorities notified more than three thousand companies in 2013 that their networks had been hacked — a huge number, but likely only a small fraction of the real total. Those were just the intrusions that the government had noticed or been tipped to by security companies. The owners of critical infrastructure are in an especially precarious position. In December 2013, Ernest Moniz, the secretary of energy, said that the majority of "cyberattacks" in the United States that year had been directed at energy infrastructure, which includes the companies that own and operate the electrical grid and that control oil and natural gas production and distribution. So far, those attacks have consisted of attempted intrusions into the networks that run energy facilities or the computers in their owners' corporate offices. But, Moniz said, "there's no question" that the United States will suffer a major attack that threatens to bring down part of the power grid. "There is certainly not an 'if' when it comes to cyberattacks. I am not willing to concede on bringing the grid down. But that's the race we are in to try to shore up our defenses. . . . We have a lot of work to do."

The government is certainly in that race, and there are things it can do to help companies keep up: share more specific, useful intelligence about where the threats are coming from; pressure Internet service providers to deny access to known hostile sources; and ultimately take offensive measures to repel an imminent attack, if it can be detected. Not all of these solutions would require new legislation. An administration could take them on as a matter of executive policy. But energy companies, just like companies that are less central to a functioning economy, would still be largely on their own when it comes to fending off the intruders who are at their gates every day, threatening to breach their defenses. There are simply too many networks spread out over too big a geographic area for the government to protect them all, even if Keith Alexander's master plan of installing a sensor in every bank's network came to pass.

The adversaries aren't relenting. From September 2013 to March 2014 there were more than three hundred denial-of-service attacks against banks, like the ones attributed to Iran that crashed websites and ignited so much panic in the financial sector. The government is well aware of the attacks — the three hundred figure came from the NSA, which tracks them. If companies are going to protect themselves, they'll have to share some information with the government about what's happening on their networks. But they have a bigger incentive to take their security into their own hands and defend themselves.

Eventually, strong security will be a selling point, a feature that banks, Internet service providers, and other companies that handle personal information use to lure customers, the same way that automakers promote airbags and antilock brakes. In fact, it's already happening. American Express, which has long sold itself not so much as a credit card but as a members-only club whose annual fee affords particular benefits (status, higher spending limits), launched a series of television and web ads in 2013 touting its "intelligent security" system, which sends alerts to customers' mobile phones the moment Amex spots a suspicious charge that might indicate fraud. One ad shows a trim, well-dressed city dweller walking beneath surveillance cameras, past the security guards in his elegant apartment lobby, and next to speeding police cars as a narrator asks, "But who looks after us online, where we spend more than two hundred billion dollars a year?" Answer: American Express does, with an algorithm that learns your personal spending patterns and spots anomalies. (The narrator, incidentally, is actress Claire Danes, who plays a CIA agent obsessed with stopping another terrorist attack in the United States in the Showtime series *Homeland*.)

Of course, credit card companies have been using fraud-detection systems for years, but they've only recently begun marketing them as a lifestyle service, in response to their customers' dawning awareness that they and their money are vulnerable online. Our hip cardholder gets an alert on his iPhone and, standing in the middle of a crowded street, informs American Express that, no, he didn't authorize that $1,245 purchase made nine seconds ago on an electronics website. He relaxes over lunch at a diner and confidently plops down his Amex card, knowing that he's "a member of a more secure world." The message is inescapable. You can be safe. (You should *want* to be safe.) But it's going to cost you.

In February 2014, the Obama administration came out with a set of voluntary cyber security guidelines and "best practices" that it encouraged companies to adopt. But it wouldn't force them to do so. "At the end of the day it's the market that's going to drive the business case" and determine whether companies follow the guidelines, said a senior administration official.

Companies will also be responsible for the most innovation in cyber security — the new tools and techniques to keep data safe, and to attack their adversaries. Cyber security companies will attract the most highly skilled employees because they'll pay vastly higher salaries than government agencies and militaries. The government will never be able to offer competitive wages to skilled technology workers. To attract talent, the government and the military will offer the promise of adventurous work — espionage, combat — and will appeal to a sense of duty and honor that has always been the allure of public service. But this won't be sufficient to address the security shortcomings that the government will face, particularly in the civilian agencies where security in some organizations is still appallingly inadequate. You're far more likely to call the Veterans Affairs Department, which has repeatedly lost track of patient information, including their Social Security numbers and other sensitive records, than you are the CIA, which practices generally good defense. And yet the places in government where citizens' information is most vulnerable are usually the least defended.

Agencies that can't hire their own defenders will hire the corporations, whose ranks are stocked with well-trained former government and military personnel, and whose leaders were once themselves in charge of so many of the government's cyber security programs and operations. Public service is already seen as a pathway to private enrichment. Government agencies and the military now plan for the fact that most new employees stay long enough to acquire training, a top-secret security clearance (an absolute requirement for cyber security work), and a base of professional contacts and acquaintances before heading off to industry. This is the classic revolving door between government and business. It will spin faster.

The US government will continue sharing classified threat signatures with Internet service providers, who will use them to scan their customers' traffic. That means your e-mail, your web searches, the sites you visit. Congress will have to enact laws for some of this security by government proxy to happen more frequently than it does now. The service providers, as well as other companies that store and transmit personal information, have demanded assurances that if they give data to the government, they won't be held liable for any privacy violations that might occur with how it's handled. Some of these companies also want to be given immunity in case they fail to respond to a cyber attack that results in physical damage or loss of information. Once those liability protections are in place, the government will look to Internet service providers in particular to mount a more forceful defense of cyberspace. These five thousand or so providers and carriers that effectively run the infrastructure of cyberspace will be expected to stop selling Internet domains to cybercriminals; to shut down service to known or suspected malicious actors; and to reroute or cut off traffic during a major cyber attack.

Some observers have likened today's cybercriminals and malicious hackers to pirates in seventeenth-century Europe. The comparison is apt and instructive. English pirates once roamed the open seas, harassing commercial traders and bedeviling more powerful sovereign navies, mainly the Spanish. Chinese cyber spies are like those pirates, operating on behalf of their government but with enough remove or obfuscation to create plausible deniability, so that the government can claim to be powerless to rein them in. At the highest levels of government, this façade is eroding. US officials have privately and publicly called on the Chinese government to end the cyber piracy all sides know it's committing. But in that same vein of piracy, governments might employ cyber privateers to combat threats. The modern equivalent of a letter of marque, or a traditional bounty system, may be employed to allow private cyber warriors to attack criminals and spies, or at least to employ the euphemistic "active defense" that is the trademark of the NSA. To be sure, the state of cyber security would have to be far worse than it is now for governments to resort to such mercenary tactics. But the companies with the requisite skills for the job are in business today. It might seem implausible, but it's not at all impossible that a government could grant special exemptions to certain firms allowing them to hack back against dangerous targets, especially during a major cyber attack that threatened critical infrastructure.

Governments will still forbid companies from launching private cyber wars — that includes hacking back as retaliation for a theft or an attack on a privately owned network. But there will have to be rules that recognize the legitimate right to self-defense. Will these rules take the form of law? Perhaps in the long run. But in the nearer term they will take the form of generally accepted norms of behavior, and they will be extremely difficult to regulate. As soon as one company hacks back in self-defense, another will feel justified in doing the same, even if the law doesn't expressly allow it. Private cyber wars are probably inevitable. Someday soon a company is going to bait intruders with documents loaded with viruses that destroy the intruder's network when opened. That provocation will escalate into a duel. Then governments will have to step in to defuse the crisis or — in the worst case — forcefully respond to it.

But to protect people from day-to-day threats, which pose less risk to life and limb, companies will create Internet safe zones. Banks have tried to get rid of the .com domain name for their websites and replace it with .bank or with their company name. They hope this will signal to customers that they're communicating with a legitimate bank and not a scam site. But companies will also build entire cyber infrastructures in which security is rooted in the foundations, and where traffic is more actively and closely patrolled than it is on the public Internet. These will be the online equivalent of gated communities. And like any private organization, its owners may restrict membership, write and enforce rules, and offer special benefits, namely, safety. Imagine all the services you rely on in your daily life — your bank, your e-mail service, your favorite stores — running in this private network, or in several of them. Inside, the owner scrutinizes traffic for malware, alerts you to a potential theft or breach of your personal information, and keeps tabs on who's trying to get into the networks and keeps out any suspicious characters. It is, in effect, like the top-secret networks the military uses. It won't be impervious to assault — neither are the military's, as the Buckshot Yankee operation showed. But they will afford a higher level of security than what you have now in the mostly ungoverned expanse of the Internet.

Who would build such a community? Perhaps Amazon. In fact, it has already built a version — for the CIA. Amazon Web Services, which hosts other companies' data and computing operations, has a $600 million contract to build a private system, or cloud, for the spy agency. But unlike other clouds, which are accessed through the public Internet, this one will be run this one using Amazon's own hardware and network equipment. Amazon hasn't historically offered private clouds to its customers, but the CIA may be on the frontier of a new market.

In the near future, you may be spending more of your time inside these protected communities. And the price for entry will be your identity. The company will need to know who you are but, more important, where you and your computer or mobile device are physically located. The ability to attribute your location will help the safe zone know whether you are more likely a friend or a foe. And it will let them kick you out should you violate the rules. Anonymity will be perceived as a threat. It will mean you have something to hide, like a malicious hacker who masks his true location by hijacking a server in a different country. You will carry a credential, analogous to a photo ID or passport, that says you belong in the safe zone, and that you consent to its rules in exchange for protection. Security in cyberspace won't be your right. It will be your privilege. And you will pay for it.

The fundamental questions facing our future in cyberspace aren't whether we should govern it or create laws and rules to regulate behavior there. Ungoverned spaces fall apart. They're unhealthy. They become safe havens for criminals and terrorists. No one is seriously proposing a future with no rules. The dilemma is how much relative weight we give to security in cyberspace, and who should be responsible for it. Which transactions, and how many of them, do we subject to scrutiny? All e-mails? All web searches? All purchases? And by whom? Should people be allowed to opt out of a more secure cyberspace in favor of one that gives them anonymity? We've never recognized a right to remain anonymous. But cyberspace affords us the capability. And for many, it is the essence of free expression that the Internet is meant to foster. The US government embraced that concept when it helped to build Tor.

And what of privacy? Our vocabulary for describing that concept has been rendered useless by the pervasiveness of the surveillance state. Most of the information the US intelligence agencies collect on American citizens consists of logs and records, so-called metadata, that are not protected by the Fourth Amendment from search and seizure. When people talk about a right to privacy online, do they really mean a right to remain anonymous? To be unrecognizable to the surveillance state? From the government's perspective, that immediately makes one suspect. A potential threat. It's why the NSA ultimately devoted so much time to undermining the Tor network. Anonymity and collective security may be incompatible in cyberspace. They will certainly remain in tension for years to come.

We should be skeptical about entrusting governments alone to make the calculations necessary to balance those competing interests. Clandestine intelligence operations aren't the appropriate means of making sound, durable public policy. The NSA conducted mass warrantless surveillance of American citizens for nearly four years, a hidden program, parts of which were almost certainly illegal, that laid the foundations for the military-Internet complex. We didn't know it was rising until it was upon us.

By its own actions, which were directed by two presidents, the NSA has in many respects made the Internet less safe. By injecting malware into tens of thousands of computers and servers around the world, the agency could introduce new vulnerabilities on machines used by innocent people, putting them at greater risk of being attacked or spied upon by third parties, including their own governments. The agency has also made it harder for American companies to do business in a global economy. IBM, Hewlett-Packard, Cisco, and Microsoft all reported falling sales in China and other key markets in the wake of the NSA spying revelations. Foreign countries now view American technology, once the gold standard for performance and innovation, as tools of American spying. To be sure, companies bear a big share of the blame for this, to the extent that they participated in government surveillance programs or knowingly allowed the NSA to install backdoors in their systems. We should be skeptical, too, of corporations deciding how to balance the competing interests of civil liberties and security in cyberspace. But they will certainly have the most direct effect on the future shape of the Internet, and they're already taking steps — largely in opposition to NSA spying — to enhance the security of their products and services. Google, for instance, has now beefed up encryption on its e-mail service, making it harder for spies to read the private communications they intercept. That counts as a win for privacy-conscious consumers. Demand for more secure, potentially more anonymous technologies will fuel a new sector of the high-tech economy: surveillance-proofing yourself in cyberspace.

But the NSA is not the enemy. It's home to indispensable expertise about how to protect computers — and the people who use them — from malevolent actors, whether they're criminals, spies, or soldiers.

The NSA and Cyber Command should build up their capacity to provide for the national defense. But the spy agency has maintained too tight a grip over Cyber Command's evolution. Cyber warfare is properly a military function, and the military, which is controlled by civilians and not soldiers or spies, should take the lead. It should be in charge of integrating cyber warfare into the armed forces' doctrine — just as every modern military in the world undoubtedly will. A future president may elect to separate the leadership of the NSA and Cyber Command, which would go a long way toward maintaining a competent and accountable cyber force.

But cyberspace is too vast, and too pervasive, to allow a single entity to govern it or to dictate the norms of behavior. There is no neat way to define cyberspace. It's not a commons. But it's not private. We have come to depend on it as a public utility — like electricity and water. But it's still mostly a collection of privately owned devices. Fortunately, we are at the dawn of a new age, not its twilight, and there is some time to consider this conundrum, which has confounded every discussion about the nature of this space to which we seem inexorably tied.

But time is running short. Governments and corporations are making the rules as they go, and their actions have had a more tangible effect than many have realized. It's incumbent on everyone who touches cyberspace — which is undeniably a collective — to find what Eisenhower called "essential agreement on issues of great moment, the wise resolution of which will better shape the future of the nation." As anxious as Eisenhower was about the emergence of powerful and potentially destructive new technologies, he was more wary of a "scientific-technological elite" who claimed to know best how to make decisions that free people could make for themselves. It was the entitlement of the military-industrial complex that Eisenhower feared most. And his reminder to remain vigilant to the "rise of misplaced power" resonates as much now as it did then. "We should take nothing for granted. Only an alert and knowledgeable citizenry can compel the proper meshing of the huge industrial and military machinery of defense with our peaceful methods and goals, so that security and liberty may prosper together."

ACKNOWLEDGMENTS

BOOK WRITING IS a solitary experience. But publishing a book is a collaborative act. Actually, it's a series of them. I'd like to mention a few people whose guidance, encouragement, support, and time was especially valuable to me along this book's journey.

I long ago ran out of superlatives to describe my agent, Tina Bennett, which, I can attest, is a common problem among her clients. She is one of the most thoughtful people I know, and a tireless advocate for her writers and their work. This is our second book together, and as with the first, she sharpened and refined my ideas and helped me realize what I wanted to say. A writer can have no better companion.

Which is why I'm absurdly lucky to have two of them. I would trust my editor, Eamon Dolan, with my firstborn, which I suppose I did. This is also our second book together, and not that I needed to be reminded of his gifts and generosity, but I was. Eamon didn't just make this book better with his graceful editing and assiduous attention to detail. He helped to conceive a frame for the story. It's not an exaggeration to say that this would have been a different book if not for Eamon — and it would have been an inferior one.

Thank you also to Tina and Eamon's colleagues. Svetlana Katz never missed a beat, answered my every question, and saved my bacon on one occasion. And Ben Hyman kept me on track for the many deadlines that come before and after one actually finishes writing a book. I'm grateful to Margaret Wimberger, who carefully copyedited my manuscript, finding plenty of figurative bolts to tighten and wrinkles to iron. Thanks also to Larry Cooper for shepherding the manuscript through production to eventual publication.

Simon Trewin at WME was an early champion for me and the book in London. He guided my proposal to Simon Thorogood at Headline Publishing Group, whose enthusiasm for this project has been unflagging. I'm so pleased that the book found a home with them, and that more people will have a chance to read it because of their efforts.

I'm grateful to my new friends and colleagues at New America, both for their support for this book and my research and for the intellectual community they've created. I've been thrilled to be a part of it, especially because I've admired the work of New America's scholars for years. Special thanks to Andrés Martinez and Becky Shafer, who so ably corraled and guided our band of fellows. Becky and Kirsten Berg also assisted with research on some crucial chapters in the book, and I'm grateful for their help. Thanks also to Peter Bergen for his kindness and all he's done to support me and my work. Tim Maurer created a series of superb discussions on cyber security that deepened and sharpened my thinking. I'm grateful to Arizona State University and President Michael Crow for their support of my research on the future of war. And thanks to Anne-Marie Slaughter, New America's president and CEO, for her leadership, encouragement, and enthusiasm.

I was the luckiest writer in town to have Denise Wills as my editor for three years at *Washingtonian* magazine, and I'm luckier still to have her as a friend. She's the dream editor — both a coach and a collaborator. So is Noah Shachtman, who brought me back to the news business at *Foreign Policy*. We had rambunctious fun in the few months we worked together, which happened to coincide with the biggest news event of 2013. Good timing, Papi.

Thanks to my colleagues at *Foreign Policy* for making me happy to come to work every day, especially Yochi Dreazen and our news team. Thanks also to Ben Pauker, Peter Scoblic, Mindy Kay Bricker, and David Rothkopf for all they've done guiding this fast-moving and fast-growing ship.

I owe a particular debt of gratitude to the voluminous and insightful reporting of several journalist colleagues whose work informed my own research, including Siobhan Gorman and Danny Yadron at the

Wall Street Journal; David Sanger, Nicole Perlroth, and John Markoff at the *New York Times;* Ellen Nakashima at the *Washington Post;* Tony Romm at *Politico;* Spencer Ackerman at the *Guardian* and formerly of *Wired*'s Danger Room blog; Kim Zetter, also of *Wired* and author of its Threat Level blog; Joseph Menn at Reuters; and Michael Riley at *Bloomberg Businessweek.* Each of them has done groundbreaking work on this terrain.

Thanks to my friend and favorite lunch companion, Ben Wittes, whose blog *Lawfare* is an indispensable destination for serious thinking about national security. Ben has been an unfailing counselor and guide to me over the years, supremely generous with his time and ideas.

Carol Joynt has been a source of fun and laughter, support and wisdom. She's a true pal, and an ace reporter, who has taught and inspired me. Thanks also to Spencer Joynt, both for letting his dear mom stay out late and for his friendship.

Dave Singleton continues to be the best friend a guy can have. It's hard to find someone who can embrace, and frequently tolerate, the many sides of yourself. We met nearly fifteen years ago, and we didn't know at the time we had something so rare. But we do now.

Christopher Kerns makes me laugh hard and think hard at the same time. His willingness to say what he means and to mean what he says has made me a sharper thinker and a stronger journalist. I cherish our conversations, whether over a drink or a long car ride.

Special thanks go to my friends Jason Kello and Jason Wilson, whose thoughtful insights into cyber security — what it looks like now and where it's going — inform so many parts of this book. Their enthusiasm for this subject is infectious. Their ability to translate technical complexity into clear, compelling language is remarkable.

My longtime mentor and friend Anne Laurent has a special place at the heart of everything I write. More than a decade ago she put me on the path of writing about the intersection of technology and security. Surely I wouldn't be here if not for her.

Thanks to my family, particularly my mother and father, Ed and Carol Harris, for being teachers and teammates, and always at the moments I needed them most. To Troy, Susan, and Madelyn Harris, thank you for reminding me every day about the constancy of family. My grandmother, Bettiann Kinney, who taught me to tell stories, continues to be a source of inspiration in more ways than I'd ever expected. To my mother-in-law, Mary de Feo, and my (now legal) extended family, thank you for bringing so much laughter and happiness into my life, and for welcoming me into yours.

Finally, to my husband, Joe de Feo, what could I possibly tell you that you don't already know? Somehow you manage to make me happier every day than I was the last. The months I spent writing this book, sitting with the two little monsters in one room and you working in the other, were some of the happiest we've shared. Thank you for everything you've done for me, and for us. Thank you for centering me. And thank you for being there when I come home. It's my favorite part of the day.

NOTES

Page

Prologue

xiii *He was an ex-military officer:* This account is based on interviews with a number of former Defense Department officials, as well as news reports.

xiv *About 7.5 million lines:* "Joint Strike Fighter: Strong Risk Management Essential as Program Enters Most Challenging Phase," US Government Accountability Office, GAO-09-711T, May 20, 2009, http://www.gao.gov/products/GAO-09 -711T.

xv *In 2006 it held at least $33.5 billion:* "Top 200 Contractors," *Government Executive,* August 15, 2007, http://www.govexec.com/magazine/2007/08/top-200 -contractors/25086/.

The spies had made off: "Computer Spies Breach Fighter-Jet Project," *Wall Street Journal,* April 21, 2009, http://online.wsj.com/news/articles/SB124027491029 837401.

xvi *The spies had penetrated:* "Security Experts Admit China Stole Secret Fighter Jet Plans," *Australian,* March 12, 2012, http://www.theaustralian.com.au/news/ world/security-experts-admit-china-stole-secret-fighter-jet-plans/story-fn b640i6-1226296400154#mm-premium.

xvii *It bore a number of design:* Andrea Shalal-Esa, "Pentagon Sees Risks, Progress on Lockheed's F-35 Jet," Reuters, April 24, 2013, http://www.reuters.com/article /2013/04/25/us-lockheed-fighter-idUSBRE93O00E20130425.

The CEOs weren't sure: Author interviews with meeting participants and others who were briefed afterward, as well as Defense Department officials who worked on the DIB program. Interviews included Robert Lentz, the deputy assistant defense secretary who oversaw the initiative; James Lewis, a cyber security expert with the Center for Strategic and International Studies in Washington, DC; and Steve Hawkins, vice president of information security solutions at Raytheon, 2009. Also air force general Michael Basla, 2013.

xviii *"A lot of people went":* Author interview with James Lewis, April 2009.

After the meeting the Defense Department: Author interviews with current and former Defense Department and Homeland Security Department officials, as well as corporate executives, 2009 and 2013.

xx *"cyber Pearl Harbor":* Panetta spoke aboard the Intrepid Sea, Air & Space Museum in New York City on October 12, 2012, http://www.defensenews.com/article/20121012/DEFREG02/310120001/Text-Speech-by-Defense-U-S-Secretary-Leon-Panetta.

Five months earlier President Barack Obama: Barack Obama, "Taking the Cyberattack Threat Seriously," *Wall Street Journal,* July 19, 2012, http://online.wsj.com/news/articles/SB10000872396390444330904577535492693044650.

xxi *FBI director James Comey:* Comey testified before the Senate Committee on Homeland Security and Governmental Affairs on November 14, 2013, http://www.fbi.gov/news/testimony/homeland-threats-and-the-fbis-response.

xxiii *In 2014 the government planned:* Chris Strohm and Todd Shields, "Obama Boosts Pentagon Cyber Budget Amid Rising Attacks," Bloomberg.com, April 11, 2013, http://www.bloomberg.com/news/2013-04-10/lockheed-to-general-dynamics-target-shift-to-cyber-spend.html.

To put that in some perspective: Federal Climate Change Expenditures Report to Congress, August 2013, http://www.whitehouse.gov/sites/default/files/omb/assets/legislative_reports/fcce-report-to-congress.pdf.

1. The First Cyber War

3 *Bob Stasio never planned:* Author interview, October 2013.

7 *In May 2007:* The account of the meeting is based on two lengthy interviews with Mike McConnell, then the president's director of national intelligence, as well as an interview with Fran Townsend, then Bush's counterterrorism adviser, and Dale Meyerrose, a retired air force general who was then a senior official in the Office of the Director of National Intelligence. The operational details of the NSA and the military's cyber activities in Iraq come from three former military intelligence officers who participated in the operations and asked not to be identified. Other officials, including David Petraeus, former commander of US forces in Iraq, have spoken publicly about cyber operations in Iraq and the contribution they made to the US victory there.

11 *The president had already okayed:* In addition to the author's own interviews with current and former US officials and computer security experts, information about the Stuxnet campaign was drawn from voluminous research papers and news articles, of which the following provided key details: Ralph Langner, "Stuxnet's Secret Twin," *Foreign Policy,* November 21, 2013, http://www.foreignpolicy.com/articles/2013/11/19/stuxnets_secret_twin_iran_nukes_cyber_attack#sthash.nq7VuMAC.8FWcquMx.dpbs; David Sanger, "Obama Ordered Sped Up Wave of Cyberattacks Against Iran," *New York Times,* June 1, 2012, http://www.nytimes.com/2012/06/01/world/middleeast/obama-ordered-wave

-of-cyberattacks-against-iran.html?pagewanted=all; James Bamford, "The Secret War," *Wired,* June 12, 2013, http://www.wired.com/threatlevel/2013/06/
general-keith-alexander-cyberwar/all/; and Jim Finkle, "Researchers Say Stuxnet Was Deployed Against Iran in 2007," Reuters, February 26, 2013, http://www
.reuters.com/article/2013/02/26/us-cyberwar-stuxnet-idUSBRE91P0PP201
30226.

12   *The prior year had been one of the bloodiest:* Casualty statistic from iCasualties
.org, http://icasualties.org/Iraq/index.aspx.
Iraqi civilian deaths: Ibid., http://www.iraqbodycount.org/database/.

13   *By September 2004:* Dana Priest, "NSA Growth Fueled by Need to Target Terrorists," *Washington Post,* July 21, 2013, http://www.washingtonpost
.com/world/national-security/nsa-growth-fueled-by-need-to-target-terrorists
/2013/07/21/24c93cf4-f0b1-11e2-bed3-b9b6fe264871_story.html.

14   *"This trend presents":* David E. Peterson, "Surveillance Slips into Cyberspace,"
Signal, February 2005, http://www.afcea.org/content/?q=node/629.

17   *Their center of operations:* The description comes from several sources, including an interview with a former senior military officer, other military and intelligence officers who worked in Iraq, and press accounts, including Priest, "NSA
Growth"; and Joby Warrick and Robin Wright, "US Teams Weaken Insurgency in
Iraq," *Washington Post,* September 6, 2008, http://articles.washingtonpost.com
/2008-09-06/world/36869600_1_salim-abdallah-ashur-abu-uthman-iraqi
-insurgents. See also David H. Petraeus, "How We Won in Iraq," *Foreign Policy,* October 29, 2013, http://www.foreignpolicy.com/articles/2013/10/29/david_
petraeus_how_we_won_the_surge_in_iraq?page=0,3; and Stanley A. McChrys-
tal, "It Takes a Network," *Foreign Policy,* February 22, 2011, http://www.foreignpolicy
.com/articles/2011/02/22/it_takes_a_network.

19   *In September 2007:* See Eric Schmitt and Thom Shanker, *Counterstrike: The
Untold Story of America's Secret Campaign Against Al Qaeda* (New York: Times
Books, 2011).

21   *The NSA also developed a tool:* Scott Shane, "No Morsel Too Minuscule for
All-Consuming NSA," *New York Times,* November 2, 2013, http://www.ny
times.com/2013/11/03/world/no-morsel-too-minuscule-for-all-consuming-nsa
.html?_r=2&pagewanted=all&&pagewanted=print.
Local Christians who had lived: Ned Parker, "Christians Chased Out of District,"
Los Angeles Times, June 27, 2007, http://articles.latimes.com/2007/jun/27/world
/fg-christians27.

22   *The operation began in June 2007:* "US Launches Major Iraq Offensive," BBC
News, June 19, 2007, http://news.bbc.co.uk/2/hi/middle_east/6766217.stm; and
"Start of 'Arrowhead Ripper' Highlights Iraq Operations," American Forces
Press Service, June 19, 2007, http://www.defense.gov/News/NewsArticle.aspx?
ID=46459.
By one account, it aided: Warrick and Wright, "US Teams Weaken Insurgency."
There were 28 bombings: Ibid.

23 *Petraeus credited this new:* National Security Agency statement on surveillance programs, August 9, 2013, http://cryptome.org/2013/08/nsa-13-0809.pdf. See also Petraeus, "How We Won in Iraq."

2. RTRG

25 *The NSA's headquarters had moved: 60 Years of Defending Our Nation,* an official NSA history, published in 2012 for the agency's anniversary, http://www.nsa .gov/about/cryptologic_heritage/60th/book/NSA_60th_Anniversary.pdf.

29 *A twenty-four-hour watch center:* The description of the so-called President's Surveillance Program and Stellar Wind is drawn from multiple interviews with former government officials, as well as a report by the NSA's inspector general, *ST-09-002* Working Draft, March 24, 2009, which was disclosed by Edward Snowden. A copy of the document is available at http://www.theguardian.com /world/interactive/2013/jun/27/nsa-inspector-general-report-document-data -collection. See also the author's book *The Watchers: The Rise of America's Surveillance State* (New York: Penguin Press, 2010).

33 *In the litany of NSA code words:* Precisely how the NSA comes up with code words is a bit of a mystery. In the 1960s a single NSA employee was responsible for selecting new code words, apparently at random, suggesting that the choice of name has little to do with what the program actually does. See Tom Bowman, "Why Does the NSA Keep an EGOTISTICALGIRAFFE? It's Top Secret," NPR News, November 10, 2013, http://www.npr.org/2013/11/10/244240199/why-does -the-nsa-keep-an-egotisticalgiraffe-its-top-secret.

35 *"This is the kind of guy":* Matt Schudel, "Pedro Luis Rustan, 65, "Pedro Luis Rustan, 65, Aerospace and Surveillance Innovator," Obituaries, *Washington Post,* July 7, 2012, http://articles.washingtonpost.com/2012-07-07/local/35486174_1_ nro-spy-satellites-national-reconnaissance-office.
In a 2010 interview with a trade publication: "Change Agent," *C4ISR Journal,* October 8, 2010, http://www.defensenews.com/article/20101008/C4ISR01/1008 0311/.

38 *"Clearly establishing in the eyes of the Iraqi people":* David H. Petraeus, "How We Won in Iraq," *Foreign Policy,* October 29, 2013, http://www.foreignpolicy.com /articles/2013/10/29/david_petraeus_how_we_won_the_surge_in_iraq? page=0,3.
The agency's elite hacker unit: Craig Whitlock and Barton Gellman, "To Hunt Osama bin Laden, Satellites Watched over Abbottabad, Pakistan, and Navy SEALs," *Washington Post,* August 29, 2013, http://articles.washingtonpost.com /2013-08-29/world/41712137_1_laden-s-osama-bin-laden.

3. Building the Cyber Army

41 *The army got in:* Author interview with former military intelligence officer.

42 *His old patron Dick Cheney informed:* The author conducted a series of interviews with McConnell in his office in 2009.

44 *Just over a month later:* The list of companies subject to Prism surveillance comes from an NSA presentation disclosed by the former contractor Edward Snowden, first published by the *Washington Post* and the *Guardian,* and subsequently republished by numerous journalistic organizations. Details about Prism surveillance also come from author interviews with current and former intelligence officials.

45 *After Senator Barack Obama won:* McConnell interview.

46 *Later, in a private meeting with Bush:* See David Sanger, *Confront and Conceal: Obama's Secret Wars and Surprising Use of American Power* (New York: Crown, 2012).

49 *To find out, on May 7, 2010:* Accounts of the Schriever Wargame 2010, and the lessons the military learned, come from three sources: author interview with Lieutenant General Michael Basla, the air force's chief for information dominance and its chief information officer; *High Frontier: The Journal for Space and Cyberspace Professionals* 7, no. 1, which was entirely devoted to describing and analyzing the game, http://www.afspc.af.mil/shared/media/document/AFD-101116 -028.pdf; and Robert S. Dudney, "Hard Lessons at the Schriever Wargame," *Air Force Magazine* 94, no. 2 (February 2011), http://www.airforcemag.com/Magazine Archive/Pages/2011/February%202011/0211wargame.aspx.

52 *But privately, some intelligence officials:* Author interviews with government officials, industry experts, and business executives. Those interviewed about China's cyber capabilities included Tim Bennett, former president of the Cyber Security Industry Alliance, a leading trade group; Stephen Spoonamore, former CEO of Cybrinth, a cyber security firm with government and corporate clients; and Joel Brenner, head of counterintelligence under the director of national intelligence. See Shane Harris, "China's Cyber-Militia," *National Journal,* May 31, 2008, http:// www.nationaljournal.com/magazine/china-s-cyber-militia-20080531.
 "The hacker was probably": Author interview.

53 *It was six years after lawmakers':* Author interviews with congressional staff and investigators, as well as a confidential briefing prepared by security experts in the House of Representatives, obtained by the author. See Shane Harris, "Hacking the Hill," *National Journal,* December 20, 2008, http://www.nationaljournal .com/magazine/hacking-the-hill-20081220.

54 *The US Chamber of Commerce:* US Chamber of Commerce officials made many comments to this effect. See http://www.pcworld.com/article/260267/senate _delays_maybe_kills_cybersecurity_bill.html.

55 *And the separate directive, known as PDD-20:* A list of Obama's presidential decision directives can be found on the website of the Federation of American Scientists, http://www.fas.org/irp/offdocs/ppd/. PDD-20, which pertains to cyber operations of the military, was leaked by the former NSA contractor Edward Snowden and published in its entirety in June 2013.

57 *"There aren't enough"*: Major General John Davis, speech at the Armed Forces Communications and Electronics Association (AFCEA) International Cyber

Symposium, Baltimore Convention Center, June 25, 2013, http://www.dvidshub
.net/video/294716/mg-davis-afcea#.UpSILmQ6Ve6#ixzz2lkc87oRy.

58   *An NSA unit known as:* Scott Shane, "No Morsel Too Minuscule for All-Consuming N.S.A.," *New York Times,* November 2, 2013, http://www.nytimes.com/2013
/11/03/world/no-morsel-too-minuscule-for-all-consuming-nsa.html.

   In a remarkable shift: See Chairman of the Joint Chiefs of Staff, *Joint Targeting,* Joint Publication 3-60, January 31, 2013, http://cfr.org/content/publications
/attachments/Joint_Chiefs_of_Staff-Joint_Targeting_31_January_2013.pdf.

63   *The attack is launched:* Lieutenant General Herbert Carlisle, then the air force's
deputy chief of staff for operations, told a 2012 defense conference in Washington about the Chinese tactics. See David Fulghum, "China, US Chase Air-to-Air
Cyberweapon," *Aviation Week,* March 9, 2012.

64   *"There is a tremendous amount":* Dune Lawrence and Michael Riley, "A Chinese Hacker's Identity Unmasked," *Bloomberg Businessweek,* February 14, 2013,
http://www.businessweek.com/articles/2013-02-14/a-chinese-hackers-identity
-unmasked.

65   *"There aren't enough":* Davis speech.

66   *"Universities don't want to touch":* Jason Koebler, "NSA Built Stuxnet, but Real
Trick Is Building Crew of Hackers," *US News & World Report,* June 8, 2012,
http://www.usnews.com/news/articles/2012/06/08/nsa-built-stuxnet-but-real
-trick-is-building-crew-of-hackers.

4. The Internet Is a Battlefield

69   *The agency's best-trained:* For more on TAO, see the work of intelligence historian and journalist Matthew Aid, who has written extensively about the unit, including "The NSA's New Code Breakers," *Foreign Policy,* October 16, 2013, http://
www.foreignpolicy.com/articles/2013/10/15/the_nsa_s_new_codebreakers
?page=0%2C1#sthash.jyc1d12P.dpbs.

72   *Edward Snowden told Chinese journalists:* Lana Lam, "NSA Targeted China's
Tsinghua University in Extensive Hacking Attacks, Says Snowden," *South China
Morning Post,* June 22, 2013, http://www.scmp.com/news/china/article/1266892
/exclusive-nsa-targeted-chinas-tsinghua-university-extensive-hacking
?page=all.

73   *According to one international study:* QS World University Rankings, 2013, http://
www.topuniversities.com/university-rankings/university-subject-rankings
/2013/computer-science-and-information-systems.

   That year they also were recognized: Matthew Aid, *Secret Sentry: The Untold History of the National Security Agency* (New York: Bloomsbury Press, 2009), http://
www.amazon.com/The-Secret-Sentry-National-Security/dp/B003L1ZX4S.

   Matthew Aid writes: Matthew Aid, "Inside the NSA's Ultra-Secret China Hacking Group," *Foreign Policy,* October 15, 2013, http://www.foreignpolicy.com
/articles/2013/06/10/inside_the_nsa_s_ultra_secret_china_hacking_group.

74   *In the second half of 2009:* This account was provided by a former employee at the Hawaii center who worked on the operation.

75   *In a top-secret summary:* The Flatliquid operation was first reported by *Der Spiegel,* based on documents provided by former NSA contractor Edward Snowden. See Jens Glüsing et al., "Fresh Leak on US Spying: NSA Accessed Mexican President's Email," *Spiegel Online,* International edition, October 20, 2013, http://www.spiegel.de/international/world/nsa-hacked-e-mail-account-of-mexican-president-a-928817.html.

78   *Several dozen clandestine:* Matthew Aid, "The CIA's New Black Bag Is Digital," *Foreign Policy,* August 18, 2013, http://www.foreignpolicy.com/articles/2013/07/16/the_cias_new_black_bag_is_digital_nsa_cooperation#sthash.XUr4mt5h.dpbs.

The CIA has also set up: Barton Gellman and Ellen Nakashima, "US Spy Agencies Mounted 231 Offensive Cyber-Operations in 2011, Documents Show," *Washington Post,* August 30, 2013, http://articles.washingtonpost.com/2013-08-30/world/41620705_1_computer-worm-former-u-s-officials-obama-administration.

But other data was: See Siobhan Gorman, Adam Entous, and Andrew Dowell, "Technology Emboldened the NSA," *Wall Street Journal,* June 9, 2013, http://online.wsj.com/news/articles/SB10001424127887323495604578535290627442964; and Noah Shachtman, "Inside DARPA's Secret Afghan Spy Machine," Danger Room, *Wired,* July 21, 2011, http://www.wired.com/dangerroom/2011/07/darpas-secret-spy-machine/.

80   *The airman, a linguist:* John Reed, "An Enlisted Airman Deciphered al-Qaeda's 'Conference Call' of Doom," *Foreign Policy,* September 18, 2013.

81   *The conference call was conducted:* Eli Lake and Josh Rogin, "US Intercepted al-Qaeda's 'Legion of Doom' Conference Call," *Daily Beast,* August 7, 2013, http://www.thedailybeast.com/articles/2013/08/07/al-qaeda-conference-call-intercepted-by-u-s-officials-sparked-alerts.html; and Eli Lake, "Courier Led US to al-Qaeda Internet Conference," *Daily Beast,* August 20, 2013, http://www.thedailybeast.com/articles/2013/08/20/exclusive-courier-led-u-s-to-al-qaeda-internet-conference.html.

After he returned from Iraq: Author interview with Bob Stasio, October 14, 2013.

5. The Enemy Among Us

83   *Alexander informed":* Siobhan Gorman, "Costly NSA Initiative Has a Shaky Takeoff," *Baltimore Sun,* February 11, 2007, http://articles.baltimoresun.com/2007-02-11/news/0702110034_1_turbulence-cyberspace-nsa.

84   *So it was hardly surprising:* For details on the NSA's operations against Tor, see Shane Harris and John Hudson, "Not Even the NSA Can Crack the State Department's Favorite Anonymous Network," *Foreign Policy,* October 7, 2013, http://thecable.foreignpolicy.com/posts/2013/10/04/not_even_the_nsa_can_crack_the_state_departments_online_anonymity_tool#sthash.1H45fNxT.dpbs; Bar-

ton Gellman, Craig Timberg, and Steven Rich, "Secret NSA Documents Show Campaign Against Tor Encrypted Network," *Washington Post,* October 4, 2013, http://articles.washingtonpost.com/2013-10-04/world/42704326_1_nsa-officials -national-security-agency-edward-snowden; and James Ball, Bruce Schneir, and Glenn Greenwald, "NSA and GCHQ Target Tor Network That Protects Anonymity of Web Users," *Guardian,* October 4, 2013, http://www.theguardian.com /world/2013/oct/04/nsa-gchq-attack-tor-network-encryption.

85 *The hackers also considered trying:* The presentation can be found at http://www .theguardian.com/world/interactive/2013/oct/04/tor-stinks-nsa-presentation -document.

87 *Under a secret program called:* Author interviews with technology company employees and experts. Also see classified budget documents published by the *New York Times,* which provide further detail about the project, http://www.nytimes .com/interactive/2013/09/05/us/documents-reveal-nsa-campaign-against -encryption.html?ref=us.

Working in conjunction with the FBI: Glenn Greenwald et al., "Microsoft Handed the NSA Access to Encrypted Messages," *Guardian,* July 11, 2013, http://www .theguardian.com/world/2013/jul/11/microsoft-nsa-collaboration-user-data.

89 *But behind the scenes:* See Nicole Perlroth, Jeff Larson, and Scott Shane, "NSA Able to Foil Basic Safeguards of Privacy on the Web," *New York Times,* September 5, 2013, http://www.nytimes.com/2013/09/06/us/nsa-foils-much-internet -encryption.html?pagewanted=all.

The noted computer security expert Bruce Schneier: Bruce Schneier, "Did NSA Put a Secret Backdoor in New Encryption Standard?" *Wired,* November 15, 2007, http://www.wired.com/politics/security/commentary/securitymatters/2007/11 /securitymatters_1115.

90 *The NSA then cited:* Joseph Menn, "Secret Contract Tied NSA and Security Industry Pioneer," Reuters, http://mobile.reuters.com/article/idUSBRE9BJ1C220 131220?irpc=932.

91 *Neuberger called NIST:* The full audio version of the Neuberger interview is at http://www.lawfareblog.com/2013/12/lawfare-podcast-episode-55-inside-nsa -part-iv-we-speak-with-anne-neuberger-the-woman-on-front-lines-of-nsas -relations-with-industry/.

92 *"NIST publicly proposed":* EPIC's findings are summarized at http://epic.org /crypto/dss/new_nist_nsa_revelations.html.

94 *In 1997, according to: Cryptolog: Journal of Technical Health* 23, no. 1 (Spring 1997), http://cryptome.org/2013/03/nsa-cyber-think.pdf.

This gray market is: Information about the zero day gray market comes from author interviews with current and former US officials, as well as technical experts, including Chris Soghoian, principal technologist and senior policy analyst with the ACLU Speech, Privacy and Technology Project. Public documents and news articles provided additional information.

95 *For instance, in 2005:* Tadayoshi Kohno, Andre Broido, and k. c. claffy, "Remote

Physical Device Fingerprinting," http://www.caida.org/publications/papers /2005/fingerprinting/KohnoBroidoClaffy05-devicefingerprinting.pdf.

A year after the paper was published: Steven J. Murdoch, "Hot or Not: Revealing Hidden Services by Their Clock Skew," http://www.cl.cam.ac.uk/~sjm217/papers /ccs06hotornot.pdf. See also Quinn Norton, "Computer Warming a Privacy Risk," *Wired,* December 29, 2006, http://www.wired.com/science/discoveries /news/2006/12/72375.

99   *"We don't sell weapons":* Joseph Menn, "US Cyberwar Strategy Stokes Fear of Blowback," Reuters, May 10, 2013, http://www.reuters.com/article/2013/05/10 /us-usa-cyberweapons-specialreport-idUSBRE9490EL20130510.

100   *In 2013 the NSA had a budget:* Barton Gellman and Ellen Nakashima, "US Spy Agencies Mounted 231 Offensive Cyber-Operations in 2011, Documents Show," *Washington Post,* August 30, 2013, http://articles.washingtonpost.com/2013 -08-30/world/41620705_1_computer-worm-former-u-s-officials-obama -administration.

101   *"Graduates of the program become":* "About the Program," Systems and Network Interdisciplinary Program, http://www.nsa.gov/careers/_files/SNIP.pdf.

The company itself has been the target: John Markoff, "Cyber Attack on Google Said to Hit Password System," *New York Times,* April 19, 2010.

6. The Mercenaries

104   *"Bonesaw is the ability to map":* Aram Roston, "Nathaniel Fick, Former CNAS Chief, to Head Cyber Targeting Firm," *C4ISR Journal,* January–February 2013, http://www.defensenews.com/article/20130115/C4ISR01/301150007/Nathaniel -Fick-Former-CNAS-Chief-Heads-Cyber-Targeting-Firm.

Internal documents show: Michael Riley and Ashlee Vance, "Cyber Weapons: The New Arms Race," *Bloomberg Businessweek,* July 20, 2011, http://www.business week.com/magazine/cyber-weapons-the-new-arms-race-07212011.html#p4.

105   *"Eventually we need to enable":* Andy Greenberg, "Founder of Stealthy Security Firm Endgame to Lawmakers: Let US Companies 'Hack Back,'" *Forbes,* September 20, 2013, http://www.forbes.com/sites/andygreenberg/2013/09/20/founder -of-stealthy-security-firm-endgame-to-lawmakers-let-u-s-companies-hack -back/.

108   *"If you believe that wars":* Joseph Menn, "US Cyberwar Strategy Stokes Fear of Blowback," Reuters, May 10, 2013, http://www.reuters.com/article/2013/05/10 /us-usa-cyberweapons-specialreport-idUSBRE9490EL20130510.

One prominent player: Information about CrowdStrike's techniques is based on author interviews with Steve Chabinksy, the company's general counsel and a former senior FBI official, conducted in July and August 2013. Additional information comes from the company's website.

110   *But in an interview in 2013:* John Seabrook, "Network Insecurity: Are We Losing the Battle Against Cyber Crime?" *New Yorker,* May 20, 2013.

111   *The firm Gamma:* Jennifer Valentino-Devries, "Surveillance Company Says It

Sent Fake iTunes, Flash Updates," *Wall Street Journal,* November 21, 2011, http://blogs.wsj.com/digits/2011/11/21/surveillance-company-says-it-sent-fake-itunes-flash-updates-documents-show/.

112 *Security researchers also claim:* Vernon Silver, "Cyber Attacks on Activists Traced to FinFisher Spyware of Gamma," Bloomberg.com, July 25, 2012, http://www.bloomberg.com/news/2012-07-25/cyber-attacks-on-activists-traced-to-finfisher-spyware-of-gamma.html.

113 *Mansoor had inadvertently:* Vernon Silver, "Spyware Leaves Trail to Beaten Activist Through Microsoft Flaw," Bloomberg.com, October 12, 2012, http://www.bloomberg.com/news/2012-10-10/spyware-leaves-trail-to-beaten-activist-through-microsoft-flaw.html.

114 *Hacking Team had any knowledge:* Adrianne Jeffries, "Meet Hacking Team, the Company That Helps the Police Hack You," *The Verge,* September 13, 2013, http://www.theverge.com/2013/9/13/4723610/meet-hacking-team-the-company-that-helps-police-hack-into-computers.

In the fall of 2010: Shane Harris, "Killer App: Have a Bunch of Silicon Valley Geeks at Palantir Technologies Figured Out How to Stop Terrorists?" *Washingtonian,* January 31, 2012, http://www.washingtonian.com/articles/people/killer-app/.

117 *The company claimed that:* Sindhu Sundar, "LabMD Says Gov't Funded the Data Breach at Probe's Center," Law360, http://www.law360.com/articles/488953/labmd-says-gov-t-funded-the-data-breach-at-probe-s-center.

According to court documents: The court document can be read at https://www.courtlistener.com/ca11/5cG6/labmd-inc-v-tiversa-inc/?q=%22computer+fraud+and+abuse+act%22&refine=new&sort=dateFiled+desc.

118 *"It is illegal":* Author interview.

In June 2013, Microsoft joined: Jim Finkle, "Microsoft, FBI Take Aim at Global Cyber Crime Ring," Reuters, June 5, 2013, http://www.reuters.com/article/2013/06/05/net-us-citadel-botnet-idUSBRE9541KO20130605.

119 *The company's lawyers had used novel:* Jennifer Warnick, "Digital Detectives: Inside Microsoft's Headquarters for the Fight Against Cybercrime" Microsoft/Stories, http://www.microsoft.com/en-us/news/stories/cybercrime/index.html.

120 *A survey of 181 attendees:* nCirle, Black Hat Survey, *BusinessWire,* July 2012, http://www.businesswire.com/news/home/20120726006045/en/Black-Hat-Survey-36-Information-Security-Professionals#.UtMp8WRDtYo.

Rick Howard: Author interview, August 2013.

7. Cops Become Spies

124 *It's called the Data Intercept Technology Unit:* Information about the unit comes from author interviews with current and former law enforcement officials, technology industry representatives, and legal experts, conducted in November 2013, as well as information on FBI websites. For more on Magic Lantern, see Bob

Sullivan, "FBI Software Cracks Encryption Wall," MSNBC, November 20, 2001, http://www.nbcnews.com/id/3341694/ns/technology_and_science-security/t /fbi-software-cracks-encryption-wall/#.UsWEOmRDtYo. See also Ted Bridis, "FBI Develops Eavesdropping Tools," Associated Press, November 21, 2001, http://globalresearch.ca/articles/BRI111A.html.

127   *"The bureau tends":* Author interview, October 2013.
      The number of counterterrorism agents: G. W. Shulz, "FBI Agents Dedicated to Terror Doubled in Eight Years," Center for Investigative Reporting, April 26, 2010, http://cironline.org/blog/post/fbi-agents-dedicated-terror-doubled-eight -years-671.

128   *"We do a lot of collection":* Author interview, November 2013.

131   *The next morning, according to:* Friedman's account can be read at http://www .stratfor.com/weekly/hack-stratfor.
      One of the hackers: Vivien Lesnik Weisman, "A Conversation with Jeremy Hammond, American Political Prisoner Sentenced to 10 Years," *Huffington Post,* November 19, 2013, http://www.huffingtonpost.com/vivien-lesnik-weisman /jeremy-hammond-q-and-a_b_4298969.html.

132   *But Stratfor wasn't:* Nicole Perlroth, "Inside the Stratfor Attack," Bits, *New York Times,* March 12, 2012, http://bits.blogs.nytimes.com/2012/03/12/inside-the-strat for-attack/?_r=0.

133   *But the hackers also:* Ibid.
      It also settled a class-action: Basil Katz, "Stratfor to Settle Class Action Suit Over Hack," Reuters, June 27, 2012, http://www.reuters.com/article/2012/06/28/us-strat for-hack-lawsuit-idUSBRE85R03720120628.

134   *In 2013 the Justice Department:* Matthew J. Schwartz, "Anonymous Hacker Claims FBI Directed LulzSec Hacks," Dark Reading, *InformationWeek,* August 27, 2013, http://www.informationweek.com/security/risk-management/anonymous -hacker-claims-fbi-directed-lulzsec-hacks/d/d-id/1111306?.
      "What many do not know": Hammond's statement can be read at http://freejeremy .net/yours-in-struggle/statement-by-jeremy-hammond-on-sabus-sentencing/.

8. *"Another Manhattan Project"*

139   *"Is there anything else?":* The account of the meeting is based on two lengthy interviews with Mike McConnell, then the president's director of national intelligence, as well as an interview with Fran Townsend, then Bush's counterterrorism adviser, and retired air force general Dale Meyerrose, then a senior official in the Office of the Director of National Intelligence, 2009 and 2010.

140   *Among the secret plans and designs:* The list of weapons and technologies is contained in a report from the Defense Science Board, *Resilient Military Systems and the Advanced Cyber Threat,* released in January 2013, http://www.acq.osd.mil /dsb/reports/ResilientMilitarySystems.CyberThreat.pdf. The list itself was not made public but was obtained by the *Washington Post* and can be read at http://

www.washingtonpost.com/world/national-security/a-list-of-the-us-weapons
-designs-and-technologies-compromised-by-hackers/2013/05/27/a95b2b12
-c483-11e2-9fe2-6ee52d0eb7c1_story.html.

143   *That in itself was an extraordinary:* See David Petraeus, "How We Won in
Iraq," *Foreign Policy,* October 29, 2013, http://www.foreignpolicy.com/articles
/2013/10/29/david_petraeus_how_we_won_the_surge_in_iraq?page=0,3.
"part sensor, part sentry": William J. Lynn III, "Defending a New Domain: The
Pentagon's Cyberstrategy," *Foreign Affairs,* September/October 2010, http://www
.foreignaffairs.com/articles/66552/william-j-lynn-iii/defending-a-new
-domain.

9. Buckshot Yankee

146   *Friday, October 24, 2008:* Details of the Buckshot Yankee operation come from
author interviews with current and former military and intelligence officials, including General Michael Basla, in June 2013, and a Defense Department analyst
who participated in the program, in November 2013. Supplementary sources include: Ellen Nakashima, "Cyber-Intruder Sparks Massive Cyber Response — and
Debate Over Dealing with Threats," *Washington Post,* December 8, 2011, http://
www.washingtonpost.com/national/national-security/cyber-intruder-sparks
-response-debate/2011/12/06/gIQAxLuFgO_story.html; Jason Healey, ed., *A
Fierce Domain: Conflict in Cyberspace 1986 to 2012* (Vienna, VA: Cyber Conflict
Studies Association, 2013); and William J. Lynn III, "Defending a New Domain:
The Pentagon's Cyberstrategy," *Foreign Affairs,* September/October 2010, http://
www.foreignaffairs.com/articles/66552/william-j-lynn-iii/defending-a-new
-domain.

147   *"In so many words":* Author interview, June 2013.

150   *"It opened all our eyes":* Author interview, June 2013.
According to a former Defense Department: Author interview, November 2013.

151   *Some officials who worked:* Noah Shachtman, "Insiders Doubt 2008 Pentagon
Hack Was Foreign Spy Attack," *Danger Room, Wired,* August 25, 2010, http://
www.wired.com/dangerroom/2010/08/insiders-doubt-2008-pentagon-hack
-was-foreign-spy-attack/.
"Alexander created this aura": Author interview with former administration official who worked with Alexander and the White House on cyber security, August
2013.

152   *"If you pulled out a USB":* Author interview, March 2012.

10. The Secret Sauce

153   *During the campaign, Obama staffers':* Michael Isikoff, "Chinese Hacked Obama,
McCain Campaigns, Took Internal Documents, Officials Say," NBC News, June
6, 2013, http://investigations.nbcnews.com/_news/2013/06/06/18807056-chinese
-hacked-obama-mccain-campaigns-took-internal-documents-officials-say.
Now, as the forty-fourth president: "Securing Cyberspace for the 44th Presidency,"

Center for Strategic and International Studies, December 2008, http://csis.org
/files/media/csis/pubs/081208_securingcyberspace_44.pdf.

Among them were: Author interviews with current and former US officials and a
technical expert who analyzed Chinese spyware, May 2008.

154 *But these and other incursions:* Author interview, 2013.

In a particularly clever: An account of the spear phishing is contained in a State Department cable published by WikiLeaks. See also the author's "Chinese Spies May
Have Tried to Impersonate Journalist Bruce Stokes," *Washingtonian,* February
2, 2011, http://www.washingtonian.com/blogs/capitalcomment/washingtonian
/chinese-spies-may-have-tried-to-impersonate-journalist-bruce-stokes.php.

155 *Also in 2009 a senior:* Author interviews with a current State Department official
and a former State Department official, 2012–2013.

Charlie Croom, a retired: Author interview, January 2014.

Obama didn't say where, but intelligence: The link between hackers and the Brazilian blackouts was first reported by CBS News' *60 Minutes,* November 6, 2009,
http://www.cbsnews.com/news/cyber-war-sabotaging-the-system-06-11-2009/.
In January 2008, Tom Donahue, the CIA's chief cyber security officer, said publicly that hackers had breached the computer systems of utility companies outside the United States and had demanded ransom. Donahue spoke at a security
conference in New Orleans. "All involved intrusions through the Internet," he
said. He didn't name the countries or cities affected.

156 *Owners and operators:* See Shane Harris, "China's Cyber-Militia," *National Journal,*
May 31, 2008, http://www.nationaljournal.com/magazine/china-s-cyber-militia
-20080531.

He was carrying: Author interview with former US official. 2013.

158 *At NSA the plan:* Author interviews with former intelligence and administration
officials, 2011–2013.

159 *Alexander told them:* Author interviews with two congressional staff members
who were in meetings with Alexander, as well as a former administration official
who worked with Alexander and the White House on cyber security issues, August 2013.

"They're pretty mad": Author interview with former congressional staff member
who was in the room, October 2013.

160 *By the time she arrived:* Information about Lute's work at the Homeland Security
Department comes from former department officials who worked with her, a
senior law enforcement official who works on cyber security issues with multiple
agencies and their senior officials, and congressional staff members who work on
committees that oversee aspects of the Homeland Security Department's mission.

Homeland Security's computer-emergency watch: Richard L. Skinner, "Einstein
Presents Big Challenge to U.S.-CERT," GovInfo Security, June 22, 2010, http://
www.govinfosecurity.com/einstein-presents-big-challenge-to-us-cert-a-2677/
op-1.

In March, Rod Beckstrom quit: Beckstrom's resignation letter was published by the *Wall Street Journal,* http://online.wsj.com/public/resources/documents/ BeckstromResignation.pdf.

161 *Practically a technophobe:* Author interview, September 28, 2012.

"Pretend the Manhattan": Author interviews with two former administration officials, September and October 2013.

162 *"There's a presumption":* Author interview with senior law enforcement official, September 2013.

"His attitude was, 'If'": Author interview with former senior security official, October 2013.

"I've been behind the curtain": Author interview with former administration official who worked with Alexander and the White House on cyber security issues, August 2013.

"I do not have the authority": Keith Alexander spoke on February 9, 2011, at the AFCEA Defending America Cyberspace Symposium. See http://www.sotera defense.com/media/events/afcea-defending-america-cyberspace-symposium -2011/. A senior US law enforcement official also provided an account of the dueling speeches and op-eds between Alexander and Lute.

163 *On February 14, three days:* Jane Holl Lute and Bruce McConnell, "A Civil Perspective on Cybersecurity," Threat Level, *Wired,* February 14, 2011, http://www .wired.com/threatlevel/2011/02/dhs-op-ed/.

He gave his speech: Declan McCullagh, "NSA Chief Wants to Protect 'Critical' Private Networks," CNET, February 17, 2011, http://news.cnet.com/8301-31921_3 -20033126-281.html.

"There's a lot of folks": Keith Alexander spoke on February 22, 2011, at the AFCEA Homeland Security Conference in Washington, DC. "CyberCom Commander Calls for Government Protection of Critical Infrastructure," *Homeland Security News Wire,* February 23, 2011, http://www.homelandsecuritynewswire.com /cybercom-commander-calls-government-protection-critical-infrastructure. The entirety of Alexander's speech can be watched at http://www.youtube.com /watch?v=Z_lLSP_1Ngo.

164 *Of fifty-two cases:* Ellen Nakashima, "Cyber Defense Effort Is Mixed, Study Finds," *Washington Post,* January 12, 2012, http://www.washingtonpost.com /world/national-security/cyber-defense-effort-is-mixed-study-finds/2012/01/11 /gIQAAuoYtP_story.html.

166 *"They thought he was an idiot":* Author interview, August 2013.

167 *"Halfway through the meeting":* Author interview with Steve Chabinsky, July 2013.

168 *"The Russians will alert":* Author interview with senior law enforcement official, October 2013.

169 *As of 2013, the NSA:* Keith Alexander provided the figures on NSA employment in public remarks at a cyber security event sponsored by *Politico* in Washing-

ton, DC, on October 8, 2013, http://www.politico.com/events/cyber-7-the-seven
-key-questions/.

11. The Corporate Counterstrike

171 *"a highly sophisticated"*: David Drummond, "A New Approach to China," Google
blog, January 12, 2010, http://googleblog.blogspot.com/2010/01/new-approach
-to-china.html.
"crown jewels": John Markoff, "Cyberattack on Google Said to Hit Password
System," *New York Times,* April 19, 2010, http://www.nytimes.com/2010/04/20
/technology/20google.html?_r=0.

172 *"Google broke in"*: Author conversation with said official, February 2013.
Google uncovered evidence: For more on Google's investigation, see David E.
Sanger and John Markoff, "After Google's Stand on China, US Treads Lightly,"
New York Times, January 14, 2010, http://www.nytimes.com/2010/01/15/world
/asia/15diplo.html?_r=0.

173 *Deputy Secretary of State James Steinberg :* Author interview with a US intelligence agency consultant with knowledge of the conversation, February 2010.
In a separate interview with Steinberg, in October 2013, he said he could not
recall if he learned the news at the cocktail party, but he confirmed that Google
approached the State Department the night before going public and informed
officials of its intentions.

174 *"It gave us an opportunity"*: Author interview.

175 *"cooperative research and development agreement"*: Siobhan Gorman and Jessica
E. Vascarellaro, "Google Working with NSA to Investigate Cyber Attack," *Wall
Street Journal,* February 4, 2010, http://online.wsj.com/news/articles/SB1000142
4052748704041504575044920905689954?mod=WSJ_latestheadlines. News of the
agreement between the NSA and Google was first reported in the *Washington
Post,* Ellen Nakashima, "Google to Enlist NSA to Help It Ward Off Cyberattacks,"
February 4, 2010, http://www.washingtonpost.com/wp-dyn/content/article/2010
/02/03/AR2010020304057.html.

176 *The government could command:* See NSA's Prism overview presentation at
http://s3.documentcloud.org/documents/807036/prism-entier.pdf.

177 *Shortly after the China revelation:* Michael Riley, "US Agencies Said to Swap Data
with Thousands of Firms," Bloomberg.com, June 15, 2013, http://www.bloom
berg.com/news/2013-06-14/u-s-agencies-said-to-swap-data-with-thousands-of
-firms.html.
A security research firm soon: Kim Zetter, "Google Hackers Targeted Source
Code of More Than 30 Companies," Threat Level, *Wired,* January 13, 2010, http://
www.wired.com/threatlevel/2010/01/google-hack-attack/.

178 *"The scope of this"*: Kim Zetter, "Report Details Hacks Targeting Google, Others," Threat Level, *Wired,* February 3, 2010, http://www.wired.com/threatlevel
/2010/02/apt-hacks/.

179 *"They indoctrinate someone":* Author interview, August 2013.

180 *"We scare the bejeezus":* Tom Gjelten, "Cyber Briefings 'Scare the Bejeezus' Out of CEOs," NPR, May 9, 2012, http://www.npr.org/2012/05/09/152296621/cyber-briefings-scare-the-bejeezus-out-of-ceos.

181 *Several classified programs allow:* Author interviews with current and former intelligence officials and security experts. See also Riley, "US Agencies Said to Swap Data."

   Microsoft, for instance: Ibid. Glenn Greenwald et al., "Microsoft Handed the NSA Access to Encrypted Messages," *Guardian,* July 11, 2013, http://www.theguardian.com/world/2013/jul/11/microsoft-nsa-collaboration-user-data

   Cisco, one of the world's: Author interview.

   And McAfee: See Riley, "US Agencies Said to Swap."

   In 2010 a researcher at IBM: Andy Greenberg, "Cisco's Backdoor for Hackers," *Forbes,* February 3, 2010, http://www.forbes.com/2010/02/03/hackers-networking-equipment-technology-security-cisco.html?partner=relatedstoriesbox.

182 *The Homeland Security Department also conducts:* The list of meetings and their agenda can be found at http://www.dhs.gov/cross-sector-working-groups.

184 *After the terrorist attacks, the NSA:* See the case documents for *USA v. Nacchio,* in particular "Exhibit 1 to Mr. Nacchio's Reply to SEC. 5 Submission," which contains FBI Form 302 Regarding November 14, 2005, Interview of James F. X. Payne, a former Qwest executive. See also Shane Harris, *The Watchers: The Rise of America's Surveillance State* (New York: Penguin Press, 2010), p. 16, which describes in further detail the interactions between Qwest and the NSA.

   To obtain the information: See the Homeland Security Department's list of critical infrastructure sectors, http://www.dhs.gov/critical-infrastructure-sectors.

185 *In a speech in 2013:* Major General John Davis, Speech to the Armed Forces Communications and Electronics Association (AFCEA) International Cyber Symposium, Baltimore Convention Center, June 25, 2013, http://www.dvidshub.net/video/294716/mg-davis-afcea#.UpSILmQ6Ve6#ixzz2lkc87oRy.

12. Spring Awakening

187 *In March of that year:* Author interviews with current and former US officials and security experts, including a spokesperson for the Homeland Security Department, May 2012. A subsequent interview was conducted in October 2013 with a former senior FBI official who worked on the case. The intrusions against natural gas companies were first reported in Mark Clayton, "Alert: Major Cyber Attack Aimed at Natural Gas Pipeline Companies," *Christian Science Monitor,* May 5, 2012, http://www.csmonitor.com/USA/2012/0505/Alert-Major-cyber-attack-aimed-at-natural-gas-pipeline-companies.

188 *But at the height of the Cold War:* See Thomas Reed, *At the Abyss: An Insider's History of the Cold War* (New York: Presidio Press, 2004).

   The alerts from companies: Author interview, October 2013.

They shared "mitigation strategies": Author interview with Homeland Security Department official, May 2012.

189 *That summer,* Homeland Security: Information Sharing Environment 2013 Annual Report to the Congress, http://www.ise.gov/annual-report/section1.html #section-4.

190 *Homeland Security, the FBI, the Energy Department:* Department of Homeland Security Industrial Control Systems Cyber Emergency Response Team, *Monthly Monitor* (ICS — MM201310), July–September 2013, released October 31, 2013, http://ics-cert.us-cert.gov/sites/default/files/Monitors/NCCIC_ICS-CERT _Monitor_Jul-Sep2013.pdf.

Shell, Schlumberger, and other: Zain Shauk, "Phishing Still Hooks Energy Workers," *FuelFix,* December 22, 2013, http://fuelfix.com/blog/2013/12/22/phishing -still-hooks-energy-workers/.

In a rare public appearance: Berlin spoke at a cyber security conference at the Newsuem in Washington, DC, on May 22, 2013.

191 *A few months after the intrusions:* Brian Krebs, "Chinese Hackers Blamed for Intrusion at Energy industry Giant Telvent," *KrebsonSecurity,* September 26, 2012, http://krebsonsecurity.com/2012/09/chinese-hackers-blamed-for-intrusion-at -energy-industry-giant-telvent/.

But the country also needs: World Bank, "GDP Growth," http://data.worldbank .org/indicator/NY.GDP.MKTP.KD.ZG

China is the world's second-largest: US Energy Information Administration, http://www.eia.gov/countries/country-data.cfm?fips=CH.

192 *At least one US energy company:* Michael Riley and Dune Lawrence, "Hackers Linked to China's Army Seen from E.U. to D.C.," Bloomberg.com, July 26, 2012, http://www.bloomberg.com/news/2012-07-26/china-hackers-hit-eu-point -man-and-d-c-with-byzantine-candor.html.

And the country has pursued legitimate paths: Ryan Dezember and James T. Areddy, "China Foothold in US Energy," *Wall Street Journal,* March 6, 2012, http://online.wsj.com/news/articles/SB10001424052970204883304577223083067 806776.

193 *By one estimate, the flow:* Nicole Perlroth and Quentin Hardy, "Bank Hacking Was the Work of Iranians, Officials Say," *New York Times,* January 8, 2013, http:// www.nytimes.com/2013/01/09/technology/online-banking-attacks-were-work -of-iran-us-officials-say.html?pagewanted=all&_r=3&.

The banks' Internet service providers: Author interview with Mark Weatherford, August 2013.

194 *"For the first two or three weeks":* Ibid.

195 *Reportedly, the Iranian regime:* Yaakov Katz, "Iran Embarks on $1b. Cyber-Warfare Program," *Jerusalem Post,* December 18, 2011, http://www.jpost.com/Defense /Iran-embarks-on-1b-cyber-warfare-program.

196 *A group of financial executives:* Author interview with senior financial services executive who participated in the meeting, November 2013.

13. The Business of Defense

199 *It occurred to Hutchins:* Author interview with Eric Hutchins, January 2014.

200 *Using the kill chain model, Lockheed:* Author interview with Charlie Croom, January 2014.

203 *"Within a couple of years":* Author interview with former military intelligence officer, July 2013.

    A security expert with close ties: Author interview with cyber security expert, December 2013.

204 *"We've already got":* Author interview with Mark Weatherford, August 2013.

    On February 18, 2013: Mandiant, *APT1: Exposing One of China's Cyber Espionage Units,* http://intelreport.mandiant.com/Mandiant_APT1_Report.pdf.

206 *Less than a month later:* Donilon's full speech, before the Asia Society on March 11, 2013, can be seen at http://asiasociety.org/video/policy/national-security -advisor-thomas-donilon-complete.

207 *"We decided it was":* Author interview with Dan McWhorter, February 2013.

    Mandiant's forensic analysts: Nicole Perlroth, "Hackers in China Attacked the Times for Last 4 Months," *New York Times,* January 30, 2013, http://www.ny times.com/2013/01/31/technology/chinese-hackers-infiltrate-new-york-times -computers.html?pagewanted=all&_r=0.

210 *Reportedly, more than a third:* Hannah Kuchler and Richard Waters, "Cyber Security Deal Highlights Threats from Spying," *Financial Times,* January 3, 2014, http://www.ft.com/intl/cms/s/0/e69ebfdc-73d0-11e3-beeb-00144feabdco.html? siteedition=intl#axzz2pM7S3G9e.

    "A lot of companies, organizations": Ibid.

211 *While working as an NSA contractor:* Author interviews with school officials and individuals familiar with the details of Snowden's trip, January 2014.

212 *They came back with a three-hundred-plus-page report:* President's Review Group on Intelligence and Communications Technologies, *Liberty and Security in a Changing World,* December 12, 2013, http://www.whitehouse.gov/sites/default /files/docs/2013-12-12_rg_final_report.pdf.

    In September 2013 a senior air force: John Reed, "The Air Force Still Has No Idea How Vulnerable It Is to Cyber Attack," *Foreign Policy,* September 20, 2013, http:// killerapps.foreignpolicy.com/posts/2013/09/20/the_air_force_still_has_no _idea_how_vulnerable_it_is_to_cyber_attack.

    And this more than four years: Siobhan Gorman, August Cole, and Yochi Dreazen, "Computer Spies Breach Fighter-Jet Project," *Wall Street Journal,* April 21, 2009, http://online.wsj.com/article/SB124027491029837401.html.

213 *A month after the air force's admission:* Aliya Sternstein, "IG: Government Has No Digital Cyber Warning System," Nextgov, November 5, 2013, http://www .nextgov.com/cybersecurity/2013/11/ig-government-has-no-digital-cyber -warning-system/73199/.

    Earlier in the year a pair: Nicole Perlroth, "Electrical Grid Is Called Vulnerable to Power Shutdown," Bits, *New York Times,* October 18, 2013, http://bits.blogs

.nytimes.com/2013/10/18/electrical-grid-called-vulnerable-to-power-shut
down/.

"There isn't a computer system": McConnell spoke at a cyber security conference
sponsored by Bloomberg in Washington, DC, October 30, 2013.

214 *Investigators concluded that the hackers:* Brian Krebs, "Target Hackers Broke in
Via HVAC Company," *KrebsonSecurity,* February 5, 2014, http://krebsonsecurity
.com/2014/02/target-hackers-broke-in-via-hvac-company/.

In February 2014 a Senate committee report: Craig Timberg and Lisa Rein, "Senate Cybersecurity Report Finds Agencies Often Fail to Take Basic Preventative Measures," *Washington Post,* February 4, 2013, http://www.washingtonpost
.com/business/technology/senate-cybersecurity-report-finds-agencies-often
-fail-to-take-basic-preventive-measures/2014/02/03/493390c2-8ab6-11e3-833c
-33098f9e5267_story.html.

At a security conference in Washington, DC: Alexander spoke in Washington,
DC, at the Newsuem on October 8, 2013, http://www.youtube.com/watch?v=
7huYYic_Yis.

14. At the Dawn

218 *A senior administration official:* Author interview with senior administration official, January 2014.

The timing of Obama's speech: Olivier Knox, "Obama NSA Speech on Anniversary of Eisenhower Warning," Yahoo News, January 16, 2014, http://news.yahoo
.com/obama-nsa-speech-on-anniversary-of-eisenhower-warning-025532326
.html. White House aides told Knox that the timing was a coincidence.

220 *In December 2013, Ernest Moniz:* "Moniz Cyber Warning," *EnergyBiz,* January 5,
2014, http://www.energybiz.com/article/14/01/moniz-cyber-warning.

221 *The government is well aware:* General Keith Alexander disclosed the number
during a speech at Georgetown University on March 4, 2014.

222 *"At the end of the day":* Press briefing by senior administration officials, February
12, 2014.

223 *Once those liability protections are in place, the government:* For a thorough examination of how Internet service providers may be tapped to better secure cyberspace, see Noah Shachtman, "Pirates of the ISPs: Tactics for Turning Online
Crooks into International Pariahs," Brookings Institution, July 2011, http://www
.brookings.edu/~/media/research/files/papers/2011/7/25%20cybersecurity%20
shachtman/0725_cybersecurity_shachtman.pdf.

224 *Some observers have likened:* Ibid. See also Jordan Chandler Hirsch and Sam
Adelsberg, "An Elizabethan Cyberwar," *New York Times,* May 31, 2013, http://
www.nytimes.com/2013/06/01/opinion/an-elizabethan-cyberwar.html.

225 *But unlike other clouds:* Brandon Butler, "Amazon Hints at Details on Its CIA
Franken-cloud," *Network World,* November 14, 2013, http://www.networkworld
.com/news/2013/111413-amazon-franken-cloud-275960.html.

INDEX